Left Brains for the Right Stuff

Computers, Space, and History

⎯⎯⎯⎯⎯⎯

Hugh Blair-Smith

Left Brains for the Right Stuff, Published November, 2015

Editorial and Proofreading Services: Gregory Crouch, Kellyann Zuzulo,
    Karen Grennan
Interior Layout and Cover Design: Howard Johnson,
    Howard Communigrafix, Inc.
Photo Credits listed on page 430

 **SDP Publishing**

Published by SDP Publishing, an imprint of SDP Publishing Solutions, LLC.

To obtain permission(s) to use material from this work, please submit a written
request to:

SDP Publishing
Permissions Department
PO Box 26, East Bridgewater, MA 02333
or email your request to info@SDPPublishing.com.

ISBN-13 (print): 978-0-9964345-3-9
ISBN-13 (ebook): 978-0-9964345-4-6

Library of Congress Control Number: 2015947856

Printed in the United States of America

For the many individuals around the world who cooperated gladly, generously, and passionately to add rocket science, navigation science, and especially computer science (electronic Left Brains) to the Right Stuff. They answered the long-sought quest for "a moral equivalent to war" and changed the world.

TABLE OF CONTENTS

INVOCATION

Creator of the Universe,

Creator of the Earth, the Sun, the Moon, the planets and the stars,

Creator also of the elegant and beautiful laws

That govern the motions of all these,

Creator, finally, of our combination of intelligence and curiosity

Enabling us to find our way around this universe:

We have but little understanding and less agreement

As to who and what You are,

But we do know what has been created, and we can agree

That it's only natural to feel and express gratitude.

And so we do.

Amen.

—HUGH BLAIR-SMITH, 2014

PREFACE

What made the Space Race possible? Rocket science, navigation science, computer science, and a lot of people who learned how to weave them all together.

What made it necessary? The rise of superpowers, entities too big and well-armed to fight a war that either side could win. They could be rivals but not enemies.

How close a race was it? Wellington's assessment of Waterloo will do: "It has been a damned [close] thing—the nearest run thing you ever saw in your life."

And what did it achieve? A giant leap in the shared consciousness of mankind, a realization that sustainability of our small blue planet depends upon a higher level of cooperation than would have been conceivable a century ago.

———⊗◗◖⊗———

Timing is everything. Born in 1935, I grew up at the best moment to live and work in the rapid development of these sciences, their nexus, and their consequences. A lifelong practice of system analysis, alternating between top-down approaches and bottom-up approaches to everything, has helped me to connect many dots. This book is a combination of large-scale history and a small-scale inside story. There are presidents and premiers, policies and projects, and pioneers of technology. Sprinkled between chapters are year-by-year Space Race Highlights with enough dates to annoy the most dedicated student, to document the progression of events, and to raise questions of causes and effects.

The histories of the three sciences have internal threads of consequences over centuries of development, and external threads connecting them to each other and to world history. In the nineteenth and twentieth centuries particularly, there are startling parallels.

I have attempted an even-handed treatment of Soviet engineers and cosmonauts, as well as American engineers and astronauts. On both sides, those groups defied national stereotypes, exhibiting an outstanding level of integrity and a passion for getting things right. Covering fields which were male-dominated through most of the period, I have been delighted to find opportunities to give some exceptional women their due.

Histories tend to be about kings and wars and dates, but they must be understood as being about people. The Space Race involved close to a million individuals around the world. My inside story necessarily focuses on the part of that world I know best: MIT and its laboratories, engineers there and at NASA and at companies we worked with.

This book is more one individual's system analysis than a conventionally researched history. I have been able to fact-check a large number of personal memories, and have not hesitated to make highly educated guesses where necessary. People with deep knowledge of the technical details will notice places where I've simplified descriptions to make them more accessible, and will undoubtedly catch me out in what I hope will be small errors.

And people who are convinced that science is false, progress is an illusion, and humanity is doomed, will find me a "cock-eyed optimist" on many points. So be it.

—**Hugh Blair-Smith**,
November, 2015

THE STARTING GUN: 1961

The telephone rang with what seemed to be a special urgency, as if it too had been galvanized by President John F. Kennedy's words to Congress on May 25, 1961 … only a few days before.

> *I believe that this nation should commit itself to achieving the goal, before this decade is out, of landing a man on the moon and returning him safely to the earth.*

The President's bold eloquence rose precisely to the significance of the moment. Over the past four years, the Congress—and the nation they represented—had been shocked by the launch of Sputnik, encouraged by President Eisenhower's creation of the National Aeronautics and Space Administration, embarrassed by repeated failures of rocket launchers, frustrated by delays in the manned Mercury program, and now humiliated by the Soviet propaganda machine's trumpeting of the triumphant orbital flight of Yuri Gagarin on April 12. It was time to pick up the Goett committee's 1960 concept[1] called *Apollo* and make it a program.

The telephone sat on a corner of a cluttered desk on the fourth floor of an old wood-framed, brick-faced factory building in the gritty industrial heart of Cambridge, Massachusetts. The hand that reached out to it belonged to a sixty-year-old man with a nearly full head of graying hair, a still-robust build, steel-rimmed glasses over blue-gray eyes—aviator's eyes, restless, missing nothing—in a ruddy face that showed his preference for keeping the top down on his Morgan Plus 4. Professor Charles Stark "Doc" Draper of MIT's Aeronautics and Astronautics Department was founder and director of the Instrumentation Laboratory, which had recently delivered computer-centered inertial guidance, navigation, and control (GN&C) systems to the United States Navy for the ultimate deterrent, the Fleet Ballistic Missile (FBM) system. Each FBM unit was a nuclear-powered submarine capable of roaming the undersea world indefinitely, kept informed of its position by inertial navigation without reference to any external signals. An FBM sub carried sixteen Polaris missiles, each with its own GN&C system operated by a micro-miniaturized digital differential analyzer, a hybrid type of digital device "dressed up as an analog computer." No air defense could jam guidance signals to a self-contained system that didn't need any. And no aggressor could be sure of taking out all such submarines in a first strike; enough would be left to exact an unacceptable price.

"Stark Draper." The voice was clear and confident.

"Hi Stark, it's Jim." James Edwin Webb had been Doc's colleague at Sperry Gyroscope years ago, and had taken over as NASA's second administrator three months earlier. Doc had no trouble guessing what the call was about.

"Hi Jim. What can I do for you?"

Webb knew well enough what Doc would say, but he had to put the questions and the answers on the record. "Can you build a GN&C system for Apollo?"

"Yes."

"When will it be ready?"

"When you need it."

"How do I know it will work?"

"I'll go along and operate it for you."

Jim Webb was amused by this last sally, and not a bit surprised. Doc had always preferred to take the hands-on approach, personally fitting airplanes with innovative instruments and then flying them himself. But everyone knew astronauts had to be test pilots, physical and psychological supermen in the prime of life, made of what Tom Wolfe called the *Right Stuff* in his 1979 book. Doc's way of expressing unshakable confidence in what his Lab would achieve was typical, but not to be taken literally.

Or was it? A couple of months later, Doc wrote a long letter to NASA Associate Administrator Robert Channing "Bob" Seamans, Jr., insisting that his age should not be an obstacle and spelling out several reasons why his role as crew would be beneficial. A nonplussed Seamans wrote a prompt and courteous reply, taking note of Doc's offer and promising to pass it along the proper channels.

That's how the deal with Doc's Instrumentation Laboratory was done. No RFP (request for proposal), no bidding cycle, no catfights among congressmen to shift torrents of federal funding into their districts. It was the first of many occasions in which the urgency of JFK's commitment made people say, in effect, "We don't have time to mess around being bureaucrats in the usual way—we've got to get this thing going!"

The Lab's main building—a factory long since vacated by the Whittemore Shoe Polish Company—had been repurposed as one part of MIT's gradual encroachment on parts of Cambridge where Lever Brothers manufactured soap, Necco turned out rolls of sugary wafers, Squirrel Brand packed peanuts, and a hundred miscellaneous products were stamped

Made in Cambridge, Mass. and shipped around the world. I had been working there as an engineering staff member for a year and a half, a very junior member in a staff of hundreds. But I carved out a nearly unique role for myself, with one foot in the digital computer hardware engineering side of the house and one foot in the programming side. Though officially in the Digital Computation Group that wrote programs for the house mainframe computer, I had also been working with the Digital Development Group that was creating a compact, low-power guidance computer to go in an Air Force space probe to Mars. The third of that series, the first to bear my design thumbprint, was instantly repurposed as the prototype Apollo Guidance Computer. Hence, my claim to have begun working on Apollo several months before it began.

Throughout the program, I functioned as a bridge, interpreting the hardware and software sides to each other. Later, my efforts in the Lab's consultative role in Space Shuttle avionics development built on that experience.

It took a lot of educated people to braid together the three technological strands of rocket science, navigation science, and computer science. My lucky privilege was to be among those whose careers as systems engineers became the fourth strand. The braiding was performed in many more places than just MIT. For manned space flight, these included International Business Machines' Federal Systems Division (IBM FSD) working with NASA and McDonnell Aircraft on the Gemini spacecraft, and IBM FSD again with NASA's Marshall Space Flight Center on the Titan and Saturn boosters.

The Lab worked under the direction of NASA's Manned Spacecraft Center, and in sometimes uneasy partnership with both North American Aviation and Grumman Aircraft

Engineering. We had to create a computer-centered suite of instruments playing a multi-faceted role in the Apollo spacecraft, connecting both Houston's Mission Control and the three-astronaut crew with essentially everything the spacecraft did.

Let's take a look at how the four strands began and how they grew up to become ready to take men to the Moon.

I

BEGINNINGS: 1100–1956

OF ROCKET SCIENCE: 1567–1914

Wan Hu knew that as a powerful mandarin in the Middle Kingdom, he was under the special protection of Heaven. With unruffled serenity, he decided to travel faster than any man on Earth. The year was known as 1567 AD to the Western world, but China had no need or use for the calendars of barbarians. Wan had a smooth wooden track built, on which he placed an elegant chair, lavishly gilded and richly upholstered in a brocade of the boldest court colors. Securely fastened to the back of the chair were forty-seven rockets, the largest size then in use as weapons called "fire arrows," their fuses neatly aligned for simultaneous ignition by forty-seven servants. Sitting in his chair, Wan Hu gave the signal by nodding gravely.

The servants carefully extended their long matches. The fuses sparked and crackled in perfect synchronism while the servants backed off to the safest distance from which they could still watch. There was a tremendous explosion. No traces of Wan Hu or his chair were ever found. Thus ended the first application of rockets filled with gunpowder for human flight. Solid-fuel rockets did not again become "man-rated" until the Space Shuttle four hundred years later, with (mostly) better results.

Writers of a scientific bent imagined human travel between the Earth and the Moon, making use of rockets and cannons—with the notable exception of Johannes Kepler's 1630 book *Somnium*. Kepler's traveler was described as a student of Tycho Brahe, the persistent Dane who mapped the heavens with unprecedented accuracy, though unaided by a telescope. Noting that Copernicus used Tycho's database to develop a mathematical model of a Sun-centered Solar System, Kepler's fictional student figured he could judge the correctness of that model by observing from the Moon.

Folklore of the time imagined Lunar demons who brought evil to Earth, taking advantage of the "bridge of darkness" that filled space between Earth and the Moon during eclipses—also getting God off the hook for the existence of evil. The student obtained his "ticket" from a deal his mother (a prominent witch) made with these demons to travel over the eclipse-bridge to the Moon. Kepler concocted this elaborate fantasy to show how the Copernican model might be verified, while giving himself full deniability for when Papal thugs came around to enforce the orthodox view of a stationary Earth at the center of the Universe. He claimed it was all a dream (*somnium*), involving nothing so realistic as rocket propulsion or cannon fire, and that one couldn't be held responsible for the content of one's dreams. This dodge worked well enough, with one hitch—the Papal thugs improvised by arresting Kepler's mother on suspicion of witchcraft.

A decade or so later, a parade of wildly improbable technologies appeared in Cyrano de Bergerac's first-person fantasy, *L'Autre monde ou les états et empires de la Lune* ("The Other

World: Comical History of the States and other Empires of the Moon"). With an instinct for what was bogus in the natural philosophy of the ancient world and its importation into his own time, the narrator (ostensibly Cyrano himself) described being borne aloft by bottles filled with dew, which everybody knew was strongly attracted by the Sun. Later, the narrator experimented with a sort of rocket sled that crashed, injuring him so he had to slather himself with beef marrow to ease the pain. Then he had to rescue the machine from a bonfire, setting off the remaining rockets accidentally. That boosted him into the stratosphere, where the exhausted rocket machine fell away, but he didn't fall. That was due to lucky timing since it was past the Moon's third quarter and, as everybody knew, the waning Moon in its last quarter is accustomed to sucking animal marrow.

"Say what??" you might ask. Cyrano the author needed a miracle to save Cyrano the character and, for that purpose, reached for what he knew was one of the most absurd superstitions of his time. Oddly, the superstition persists into our own time in slightly more abstract form: you can find online forums on witchcraft arguing over whether the waning Moon is a time of "negative energy." Cyrano the author manhandled this fantastic notion into the shape he required, making the Moon's "sucking" energy pull his character's slathered body to where the Moon's gravity balanced the Earth's. Cyrano stated this distance as well over three quarters of the way—not a bad guess, since the right answer is 71%. He landed safely on the Moon and logged many cockeyed adventures, finally returning home by supernatural means. Cyrano's is the funniest concept of Earth-Moon travel, and it's no surprise that scholars consider it the inspiration for Jonathan Swift when he wrote *Gulliver's Travels* nearly a century later.

In 1650, a Polish-Lithuanian military engineer, Kazimierz Siemienowicz, made a drawing of a three-stage rocket to propel a warhead toward a target many miles away, but did not leave any account of how it might be guided. His drawing joins many of da Vinci's works in portraying a carefully engineered design that had no hope of being realized in his lifetime. Still, the proportions of the three stages to each other is a fair approximation of the corresponding proportions in Apollo's Saturn 5 booster.

A more practical form of military rocket was developed, not in Europe, but by anti-Raj rebels in India, who deployed it to rout a considerable British Army force at Guntur in 1780. Jolted from complacency, Whitehall backed Colonel Sir William Congreve in his 1804 development of rocket weapons with a four-mile range. Congreve rockets were used against Napoleon in 1806, and against our own Fort McHenry in 1814 with less effect but more fame, thanks to Francis Scott Key.

In the midst of all this belligerent rocketry was an attempt at a peaceful—well, sort of peaceful—use of rocket propulsion for human flight. An Italian, Claude Ruggieri, undertook experiments rocketing animals outfitted with parachutes high in the air. Hoping to top these feats in 1806, he persuaded a small boy in Paris to be the next payload, but the gendarmes wouldn't let it happen.

By 1865, authors imagining the uses of peaceful rockets had acquired a modicum of scientific sophistication. Jules Verne's tale, *From the Earth to the Moon*, inspired just about everybody who later contributed to the art, and even demonstrated a correct understanding of weightlessness in space flight. Four years later, Edward Everett Hale anticipated by a full century the Global Positioning System (GPS) in his short story *The Brick Moon*. Hale imagined a large and highly visible satellite, boosted into polar orbit around the Earth to provide ships at sea with a direct observation of longitude. Hale's bricks were intended to absorb and dissipate the heat of re-entry, anticipating the Space Shuttle's skin of thermal tiles.

In the 1914 twilight of the *Pax Brittanica*, Congreve rockets turned to peaceful purposes, carrying breeches-buoy ropes to wrecked ships and saving a thousand sailors.

OF NAVIGATION SCIENCE: 1100–1802

The birds and the bees do it, and so do butterflies. They navigate over long distances, using built-in biological instruments that we are struggling to understand. Humans have had to invent inorganic navigational instruments to guide them to places they cannot see. The earliest one that deserves the name of "instrument" is the magnetic compass, invented in China over two thousand years ago, though not applied to wayfinding until about the year 1000. Even then, its use was in land-based orienteering as part of military training for a hundred years before becoming standard equipment for ships. European mariners adopted this technology from Chinese vessels at once, recognizing it as a huge advance over the polarized-light-sensitive "sunstone" crystals used by Vikings to find the direction of the sun on cloudy days.

An instrument to measure speed through the water came next, using a reasonably accurate interval timer in the form of a half-minute sandglass, rather than an hourglass. A triangular piece of wood called a *chip log*, with its corners tied to the end of a rope in which evenly spaced knots are tied, remains nearly stationary in the water after being dropped from the stern, if the rope is paid out freely. The number of knots paid out before the glass runs out is the speed in nautical miles per hour, or "knots" for short.

Combining the compass and the log with a reasonably accurate clock allowed for *dead reckoning*, the art of calculating both distance and direction through the water without visual reference to land or even to celestial bodies. In parts of the ocean without substantial currents, dead reckoning was at least as accurate as the charts of the medieval and Renaissance eras. But since there was no way to measure currents, knowledge of ocean currents like the Gulf Stream had to be collected into books for navigators' use.

Direct finding of a ship's position in the northern hemisphere, where almost all shipping takes place, is aided enormously by the North Star, Polaris. Many devices were developed to measure the angle between the northern horizon and Polaris, including cross-staffs, octants, and sextants. The angle observed is the vessel's latitude within one degree. Near the Equator, it's a small angle of just a few degrees. Standing at the North Pole, it's 90°—directly overhead. And in Venice or Minneapolis, it's about 45°.

In the southern hemisphere, none of the naked-eye stars are anywhere near as helpful, so the Polynesian navigators of the South Pacific had to create sophisticated and lengthy oral traditions to interpret the star fields at various times of year.

For daytime navigation in either hemisphere, the angle the Sun makes with the horizon at noon provides a very accurate latitude if the navigator has a book giving the Sun's "declination" for each day of the year. Since the Earth's axis is inclined 23.5° to the axis of the Earth's orbit around the Sun, a navigator at latitude 23.5°N will find the Sun directly overhead on June 21. Returning to the same place on December 21, the navigator will find the Sun only 43° above the horizon. The books that record these predictions, called nautical almanacs, have gradually been improved to match the greater accuracy of angle measurements by modern sextants, better than one-hundredth of a degree.

Finding longitude—position in the east-west direction—is a very different matter and requires another instrument, the chronometer, a clock so accurate as to give the correct time to within a second or two. The Earth's rotation on its axis—producing the illusion of Sun, Moon, planets, and stars apparently circling the Earth once per day—needs that accuracy to predict where each celestial body will appear. Until recent centuries, navigators had to combine direct measurement of latitude with a dead-reckoning estimate of longitude, augmenting the latter with whatever knowledge they possessed of currents. Dead reckoning accumulated errors rapidly, partly because the navigator was depending for speed data on the skill of the men trailing and timing the chip log, and depending for direction data on the steadiness of the man at the wheel as well as the quality of the compass. Very little quantitative data on currents was available, even when Benjamin Franklin made his amateur measurements of the Gulf Stream on his many voyages to Europe.

In 1707, this problem proved tragic for a homeward bound—and fogbound—Royal Navy fleet under Admiral Sir Cloudesley Shovell. His navigators *knew* they were south of the latitude of the English south coast, and north of the latitude of Brittany's Ushant Island. They *calculated* they were miles east of the sharp-edged rocky Isles of Scilly, which stick out like monstrous daggers from Land's End, the southwestern corner of England. But the calculations, based on inaccurate estimates of when sextant measurements were made (before the fog rolled in), were badly off. The navigators' northeast course was intended for Falmouth, but instead took the whole fleet into those rocks.

The catastrophic loss of over a dozen ships and two thousand sailors prompted Parliament to offer the monumental prize of £20,000 for a solution. At $4 million in modern terms, it was so handsome that the Admiralty's Board of Longitude couldn't, half a century later, bring themselves to pay it to a simple Yorkshire clockmaker, John Harrison, who had spent those decades developing a chronometer. Harrison's clock ran steadily in hot weather and cold, at whatever angle the ship's deck was canted, even absorbing the shocks of heavy waves. The Board claimed that only luck and coincidence could have given the sea trials of his chronometer more success than the methods favored by the empire's greatest astronomers. In the end, Harrison got some of his money by going over their heads and getting an interview with King George III. The King tested an advanced model at the palace for ten flawless weeks and, exasperated with the Board, told the inventor, "By God, sir, I'll see you righted!"

Even with accurate time, navigators had to perform some complicated arithmetic (including spherical trigonometry) when working up sextant sights. At sea especially, it required large books filled with tables of numbers to do all the arithmetical heavy lifting, leaving only adding, subtracting, interpolation, and careful plotting for the navigator to do. Harrison's chronometer was the solution to the longitude problem *if* accompanied by accurate mathematical tables.

That was a big *if.* To produce these books of tables, bored tired men sitting on high stools did the calculations by hand, copying the results on paper with their quill pens. Bundles of the papers went to a print shop where apprentices—young "printer's devils"—set the type (necessarily in mirror image and sometimes upside down as well), copying digits that had no meaning for them. The opportunities for omissions, duplications, transpositions, 2s confused with 5s, and 6s confused with 9s, were infinite. Short budgets of time and money, as well as pressure to get the volumes out, curtailed proofreading.

In the first years of the American republic, a patient slight-built youngster, Nathaniel Bowditch of Salem, Massachusetts, passed up playing vigorous games with his schoolmates because he much preferred examining and correcting the error-ridden tables used by his seafaring family. His book, *The American Practical Navigator*, became the ninth title published by the United States Navy's Hydrographic Office, and a much updated "HO-9" is still a bestseller in the nautical world.

OF COMPUTER SCIENCE: 1642–1907

Like Nathaniel Bowditch a generation earlier, Charles Babbage corrected entries in large books of mathematical tables for use in celestial navigation. Unlike Bowditch, who was doing what he loved for the family business, young Babbage was working at a job, in his native London, for which he was absurdly overqualified. Bored and frustrated, he longed to make use of the pinnacle of technological innovation of his time. "I wish to God these calculations had been executed by steam," he exclaimed.

Babbage became the first to attempt development of steam-driven calculating machines. I suspect there could have been earlier large-scale machines, driven by the windmill or watermill technologies that had been grinding wheat into flour for centuries. And if such machines could have existed, why didn't they? One surprising answer is an invention in the last third of the seventeenth century by two mathematical giants, Sir Isaac Newton in England and Gottfried Leibniz in Germany. Newton (with an astronomical orientation) and Leibniz (with a mathematical orientation), simultaneously invented a new analytical approach to physical problems, making large-scale calculating machines unnecessary for over a century.

Their advance was called calculus—differential calculus to generate formulas for rate-of-change problems, and integral calculus to generate formulas for the accumulated effects of varying forces. They built on René Descartes' development of analytical geometry, applying his system of perpendicular coordinates (with a numerical scale along each axis) to expressions for smoothly changing variables such as the motion of planets through space. In schools and colleges today, analytical geometry is fittingly called "precalculus."

The value of the "differential calculus" lay in the ability to express differentials or derivatives—the rate of change of one variable with respect to another—in the same sort of algebraic formulas that describe the behavior of the original variable. That made them computable with small-scale manual adding machines like Blaise Pascal's "Pascaline" of 1642 or Leibniz's "Stepped Reckoner" of 1694.

The "integral calculus" part of their invention conferred a similar benefit on the reverse process, deducing the formula for an underlying variable from an expression for its rate of change. For fairly simple functions, these operations can be performed by devices that we don't even think of as computers. Dashboard instruments in twentieth-century cars perform mechanical differentiation of a wheel's rotation to position a speedometer needle, and equally mechanical integration of the same variable to drive an odometer's number wheels.

The tedious labors of young Babbage took place at a time when the demand for more accurate calculations was undergoing explosive growth. The practical limits of calculus had been reached in two areas, both relating to celestial observations of Sun, Moon, planets, and stars. One, which we'll meet later in spacecraft navigation, was the famously intractable three-body problem, where the motions of a body significantly attracted by the gravity of two or more other moving bodies cannot be expressed in a neat algebraic formula. The other was the complexity of navigational arithmetic.

Babbage was born into London banking money and access to all the stars of the British Enlightenment. At Cambridge University, he found the programs in mathematics badly inadequate and sought to raise the level of intellectual stimulation by forming the Analytical Society with some brilliant friends. This society served as the platform for Babbage's bold arguments about the best notation for calculus, couched in the elegant elaborate puns for which Cambridge is famed. Babbage tagged Leibniz's notation (exemplified by representing the rate of change of a variable **x** with respect to time as **dx/dt**, pronounced *dee-ex-dee-tee*) "d-ism" as a riff on the religious philosophy of Deism so characteristic of the Enlightenment. He dismissed Newton's notation (exemplified, for the same purpose, by $\dot{\mathbf{x}}$, pronounced *ex-dot*) as "dot-age."

Taking a degree in 1814, Babbage married in defiance of his father's objections and began his career while raising a family of nine children. Seeking a route to calculation "by steam," he studied small-scale calculating devices and Johann Müller's design for a "difference engine" of 1784. In 1822, he persuaded the Royal Astronomical Society to back construction of his own design of a difference engine to calculate entries for mathematical tables. The name comes from use of the "differences method," a basis for the method of "difference equations" used for calculating positions and velocities of spacecraft in the twentieth century.

Construction began in 1823 and quickly ballooned into a mega-project requiring revolutionary advances in building machine tools to form the engine's parts and, like Apollo over a century later, in project management. After production of only a small proof-of-concept model and a decade of ever-increasing problems with contractors, politics, and funding, Babbage was forced to halt his development project in 1832. It had consumed £17,000 of government money and £6,000 of his own, totaling approximately the sum used by John Harrison over a lifetime of developing chronometers, but with less result.

Overcoming his great "disgust and annoyance" with the failed project, Babbage in 1834 conceived a higher vision, a machine that would "eat its own tail," his phrase for feeding the outputs of some of the calculations back as inputs to other calculations.* After five years of research and development, he faced the new model's need for a systematic approach to programming. Fortunately, he had only to look at a new silken portrait of Joseph Marie Jacquard on his wall to find a ready technology.

In 1801, Jacquard had invented programmable automatic process control. His automatic tapestry loom used stiff-paper cards, about 5″ × 30″, with places for hundreds of holes corresponding one-for-one with the threads of the warp. A mechanical linkage "read" each card by poking probes at every hole position. Where there was a hole, the probe passed through

---

*It seems likely that "eat its own tail" is a Bowdlerized Victorian version of what Babbage actually said. A more accurate image, more likely to have been used by this rough-mannered genius, is "eat its own shit." Babbage must have been aware of Vaucanson's automaton of 1739, the *Canard Digérateur*, a mechanical duck that ate and defecated, and was claimed (falsely) to digest. The duck remained on display in a Paris museum, with hidden machinery capturing the swallowed grain and supplying synthetic poop, until 1879.

by an inch or so, lifting the corresponding warp thread. Where there was no hole, the probe was blocked and the corresponding warp thread stayed put. Then the operator sent a weft thread across on a flying shuttle below the lifted warps, reset the probes to home all the warps, and brought the next card into position by pulling on a pair of strings. Rube Goldberg would have died of joy to watch it.

What hung on Babbage's wall was an exquisitely detailed 1839 portrait of M. Jacquard, a nineteenth-century "selfie" automatically woven in silk under control of 24,000 punched cards as a bravura demonstration of the technology. Babbage figured out how to make the Jacquard warp lifters control his new model, enabling it to perform more general forms of processing than just polynomial equations. This "analytical engine" would transcend *calculation*, arithmetic done on numbers representing measurements such as distance, time, speed, and money. Processing of all forms of information, including text, sound, and pictures as well as numbers, became known as *computation*.

Ada Lovelace (Augusta Ada Byron, Countess of Lovelace, to give her full name and title) was quick to see the possibilities. In an age when offering women any significant education was abnormal, the romantic poet Lord Byron trained his only legitimate daughter in mathematics from childhood. He even took her, as a teenager, to a presentation by Babbage of his difference engine. She was so impressed that she cherished the memory through a dozen dutiful years as a wife and mother. As soon as the day-to-day pressures of that role eased off, she sought out Babbage again. Applying her well-furnished mind to the burgeoning science of mathematical logic, she worked with him on the analytical engine. He was then among London's leading social lions, in demand not only for his brilliance in developing dozens of different inventions but also for his ill-tempered and articulate impatience with non-geniuses. Charles Babbage was the premier "badly socialized nerd" of the early Victorian era.

As they worked together—he, for the most part, on the mechanical details of the engine; she, for the most part, studying a notebook full of his program code—the silken portrait of M. Jacquard looked down from the wall. A fly perched on that picture, on a certain day, must have seen and heard something very like this:

Ada looked up at Babbage, then back down at the page, up again, took a deep breath, and spoke. "I say, Mr. Babbage, this part isn't going to work in the Southern Hemisphere, where you give the latitude in negative numbers."

He continued scratching away at drawings of the special gearing for long division. "Bugger the Southern Hemisphere; nobody sensible goes there."

She sipped at her cup. "How then, sir, are we to get our tea from India, but by doubling the Cape of Good Hope?"

The scratching only became more feverish. "Tea!" he snorted.

With a twinkle in her eye, she topped up his cup and pressed her point: "And how shall we navigate, to transport such ruffians as yourself to Australia?"

He sighed and looked up. "Mind your saucy tongue, mistress, or I'll ..." He paused, squinted as if at something far away, snatched the notebook from her hands and glared at the page. "Damn me! I suppose you mean this one, that I called iota-2." She nodded, but he did not see, nor need to. He muttered aloud to himself, "That wretched little angle does have to keep the sign of the latitude, don't it?"

He looked up as if seeing her for the first time, cocking his head to one side. "Ada—my very dear Ada—" He ignored the sudden elevation of her left eyebrow and continued, "Your father raised you to bear the title, Princess of Parallelograms. Today I promote you to Empress of Hemispheres. You must run your curry-comb through all my programming. Only ... you won't tell Mrs. Babbage about this, will you?"

She smiled serenely and reassured him, "Nary a word, Mr. Babbage, nary a mumbling word."

He smiled back, an effort in a face unused to it. "And never mind about 'Sir' and 'Mr. Babbage' now. 'Charles' will do nicely."

Scholars differ over whether Ada actually created any code, which would make her the first female programmer, but there can be no doubt she was the first person to specialize in what we now call software. Italian Luigi Menabrea was so impressed by the design of the analytical engine that he wrote a paper on it in French to make his subject available to the largest number of educated people. Ada translated it into English, adding her own notes which included the first description of computer programming ever published. She combined vision—great enough to see that a computational machine might compose music—with a talent for communicating to the world the facts and significance of the analytical engine. It would have been the world's first general-purpose computing machine if its designer had been able to build any substantial part of it. How might the British Victorian computer industry have developed if Babbage could have tempered his intellectual hubris with some of Ada Lovelace's communications savvy, and practiced enough courtesy with officials to get funding for advanced development? A novel, *The Difference Engine,* by William

Gibson and Bruce Sterling, speculates at length on this point for a fascinating alternative history.

Up through the nineteenth century, "engine" meant any ingenious device, not just a steam engine—though the friction of numerous metal gears would have required steam power for the analytical engine. Shakespeare has Hamlet use the word's military sense (seeming to foreshadow Saturn rocket engines, and to cast Rosencrantz and Guildenstern as doomed astronauts):

> *... Let it work;*
> *For 'tis the sport to have the enginer*
> *Hoist with his own petar'; and 't shall go hard*
> *But I will delve one yard below their mines*
> *And blow them at the moon.*

By the twentieth century, "engine" had become tied almost exclusively to locomotives and the motors of other vehicles, so "computing machine" and eventually "computer" took over.

But many key issues remained the same. Defining a coded expression of the steps to a solution—programming—was a design issue for the Jacquard loom-cards of the analytical engine, and remains so today. The practice of program code inspection introduced by Ada Lovelace is still a valuable tool in software development, and the uneasy relationship between precision and accuracy has persisted. One pragmatic nineteenth-century soul complained about Babbage's insistence on keeping forty or possibly even fifty digits of *precision* for each number, when the achievable *accuracy* of measurements didn't generally surpass one part in ten thousand or maybe a hundred thousand, that is, four or five digits.

Quite aside from such long numbers making a full-scale

analytical engine impossible to drive (because the required brute force of steam power would have overwhelmed the brass fabric of the gears), it was a monumental waste of resources to calculate and store so many digits that couldn't possibly mean anything. Today, *accuracy* still means "how exactly do I really know this quantity" and *precision* still means "how many digits will I use to express it."[2]

The application of electricity to projecting information and action over a distance also began in the nineteenth century. First came *action*, what we now call remote control. In 1800, Count Alessandro Giuseppe Antonio Anastasio Volta was looking for a way to demonstrate the power of his new invention, the Voltaic pile, or battery. Knowing that a novel military device would get the most attention, he thought of Sir William Watson's 1748 demonstration that electricity would travel through a two-and-a-half-mile wire (apparently) instantly, and devised a remote control to fire a gun. In the next town, thirty miles away, he set up a flintlock musket with one copper wire, thirty miles long, attached to the barrel. He rigged a second thirty-mile wire so that its end hung just above the gunpowder in the musket's flash pan, and told the assembled dignitaries to watch the gun carefully when the church bell struck noon.

He raced back on his best horse, on the road along which the wires were laid out, to his home town of Como, where one wire was attached to the bottom of the biggest Voltaic pile he'd built. When the Como church bell struck noon, he slapped the other wire down on top of the pile and prayed—as engineers have always prayed—for the flawless operation of his prototype. The voltage set off a spark in the musket's flash pan, thirty miles away, firing the gun just as the flint striking the steel would normally do.

With battery technology thus established, Samuel Finley Breese Morse achieved *information* at a distance by exploiting the principle of electromagnetism, published in 1826 by André-Marie Ampère. One could make a piece of non-magnetic iron into a temporary magnet by passing an electric current through a wire wrapped around the iron, empowering magnetic force to move metal objects under precise electrical control. During the 1830s, Morse applied this technique to move a pencil over paper in response to a voltage pulse in a wire, hence the name *telegraph* (distant writing). He represented information by a digital code composed of four types of signals: short pulse (dot), longer pulse (dash), short pause (between pulses within one letter code), and longer pause (between one letter code and the next). Note the different pauses in the best-known Morse code message, the distress call "SOS": **dot-dot-dot—dash-dash-dash—dot-dot-dot**.

Soon he substituted a *telegraph sounder* for the unreliable pencil mover when he discovered that operators could interpret its audio dots and dashes in real time. Extending this technology to distances longer than a few hundred miles became a problem because of the amount of energy converted to useless heat by the resistance in the wire. Morse developed repeaters that used a weak incoming signal to actuate an electromagnetic switch—a *relay*—to send a refreshed signal on to the next station.

Coast-to-coast telegraph communication in the United States was established on October 24, 1861, just in time to assure President Lincoln that Utah would not secede from the union. The hopelessly outclassed Pony Express went out of business two days later.

Morse can be called the grandfather of electrical/electronic computing because his relay, which could be configured to perform other digital logical functions (AND, OR, etc.) as well as simple repetition, would be recognized as the first *amplifier* of electrical signals. The relay became the basis for electrically driven computers almost a century later.

Morse can also be called the grandfather of not telephones, but telephone exchanges, a very different invention. While Alexander Graham Bell's 1876 telephone was the first analog device, making variations in an electrical signal follow sound waves and restoring the sounds electromagnetically at the receiving end, it was a point-to-point communicator with no switching, that is, no digital function. Switching was introduced in 1877 with the invention of a relay-technology telephone exchange by Thomas Edison's Hungarian associate, Tivadar Puskás. It was built by the Bell Telephone Company in Boston, Massachusetts.

The art of electronics began right after the turn of the twentieth century, as a way to project *sounds* over distances too great for simple telephone technology. Engineers sought a way to exploit the Edison Effect to achieve wireless telegraphy, now called radio communication. In London in 1904, John Ambrose Fleming invented the thermionic diode, in which an internally heated cathode loosened electrons from their normal orbits, and a nearby anode collected them—sometimes. If the circuit to which these two electrodes were attached put the anode at a positive voltage relative to the cathode, electrons would flow to complete the circuit. If the voltage was negative, nothing would flow and the circuit would stay open. The device did for electric currents exactly what a check valve does for liquid currents in a hose, allowing flow in only one direction, which was an essential first step in detecting radio waves and converting them to sound waves. That's why it was called a *thermionic valve,* a term that long survived in British use for the whole class of devices that work by making electrons leap from cathode to anode. All such devices work best if enclosed in a glass or metal tube from which nearly all the air has been evacuated, leading to the American term *vacuum tube.*

An Iowa-born American, Lee De Forest, patented his refinement of the diode in 1906 as part of his extensive pioneering of radio technology. What bothered him was the fact that it did nothing to strengthen the signal, as Morse's relay did for wire telegraphy. Suddenly he realized that Morse's use of a battery for an energy source could be applied to Fleming's valve, maintaining a positive voltage at the anode, if he interposed a third element between the cathode and the anode to regulate the flow of electrons. De Forest's "grid"—so called because it was a metal screen with plenty of open space to let electrons through—could cut off the flow with a fairly small negative voltage or let it pass through to the anode with a fairly small positive voltage.

Combined with a "load" resistor between the anode and the battery voltage, his tube amplified a small or weak electrical signal into a larger more energetic copy of the signal. De Forest patented his *Audion* tube in 1907, a dozen years before it acquired the generic name of *triode.* The best part was that the output voltage would be quite accurately proportional to the input voltage, if the grid voltage was never so negative as to cut off the electron flow entirely nor so positive as to let it flow as copiously as the cathode heating would support. This hugely desirable property, *linear* amplification, accurately restored the energy lost to space in the radio transmission of the rapidly varying electrical signals created by Alexander Graham Bell's microphone, much as Samuel Morse's relays restored energy lost to heat in using long wire runs to send dots and dashes.

Linear amplifiers became so important for radio purposes that electronic engineers made sure in their designs never to put enough positive voltage on a grid to pass the maximum current through. This principle arose not from any concern for damage, but because "driving the tube into saturation" would violate the holy grail of linearity. That was still taught when I studied electronics in college. The emphasis on linearity made it harder for many engineers to appreciate how the same tubes, operated in saturation or cutoff, could strengthen ones and zeros in digital logic and computing.

OF A SYSTEMS ENGINEER: 1939–1956

My earliest memory of an engineering orientation was getting a perfect present on my fourth birthday: a set of smooth wooden blocks plain in color but shaped like various parts of a car body. I could put them together one way to make a stately 1930s touring car, another way to form a snazzy roadster, or a pickup truck ... just about anything. My parents had a problem at bedtime that evening. I was quivering with the excitement of designing and had to be persuaded that it would be waiting for me in the morning.

Practical grounding in systems engineering began on my twelfth birthday, in the form of a kit to build an HO scale steam locomotive. It was a modest little engine, whose prototype was a Baldwin switching engine used by the Baltimore and Ohio Railroad. Its wheel configuration was "0-4-0," meaning two axles for a total of four driving wheels and no leading or trailing "truck" wheels. No tender was required, since the prototype had a saddle tank for water and enough of a coal bin to supply short runs around the marshalling yard. Where there's an engine, there must be tracks and cars and other types of engines. Where there are tracks, there must be a layout with buildings and scenery, and a power supply to deliver up to 12 volts DC through the tracks to the engine.

Soon, I had a plywood table eight feet square with all those features, including a tunneled mountain made of furnace cement, a lake made of water-glass, a small town of cardboard-kit buildings and some outlying settlements, plus a collection of lead people three quarters of an inch high. The control station featured an auto-transformer with a silicon bridge rectifier to vary the train's speed, and mechanical remote controls for switches, made from choke cables from the auto parts store. If you want to know if you have an engineer in the family, that's not a bad way to go about it. As an incidental benefit, a 12-volt short circuit through the fingers will educate, but not actually kill, a child.

My six years of boarding-school experience at Middlesex School in Concord, Massachusetts, while excellently instructive in the liberal arts and math and science, was entirely innocent of rockets *and* computers. The nearest thing to Boolean Logic was the electrical and mechanical design of the school's model railroad club. Three of the teachers were called by the students Bull, Zoom-Zoom, and Dingbat.

William Alexander was "Bull" because he looked like the rough-spoken football coach he was. He had a good eye for mathematical talent and wasn't a bit shy about expressing his expectations. "Blair-Smith," he growled at me just before a class in first-year algebra, "you are going to get a hundred on this test or I will wring your scrawny neck." "Yessir," I said. And I did.

John de Quedville Briggs was "Zoom-Zoom" for his brisk style of walking, talking, and everything else. He was as elegant as Bull was plain. He convinced me that developing a skill in writing, and building a vocabulary to support it, was among the best favors I could do for myself and was by no means incompatible with my inclination toward engineering.

Arthur Motter Lamb was "Dingbat" for his collection of models of trains, dramatic figures, and toys for all ages. He was the music department, played the organ at assembly and chapel, directed the glee club and the annual Gilbert & Sullivan, ran the model railroad club, retrofitted cool gadgets to his car, occasionally rode a unicycle, tied his necktie with one hand while doing something else with the other, and generally made it clear that specialization was no reason to be less than astonishingly good at a variety of other things. There couldn't be a more multifaceted role model than the sum of those three characters.

My first three years at Harvard were similarly devoid of rockets and digital electronics, though I did have a short-term summer job one year as … a "computer!" That term was still in use (though rapidly becoming archaic) to denote a human being who operated a desktop calculator. The task was to make statistical calculations for some professor's research project, and while I never learned to love statistics formulas, the Friden calculators were great fun. They were the size and shape of overgrown typewriters and handled ten-digit decimal numbers, holding them in electromechanical number wheels like those of an old-style odometer. They had a keyboard comprising a ten-by-ten array of keys to enter the numbers, plus a few keys to command the usual functions, and they made a lot of noise.

———— ∞∞∞ ————

Majoring in Engineering and Applied Physics, I augmented my academic education with a 1955 summer job at Electronics

Corporation of America. The project, at ECA's Erie Street plant in Cambridge, was building a parachute-borne aerospace probe for some darkly military purpose. The first—and most ironclad—rule impressed on new employees was never to take a ruler anywhere near the side of the factory floor where the long antenna assembly was being fabricated. Two copper wires were spaced apart at intervals by transverse clear-plastic standoffs, and I suppose the length of the standoffs was a quarter of the wavelength, something the Soviets mustn't learn.

A lot of the inspection of incoming parts involved fairly ordinary-looking hardware with special features for mil-spec compliance, such as cadmium plating. Several times, I found the cad-plating peeling off (good thing I didn't put any in my mouth, as cadmium is now regarded as a toxic metal to be avoided or surrounded by safeguards). We also looked for defects such as burrs on nuts and bolts, in which connection one of the old hands put to me the standard riddle for inspectors: "Did you ever see a burred screw?"

II

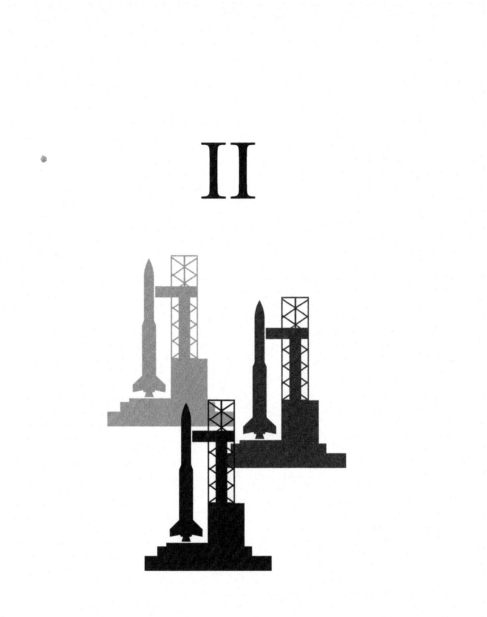

Growing Up: 1897–1961

OF ROCKET SCIENCE: 1897–1961

The story of rocket science as we understand the term today begins around 1897 with Konstantin Eduardovich Tsiolkovsky in Russia. Although he never built a rocket, his mathematical thinking and technical writing on the principles of aviation and space flight created a rigorous science studied by Robert Goddard in America and Wernher von Braun in Germany.

Tsiolkovsky's achievements formed the largest grain of truth underlying the hyperbolic claims by Soviet overlords that everything worthwhile was invented in Russia first. (*Star Trek* fans may recall the Enterprise's crewman Chekhov parroting this line occasionally.) Apollo's deflation of those claims, which were central to the Soviet Union's pretensions to be the only true way to the future of all mankind, can be considered a decisive factor in the Cold War.

Robert Hutchings Goddard played the all-American tinkerer to Tsiolkovsky's bookish nerd, launching the first liquid-fueled rocket at Auburn, Massachusetts, in 1926. It burned gasoline, but couldn't get oxygen from the air fast enough, so he had to build in a tank of liquid oxygen (now called "LOX"). Goddard was also a talented professor and writer, documenting his thoughts and discoveries in aviation, electronics, and space travel. In that connection, he drew an avalanche of ridicule for suggesting that rocket propulsion could take a payload to the Moon or even Mars. Everybody knew that a rocket engine needed air to push against ... but everybody was wrong. Goddard's proof that rockets work by pushing against the *forward* end of the combustion chamber remains the first thing students of rocket science must learn. Sergei Pavlovich Korolev followed in Goddard's footsteps, building similar rockets at a government institute in the Soviet Union in the early 1930s, and equipping them with gyroscopic stabilization for use as cruise missiles.

In Germany, Hermann Julius Oberth had a similar fascination with liquid-fueled rockets, self-publishing his proposed doctoral thesis *Die Rakete zu den Planetenräumen* ("By Rocket to Planetary Space") in 1922 because Göttingen University wouldn't touch anything so unrealistic. In 1929, his consulting role helped *Frau im Mond* ("The Woman in the Moon"), the first movie with outer-space scenes, to become a force popularizing rocketry and space travel. In 1930, his eighteen-year-old student Wernher Magnus Maximilian, Freiherr [Baron] von Braun, learned well and later called Oberth "the guiding star of my life."

During part of World War II, they worked together at Peenemünde, developing the V-2 rocket weapon to wreak vengeance upon England in a lunatic tantrum for a lost war. The "V" designation, shared with the V-1 flying bomb launched by steam catapult and powered in flight by a simple pulse jet engine, was a name change forced by Hitler in his burgeoning madness.

It stood for *Vergeltungswaffe*, or Retaliatory Weapon, translating to the appropriate English word Vengeance.

Kenneth Northcott, my English brother-in-law, had many connections with the wartime British intelligence organizations. His older brother Eric was a sort of small-scale "M," running spies all over Nazi-occupied Europe. His University of London mentor in Germanic Languages, Professor Frederick "Bimbo" Norman, was involved in the interpretation of Ultra intercepts at Bletchley Park (mentioned in R.V. Jones's *The Wizard War*). Bimbo got his nickname from fellow POWs in World War I, Italians who called him "Bambino" as the youngest prisoner in the camp. He told me some tales of how the development of the V weapons looked to the British wizards.

The Germans, having put all their own factory hands in uniform with rifles, had to staff Peenemünde's fabrication lines with slave labor from the Benelux countries. Because the morale of these workers had to be maintained, the Germans allowed them vacation leave at home, where they instantly looked up their neighborhood British spies and told all they'd seen. For a long time, this flood of information was frustrating and baffling to Allied intelligence, until they figured out that two very different weapons were being developed in the same facility. Once they realized that the V-2 was a pure rocket weapon with some sort of guidance system, they focused on that. It wasn't necessarily the best choice because the crude low-tech V-1 was a more effective weapon, "landing" horizontally in a London street and exploding while still moving fast, thus collapsing twenty or so buildings at a time. The more elegant high-tech V-2 came straight down and pulverized one or two buildings, leaving their neighbors standing.

They learned that V-2 guidance was the job of an officer at

the launch site, directing the pitchover from vertical launch with an airplane-style joystick while looking through an artillery-type sighting grid. And they learned of a training incident with an inert warhead, in which the trainee was so awed by the ascending rocket that he unconsciously pulled back on the stick, sending the practice missile backward into Poland. Partisans there handed it to *their* neighborhood British spies.

In the 1945 Nazi Götterdämmerung, Oberth and von Braun and most of his team made sure to come under the control of American forces. Some other Peenemünde engineers, who were less resourceful, less lucky, or perhaps leaning toward communism, wound up in the Soviet Union. Both sides found it possible to quietly forgive such engineers their ingenious contributions to the Nazi cause, provided they started making equally ingenious contributions to what was soon to become the Cold War. Oberth thus became one of "our Germans." Unlike von Braun and many others, however, he did not complete the immigration and assimilation process. He divided his time between the U.S. and Germany, retiring to Germany and living just long enough to see the Berlin Wall come down and reunification begin in 1989.

Just after the war, the general enthusiasm for denazification required that our Germans be kept under wraps, working quietly at remote southwestern desert sites on V-2 clones like the WAC Corporal. Operation Paperclip was an ingenious end-run around an executive order by President Truman, barring any German whose participation in Nazi party affairs was more than purely nominal. The U.S. Army simply made up sufficiently denazified biographies of the rocket scientists and "paperclipped" them to their files. As a pre-teen in those years, I saw news articles and newsreels about the WAC Corporal and similar systems, but had no way to know that these feats of American ingenuity were in fact "master classes" in rocketry taught by our late enemies.

———∞∞∞———

Siegfried Fred Singer, an American physicist born in Austria, was ahead of his time in researching the potential payloads these rockets might carry. While stationed at the U.S. Embassy in London in 1951, he and British Interplanetary Society leaders Arthur C. Clarke and A. V. Cleaver put together a design for MOUSE—Minimal Orbital Unmanned Satellite, Earth—to carry a variety of instruments for scientific observation of the Earth. Pictures of their model show a cylindrical shape with two antenna poles mounted axially. Appearing like a spool of thread with a Tinkertoy dowel sticking out both ends, the MOUSE looks too heavily built to be orbited by contemporary rockets.

A few years later, Singer was on a team of University of Maryland physicists who built lightweight *Oriole* rockets, costing about $2,000 each, that could take scientific instruments to 50,000 feet. In recent years, he has become a notorious dissenter against nearly everything that responsible peer-reviewed journals have published regarding sunscreen, the ozone hole, second-hand smoke, and global warming. The MOUSE concept, publicized in an article in *LIFE* magazine which I saw as a teenager, was the first thing to give me the idea that putting things in orbit would be a useful and interesting thing to do. But Singer's design was not pursued. American designers of *Vanguard,* and Soviet designers of *Sputnik,* chose a spherical shape to enclose the greatest volume in the least structural material.

———∞∞∞———

As noted in Chapter 1, solid-fuel rockets, burning first gunpowder and then more sophisticated substances, had no role in actual human transportation until they appeared as strap-ons for the Space Shuttle's boost configuration. Their utility is sharply limited by two factors: steering and stopping.

Most approaches to steering the thrust of solid-fuel rockets involve moving rudder-like vanes to block one side of the exhaust—not a very elegant approach, though it served well enough for the Polaris missiles mentioned in the prologue. There is no way to stop a solid-fuel burn so that it could be restarted. The closest approach to stopping it at all is to eliminate nearly all the thrust by destroying the rocket, as range safety officers must occasionally do, leaving the remaining fuel to burn uselessly. Both of the Space Shuttle's strap-ons were cast off when either ran out of fuel, with small auxiliary rockets steering them away from the vehicle so the other strap-on's fuel could safely burn to exhaustion during the long parachute drop to the ocean, where they were recovered and reused.

All other rocket engines involved in twentieth-century manned aerospace vehicles were liquid-fueled, of two major types. In a *fuel-oxidizer* engine, valve openings deliver a mixture of fuel (kerosene for heavy launching, hydrogen for on-orbit thrusting) and liquid oxygen to a combustion chamber where an ignition device starts the burn and valve closings stop the burn. Gimbaled nozzles in some of these achieve steering by directing the thrust, much like the jet nozzle of a personal watercraft or the lower unit of an outboard motor. The *hypergolic* type of engine mixes special combinations of chemicals like hydrazine and dinitrogen tetroxide, which are scary enough by themselves for their toxicity and corrosiveness, and ignite explosively as soon as their feed-pipe valves put them in contact.

Making the liquids flow to the right places is simple enough on the ground, but gets much trickier when starting a burn in the zero-gravity of space travel. Fuel tanks for hypergolics contain membranes flexed by gas pressure to force the chemicals toward the valves, so hypergolic systems tend to be small. Fuel-oxidizer engines need a spurt of artificial gravity to move the liquids to the valved end of their tanks. The trick is to supply a brief acceleration by firing hypergolic engines that are aligned with the main engines, an operation quaintly called *ullage thrust.* As every wine expert knows, ullage is the space in the bottle not occupied by wine, so the term suggests that the ullage in the fuel and oxidizer tanks is being pushed forward by the force of the hypergolic engines. A less poetic phrasing would describe the valved end of the tanks being pushed against their liquid contents. Once the main engine has fairly started, it then automatically supplies its own ullage thrust for as long as it runs.

───── ∞∞ ─────

In terrestrial travel, the bad news is that you're always moving though a medium, needing continuous motive thrust to keep going. The good news is that the properties of the medium help with the steering and (except for aviation) stopping. Turning the front wheels of a car makes the friction of the road against the tires impart a sideways acceleration to the vehicle's front end. Turning a boat's rudder makes the drag of the water against the rudder impart a sideways acceleration to the vessel's back end. Making a banked turn in a plane uses the drag of air against the banked wings to do most of the turning work. In all cases, returning the controls to neutral allows the flow of the medium to align the vehicle's orientation with its new velocity, "pointing forward."

Traveling in space is both simpler and more complex than that. It's simpler because once you've achieved the optimal velocity, the engines can be shut off and the spacecraft will coast indefinitely through the utter lack of medium in perfect silence, unaffected by drag or friction of any kind. (Thank you, Dr. Newton, for that hugely favorable First Law!) It's more complex because the coasting is never in a laser-straight line but is affected by gravitational attractions that can't be measured by any internal instrument, since gravity acts on every atom in the spacecraft the same way. The complexity doesn't amount to much in a circularized orbit around the Earth because the optimal velocity is a simple function of the altitude you want to maintain, just enough so that the tendency to fly off on a centrifugal tangent is exactly balanced by the acceleration of gravity at that altitude.

The phrase "free fall," first used to express this circular-orbit situation around Earth or any celestial body, is still appropriate when traveling between massive celestial bodies. But in that case, the gravitational complexities become daunting. To get a feel for it, imagine a magical golf course with an enchanted green that is not merely uneven but dynamic. The hole spontaneously moves around in a predictable way, altering the rises and dips of the green as it goes. Whatever velocity the ball has when it leaves your putter must be the optimal one to take it up hill and down dale, breaking left and right, to the place where the hole will be when the ball gets there.

The amazing thing is how effectively the elementary computers of the 1960s could use Newton's laws of gravity and inertia to calculate these optimal velocities, happily without having to get into Einstein's relativistic refinements. Pointing a rocket engine in the right direction to drive to such a velocity, analogous to orienting the face of your putter, was done to within a hundredth of a degree, hundreds of times better than you can hand-steer a boat in a given compass direction. Controlling the amount of energy applied by firing the engine, analogous to the force you apply with the putter, is a mixture of predicting how long the engine must fire, measuring while it's firing how much velocity is added every second or so, even calculating a throttle setting for an engine so equipped. The actual velocity attained matches the optimal velocity precisely but not quite exactly, so there has to be provision for mid-course corrections, which are brief engine firings to tweak the velocity as required. In the magical golf course model, imagine the wriggling "body English" (that we all do instinctively while a putt is en route) actually affecting the ball's course—that would be a mid-course correction.

Understanding rocket dynamics in two dimensions, the north-south axis and the east-west axis, is facilitated by comparisons to motorboats and magical greens. Such visualization in the three dimensions of space is enough to pop a mental circuit breaker, even with some education in engineering. We had to handle them mathematically, using multiple numbers to refer directions to three mutually perpendicular axes in space. Aviation and ocean diving are the most common terrestrial activities needing three-dimensional analysis; however, the up-down dimension is used in a relatively restricted way. Air and undersea vehicles roam freely through the north-south and east-west dimensions, but tend to remain for long periods at a constant altitude or depth, navigating in two-dimensional space except when it's time to make a carefully controlled change

Figure 5-1. Three-dimensional Cartesian coordinate system[3]

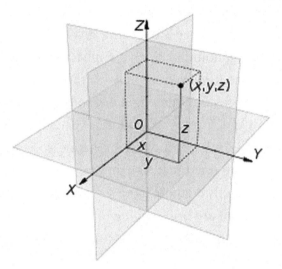

Axis lines X, Y and Z, with origin O, showing where $x = y = z = 0$. The tick marks on the axes are one length unit apart. The large dot shows a point with coordinates $x = 2$, $y = 3$, and $z = 4$, or (2, 3, 4).

in the up-down dimension. In space, "up" and "down" are meaningless and all three axes are treated alike, named X axis, Y axis, and Z axis (Figure 5-1). Fighter pilots and test pilots are the only people who learn to react quickly and decisively when controlling a fast vehicle in all three dimensions, making them the obvious choice for the first astronauts.

Space guidance engineers use several systems of axes, some conceptually attached to (and rotating with) the places the travelers belong to or are visiting. The granddaddy of them all is the non-rotating system for *inertial space*. The X axis points to a place in the star field called "the first point of Aries," the Vernal Equinox, where the Sun appears to cross the celestial equator from south to north each March 21. The Z axis points to the celestial North Pole, around which the North Star circles closely, and the Y axis is perpendicular to both X and Z. The position of a spacecraft that has left the Earth on its way to the Moon or another planet is expressed by three numbers specifying how far it is from the center of the Earth along the X axis, the Y axis, and the Z axis. Similarly, its velocity is given by three numbers specifying how fast it's going along each of those three directions. Such sets of three numbers, called *vectors*, express both the magnitude and direction of something. In Figure 5-1, an imaginary line from the origin O to the black dot would be a vector with components 2, 3, and 4. This line's own length is called the *magnitude* of the vector, the square root of $(x^2 + y^2 + z^2)$ or $(4 + 9 + 16 = 29)$, about 5.39 units, since the Pythagorean theorem for the hypotenuse works in two, three, or any number of dimensions.

Such a vector may express a spacecraft's distance from an arbitrary origin such as the center of the Earth, or it may express the velocity, or the acceleration. What it doesn't say anything about is which way any part of the vehicle is facing. An astronaut seated in a comfortable tailor-made couch may be facing forward, back, sideways, or some random angle—it makes no difference to the quality or efficiency of the flight. We use the term *attitude*, borrowed from aviation, for this orientation. An airplane can have a pitch-axis attitude (nose-up or nose-down relative to straight ahead), usually not very much but unlimited when looping the loop. A plane's roll-axis attitude relative to level flight is substantial but limited while in a banked turn, or unlimited while doing a victory roll. There had better be limited yaw-axis attitude (nose-left or nose-right relative to straight ahead), since substantial yaw angles can put the airplane into a dangerous, potentially deadly, tailspin. The three *body axes* to which these attitudes are referred are mutually perpendicular, and are accordingly labeled X, Y, and Z just like the position/velocity axes of space. By contrast, the attitude of a spacecraft is usually not related to "straight ahead," since that concept means so little in space. Instead, it's a measure of how the vehicle's three body axes are related to the three axes of inertial space. It can be expressed as simply as a vector of three numbers, one for each of the axes. Sometimes it's more convenient to express it as a three-by-three *matrix*, a sort of super-vector made up of three vectors.

We use the term *maneuver* to mean the process of changing a vehicle's attitude without affecting its position or velocity. There are a variety of reasons to do that, but we'll focus on pointing the spacecraft so that the next burn of its main rocket engine will add velocity in the desired direction. Many, usually sixteen, small hypergolic rockets are mounted around a spacecraft's periphery to control rotation, constituting a *reaction control system* (RCS). With a curious disregard for technological truth, these rockets are called "RCS jets" even though there is nothing jet-like about them. To execute a maneuver, they are fired in opposite pairs, much like turning a twin-engine boat by running one engine in forward and the other in reverse.

Calculations in vector-matrix algebra are used to select pairs of RCS jets to fire. Within the computer, the vector for the current attitude is combined with the vector for the desired attitude so that the rotations required for a maneuver are expressed as a nine-number matrix, all cosines of the angles for the rotations. The calculations are used first to fire selected jets to start the turning, and then to fire the oppositely directed jets to stop the turning when the desired attitude is achieved.[4]

Here's how the different rockets work together to execute a mid-course correction of a vehicle like Apollo, where the thrust is provided by a rocket engine that is steerable relative to the vehicle.

First, the computer calculates a vector representing the desired velocity and subtracts the vector for current actual velocity. The result is a new vector called *delta-V*, the required change of velocity. Its direction can be anything ... forward if the vehicle needs to speed up, backward if it needs to slow down, or whatever other direction will produce the desired change.

Second, the computer tweaks the two engine-steering gimbals to make the main engine's thrust vector pass through where it estimates the vehicle's center of mass is. That will minimize the turning force produced by the main engine.

Third, it calculates and commands the two steps of a maneuver using the RCS jets to put the vehicle into the attitude where that thrust vector is also aligned with the delta-V vector.

Fourth, it fires the main engine to start the burn. Because the estimated location of the center of mass usually isn't exactly correct, and because that location changes as fuel is consumed, the computer may notice some rotation. To minimize fuel usage, it may have to perform further gimbal tweaking and RCS jet firings to null out the rotation.

Fifth, instruments in the vehicle's GN&C system monitor the changes of velocity, and the computer shuts down the engine when the new velocity is reached.

Sixth, the computer calculates and commands another maneuver to change the vehicle's attitude to whatever the crew wants during coasting flight, say, a good view of the Moon.

It all sounds much more elaborate than its Earth-bound equivalent of "Turn right onto the expressway and step harder on the gas until you reach the speed limit," but conceptually it's the same thing. However, it's not hard to see why even the most control-minded astronauts are content to let the computer work out the vectors and matrices in three-dimensional space and perform the intricate coordination of the many rocket engines involved. That division of responsibility, in a nutshell, is why rocket science, navigation science, and computer science had to be braided together.

OF NAVIGATION SCIENCE: 1911–1959

At its beginning, air navigation adopted magnetic compasses and still uses them. But none of the ways to measure a boat's speed through the water were practical for measuring speed through the air, a more critical parameter since airplanes must keep up a minimum airspeed or stall and drop into a dangerous spin. To make matters more difficult, even an experienced pilot cannot easily judge airspeed just by looking at the ground. Air navigation also introduced a third dimension that had to be tracked carefully: altitude above the ground and its rate of change (ascending or descending).

Illustrating how French engineers dominated early aviation, measurements of altitude and airspeed were addressed by aerodynamic principles worked out in 1732 by Henri Pitot. He understood how atmospheric pressure decreases with altitude, making it possible to deduce the altitude by measuring the pressure with a static port, just a hole in a vehicle's skin covered by a diaphragm. Based on Bernoulli's research into the flow rates of fluids in narrow tubes, he designed an L-shaped tube sticking out of a vehicle's side and presenting a narrow opening that faces forward. The other end of that tube is also capped by a diaphragm, and the deflections of the diaphragms are measured by a mechanical linkage that drives pointers to show both altitude and airspeed. Working 170 years before airplanes were invented, Pitot understandably began by measuring water in rivers and the speed of boats, but seems to have understood how the principles translated readily to air. In airplanes, including the Space Shuttle, these instruments comprise a "pitot-static system." The gadget that transforms the diaphragm deflections into pointer angles on cockpit dials has become more sophisticated and is now dignified with the name of "Air Data Computer." Connected to a clock, it can also show altitude rate, the speed of increase or decrease in altitude.

Regarding which spot on Earth a plane is over, the combination of airspeed measurement, a magnetic compass, and a clock or watch allowed aviators to use the same art of dead reckoning as waterborne vessels whenever the ground was hidden by clouds, fog, or night. But it's more challenging to do while flying a small plane, and it's subject to larger errors since winds flow faster and more variably than ocean currents. Fortunately, radio technology developed just steps ahead of aviation and quickly provided enhancements. Radio beacons were established in many known locations, emitting signals coded to identify the beacon. Rotating a receiving antenna on the plane showed the pilot the beacon's bearing relative to which way the plane itself was heading. Two such bearings, obtained at close to the same time, determined the position—exactly as a ship can determine its position when two lighthouses are in view. Many more radio-based aids to navigation, including radar, were created throughout the twentieth century. In one early use of radio voice communications, airport controllers gave approaching pilots updated wind conditions on the ground, selecting runways accordingly.

Magnetic compasses have a weakness called *variation*, an offset caused by the Earth's magnetic North Pole being some distance away from the geographic North Pole. At any place on earth, the variation depends on whether a straight line to magnetic north is east or west of a straight line to geographic north, and by how big an angle. It's also affected by masses of iron concentrated underground. Ships have little problem with variation in most parts of the world, because they're slow and have plenty of time to look up where it changes. Airplanes, being much faster, fly through changes in variation more frequently. What's more, they can fly over the magnetic north pole in the Canadian Arctic, where a magnetic compass needle tries to point straight down.

First naval engineers and then airplane designers focused on the intriguing directional stability of gyroscopes as a way to overcome magnetic problems. One invention, the gyrocompass, is unaffected by masses of iron and indicates true geographic north by sensing the rotation of the earth. Gyrocompasses were installed on Kaiser Wilhelm's Imperial Navy ships for use in World War I. Later, as airplanes became larger and more able to carry such bulky and power-hungry devices, they too benefited from gyrocompassing.

But gyros are by no means a one-trick pony. The interesting angular stability of gyroscopes was first applied to aeronautical control problems in 1912. Elmer Sperry's two-axis *autopilot* gained widespread acceptance when Elmer's son Lawrence demonstrated it at a Paris air show in 1914. His plane maintained straight and level flight while Lawrence's hands were in view outside the open cockpit, signaling "Look, everybody, no hands!" One gyro, oriented to be sensitive to changes in heading, was connected to the rudder control cables to assure straight flight, thereby stabilizing the yaw axis. The other gyro, oriented to be sensitive to changes in "nose up/nose down" attitude, was connected to the elevator control cables to assure level flight, thereby stabilizing the pitch axis. Changes in the roll axis were inherently self-correcting because of the way the wings were mounted. That was the beginning of the Sperry Gyroscope Company, which branched out into other devices for aircraft control and became known as Sperry Corporation by the time Doc Draper and Jim Webb got to know and trust each other there.

Until fairly recently, the term "autopilot" referred only to devices to keep flying straight and level, though later wing designs required the addition of a third gyro to stabilize the roll axis. It's easy to be misled by the word into thinking that it has many more talents, especially if influenced by the movie *Airplane*. Otto, the movie autopilot, was a man-shaped inflatable artifact capable of everything a human pilot could do, including improper behavior with a stewardess. In reality, the functions and limitations of autopilots are still illustrated by the occasional instances of flights continuing past their destinations while both pilots are asleep or totally distracted. The classical autopilot performs only the control aspect of the full-scale GN&C system (Guidance, Navigation, and Control). More advanced autopilots became capable of a very basic guidance function, homing in on a radio beacon, even in crosswinds.

With war clouds thickening over Europe in the 1930s, Doc Draper, an active aviator as well as a professor in MIT's

Aeronautics Department, sought better ways of navigating aircraft in adverse conditions. High clouds could hide stars from aviation sextants, ice could block pitot tubes, and radio beams could be degraded by natural forces or even enemy jamming. Looking around for useful tools, Doc noticed how the familiar gyros of autopilots and gyrocompasses could also be rigged as accelerometers to measure accelerations along the X, Y and Z axes, and how crystal oscillators, already established as electronic frequency standards, had been elaborated into digital clocks. He founded MIT's Confidential Instrument Development Laboratory to combine these elements into what he called *inertial reference units (IRU)*, later *inertial measurement units (IMU)*. This suite of instruments had to elevate the ancient art of dead reckoning to an electro-mechanical navigation system with enough precision to navigate warplanes through unfriendly skies. He called it *inertial navigation.*

Like watercraft dead reckoning, inertial navigation of aircraft is simple enough in principle: If you know where you were at a certain time and you carefully keep track of all changes of heading and velocity, you can calculate where you are at any time during your trip. In aircraft, however, headings can have a third dimension (up or down) as well as horizontal, and the changes occur too quickly in a maneuvering airplane to keep track of by manual methods. In a boat that heels or a ship that rolls, two hinged rings called gimbals are enough to *allow* the compass card to be level under all conditions, and the mineral oil filling the compass dome slows down its motion and so tends to *keep* it level. That combination produces a stable platform for the magnetic needle attached to the pivoting compass card. The corresponding situation in a vehicle in the three dimensions of air or space is a stable platform holding the gyros and accelerometers.[5]

With gyros rigged to create electrical signals encoding the three-dimensional heading, accelerometers rigged to create electrical signals encoding changes in the three-dimensional velocity, and electrical time signals from a digital clock, it was still quite challenging to integrate the signals into an indication of the aircraft's latitude, longitude, and altitude. Analog circuitry could produce an approximate display, but without digital computation in real time, the results weren't very satisfactory. That's how Doc Draper joined the "club" of scientists who urgently needed the development of digital computers.

But Doc and his colleagues were already looking beyond this sort of aircraft navigation to the development of a full-capability autopilot that could apply the new navigation function to *guidance*—changing the intended velocity in accordance with high-level requirements like a new destination or avoiding weather—while still providing the control functions of a classical autopilot. They could logically have abbreviated this combination as NG&C, for Navigation, Guidance, and Control, but the phrasing that rolled more easily off the tongue was GN&C, for Guidance, Navigation, and Control.

And beyond aircraft GN&C lay the tantalizing prospect of applying the same art to space travel, a hot topic in that decade, as evidenced by the progress in rocket science—not to mention the popularity of the *Buck Rogers* comic strip. The inertial approach to GN&C would be essential in the absence of air because no direct measurement of speed is possible, and steering wouldn't have any medium to push against. No lift, no drag, no weight: just Newton's laws of mass, velocity, and acceleration … and gravity.

In either air or space, however, inertial navigation has the same limitation as dead reckoning for ships. Progress through the medium can be tracked well enough, but what if the medium itself is moving? Ships need an independent data source for two-dimensional ocean currents to refine their dead reckoning results, and airplanes need an independent data source for three-dimensional winds. Space is not a moving medium in the same sense, but gravitation bends it into curves that have essentially the same effect: spacecraft need an independent data source for gravitational fields. In all types of vehicle, databases and mathematical models in computers are ideal sources.

The art of GN&C, as conceived by Doc and his colleagues, was thus hobbled for about a generation, until computer science could provide not merely calculating machines but *control computers*—small enough to fit, light enough to carry, fast enough to keep up with the dynamics of the vehicles, efficient enough to work without guzzling energy, and reliable enough to stake lives on.

Doc's Confidential Instrument Development Lab was not hobbled, however. They had plenty to do before and during World War II, developing gyro-stabilized gun sights, bombsights, and other highly secret items. After the war, they simplified the name to Instrumentation Laboratory.

———————

In the early 1950s, a typical Doc Draper feat showed his flair for the dramatic. Having led the development of a large inertial navigation system he called "SPIRE," for SPace Inertial Reference Equipment, which had an analog computer at its heart, he wangled an invitation to a 1953 conference on the theme "When will inertial navigation become feasible for aircraft?" The Lab fitted out a B-29 bomber (the same long-range type used to drop atomic bombs on Japan in 1945) with a

2700-lb SPIRE and flew it from Boston to Los Angeles for the conference. The pilot had to perform the minutiae of control for takeoff and landing, but was able to rely on SPIRE for all navigational functions during the twelve-and-a-half-hour flight. Doc and a dozen of his associates were on board, and presented themselves to the conference as living proof of their system's operation. It brought down the house.

And it cannot have been lost on the aviation-oriented attendees that the system's name featured the word "space" rather than anything to do with aircraft.

OF COMPUTER SCIENCE: 1936–1954

As a graduate student in the 1930s, Howard Hathaway Aiken got irked and frustrated in his physics research. Even with his new Keuffel & Esser slide rule (a state-of-the-art *Log Log Duplex Decitrig*), working through the long formulas required to predict and interpret experimental results was tedious, fussy work. Trying to keep even three digits of valid precision in his answers—one part in a thousand—was worrisome and not always possible. Why, he wondered, can't IBM machines do this?

International Business Machines (IBM) was making useful and highly reliable devices then for enterprises worldwide, but those devices were not computers. Its tabulating machines used decimal number wheels (like those of Pascal, Leibniz, and Babbage), which IBM electrically drove and sensed with motors and relays. Aside from a few internal number-wheel adders forming totals and subtotals to print, all data storage was in the form of punched-card "unit records" holding 80 characters. A unit record held one employee's payroll data, for example, or sales data for one product line. Its capacity was not large, but it *was* more than half the capacity of a Tweet. These cards, much smaller than those used in Jacquard looms, measured 7⅜ × 3¼ inches with a corner lopped off to make it obvious if any were upside-down or backwards. They became known worldwide as "IBM cards."[6]

In one way, Aiken's wondering was premature. Over a decade and a world war would pass before IBM designed a machine for scientific computing. In another way, his query was prescient. Aiken himself would become a bridge between the old IBM—content to build plugboard-programmed unit-record machines—and the versatile postwar powerhouse that made "IBM" many people's ordinary word for "computer."

Aiken's issues with scientific calculations were far from unique. The first third of the twentieth century produced a torrent of scientific and engineering innovation, all of which demanded computation on an unprecedented scale: more reliable, more precise and, above all, faster. Some disciplines, like designing efficient airfoil shapes for airplane wings, required systems of simultaneous differential equations, straining the tools of calculus beyond what Newton or Leibniz could have imagined.

The transition from *electrical* devices, with their macro moving parts like rotors and switch armatures, to *electronic* devices, with no moving parts bigger than electrons and molecular-scale magnetic domains, produced both new problems and elegant solutions. With their accurately linear amplification, electronic devices supplied a way to perform fairly precise calculations in a way that worked to postpone the necessity for digital computers. Voltage levels of electronic signals could be made to imitate smoothly changing variables of many kinds, like the path of an airplane. Such voltages were *analogous* to the variables they were imitating, hence the term "analog computing." Autopilots and many other types of control systems were thus able, for a while, to keep up with some of the new demands without requiring the development of digital computing.

But not all physical variations change smoothly. Consider, for example, the abrupt changes of state in subatomic (nuclear) reactions, even in simple radioactive decay. And many systems have behaviors that are too complicated and have too many variations to model by creating a specialized combination of analog circuits for each one. After all the mathematical and electronic innovations that had held off the requirement for infinitely flexible high-speed computing reached their limits, the time had come. For Howard Aiken and Doc Draper, for physicists and engineers throughout the world, electrical/ electronic digital computing *had* to be invented in the 1930s. In several places around the world, this happened more or less simultaneously.

The first tool the inventors reached for was the one placed on the bench by Samuel Morse, elaborated by two generations of tinkerers into a discipline called switching theory. Morse's relay, just a gadget that used an electrical signal to break one electrical contact and make another, was a building block. Put enough of them together, backwards or forwards, in series or in parallel, and you can fabricate any imaginable logical function—any rule that produces results that are binary, on or off. All such functions are expressions of switching theory. From the beginning of the century, IBM had led the way in exploiting this tool.

That left one major problem to be solved: storage of data. And the inventors took a variety of approaches to it. A century earlier, Babbage had wanted his analytical engine to be able to "eat its own tail," preserving the results of some calculations until they could become inputs to other calculations. He had to rely on geared wheels maintaining their angular states while disengaged from the steam-driven gears running the rest of the machine. Switching theory itself provides an arrangement called a "flip-flop," two relays (or any type of amplifier), each feeding its output back negatively to the other's input, forcing their outputs to be mutually opposite. That state persists while the power is on, until a new incoming pulse upsets the balance in such a way as to reverse both outputs. Electric charge can be stored for a while in a device called a condenser or capacitor, but it leaks away and has to be refreshed at regular intervals, usually less than a second. Magnetic fields had been storable, in a way, ever since Valdemar Poulsen's 1899 development of magnetic wire recording, which was Denmark's creation of the stealthy art of "wearing the wire." To record or play back, the wire had to be in motion, an inconvenient method of storing data in an "edible tail," though usable for bulk storage in the form of tapes.

Who *was* the first to invent the electrically driven computer as we know it today? Take your favorite theory into a bar full of technology historians, and you'll soon have a fight on your hands.

In Germany, Konrad Zuse built his first experimental electro-mechanical computer between 1936 and 1938. With logic performed by sliding metal bars driven by a motor (the only electrical part of the machine), he called his Z1 the first "freely programmable" system. One might suppose such pioneering creativity was instigated and funded by the presumed hyper-discipline of the still-young Nazi regime … but no. Zuse was an odd duck who worked alone in his parents' Berlin flat. Drafted in 1939, he parlayed his achievement—and his experience doing aircraft design calculations at Henschel—into a one-man project to re-implement his design with discarded telephone relays, resulting in Z2, a much more reliable machine that filled several rooms in that spacious flat.

He presented Z2 to DVL (*Deutsche Versuchsanstalt für Luftfahrt,* or German Research Institute for Aviation, which corresponded approximately to our National Advisory Committee for Aeronautics) in 1940. DVL then set him up in business as *Zuse Apparatebau* to manufacture computers in a workshop across the street from his ever-supportive parents. In a few months, he completed Z3, an advanced model more deserving of the phrase "freely programmable" than Z1. As early as 1937, one of his rare colleagues urged him to use all-electronic vacuum tubes instead of relays, but Zuse rejected such a *schnapsidee* (crackpot idea).[7]

Allied bombers shattered Z3 and burned all of its design documents in a 1943 raid on Berlin before it could be really put to work. In early 1944, another raid destroyed his parents' flat, along with Z1, Z2, and their documentation. Construction of a further upgrade, Z4, began in a safer place, but even that area was so thoroughly bombed in early 1945 that the Z4 project was moved to the university town of Göttingen by March, barely ahead of the advancing U.S. Army. Those raids were lucky shots indeed, since such machines could have helped Hitler's atomic scientists build the first nuclear bomb. Britain's Sir Arthur "Bomber" Harris has sometimes been criticized for pushing carpet bombing of Nazi Germany with little assurance of destroying strategically valuable resources, but I think he can take a bow for those raids.

In 1937, Aiken responded to his difficulties with physics calculations by making an arrangement with IBM founder

Thomas J. Watson to experiment with IBM's reliable electromagnetic number wheels and other standard parts. Aiken's goal was to make a modern equivalent of Babbage's Analytical Engine concept, primarily for solving physics problems. Without backing for the construction of a complete computer, Aiken developed high-quality subsystems for arithmetic, storage, and input-output over five years. In an era when every component— number wheels, relays, even resistors and capacitors—added materially to the bulk, power consumption, and cost of logical devices, he became notable for swift design of such subsystems with minimal part counts.

In 1940, George Robert Stibitz of Bell Laboratories demonstrated his relay-technology Complex Number Calculator (CNC) at a Dartmouth College mathematics conference as a way to calculate electromagnetic wave problems. The CNC, too large and delicate to move, wasn't present. It was at home in New York City, and Stibitz operated it by Teletype, sending commands and receiving results over standard telephone lines—an "Internet" far ahead of its time.

Germany's Wehrmacht had exploited relay logic to build their challenging encryption machines, first Enigma and then Lorenz. Fortunately, an early Enigma model fell into the hands of Polish mathematicians who developed some basic decryption logic, but couldn't keep up with the frequent key changes as the war approached. They turned the machine and their research over to two specialists from Britain's Government Code and Cypher School (GC&CS) in July 1939. By 1941, that establishment at Bletchley Park, so secret that the letters were claimed to stand for "Golf, Cheese and Chess Society," had an all-star cast of wizards led by the immortal Alan Turing, and built relay-logic devices called "Bombes" to achieve the Ultra decrypts.

America's own odd duck, only slightly more "establishment" than Germany's Zuse, was Professor John Vincent Atanasoff at Iowa State College, who takes the prize for creative distracted driving. On a road trip to Rock Island, Illinois, in early 1938, he had an enormous insight: What if operating vacuum tubes in cutoff or saturation was a Good Thing instead of a Bad Thing? They'd act just like relays, only very much faster. He saw (still while driving) how to make a digital computer out of vacuum-tube logic, with data stored as electrical charge on capacitors. That charge would slowly leak away, but fast vacuum-tube logic could read and refresh it in plenty of time. Traffic must have been light, for he returned safely home in spite of the on-road revelation. Working with graduate student Clifford Berry, Atanasoff had a working model the next year and called it the Atanasoff-Berry Computer (ABC).

At a 1940 conference, he invited John Mauchly, later of Univac fame, to visit him for several days and examine the ABC. Now if you want to get into another fight in that bar full of historians, pick whichever side you like of the proposition that Mauchly deliberately and secretly stole the invention of the computer from Atanasoff and patented it while developing the ENIAC (Electronic Numeric Integrator And Computer) at the University of Pennsylvania. Thirty years later, Minneapolis Honeywell and Univac builder Sperry Rand traded patent-related lawsuits in a trial where Atanasoff served as an expert witness. It dragged on to 1973, when Judge Earl Larson ruled, "[J. Presper] Eckert and Mauchly did not themselves first invent the automatic electronic digital computer, but instead derived that subject matter from one Dr. John Vincent Atanasoff."[8]

Back at Bell Labs, George Stibitz took his Teletype computer interface to the next level. He configured his 1943 Relay

Interpolator so that it got its program commands by reading code from a paper tape, using the electromechanical reader on the Teletype machine. Such tapes are logically divided into five or six (or, more recently, eight) longitudinal channels, in which patterns of holes across the channels represent alphanumeric characters. As each row of holes comes up to the reading station, metal fingers seek electrical contact with a metal roller under the tape, but actually make contact only where there are holes. Since Babbage had never fulfilled his plan to build his Analytical Engine and its device to read code from Jacquard-loom punched cards, Stibitz was the first to introduce a working editable medium for computer program code—not easily editable, but manageable.

Wartime President Franklin Delano Roosevelt had been first a Harvard man and then Secretary of the Navy, so it's not surprising that he looked to Harvard for innovative technology for naval use. In the computer area, that meant recruiting Howard Aiken into the Navy in 1942 to work with IBM. Having lived so long with number wheels and relays and experienced their high reliability, Aiken felt no urge to experiment with using vacuum tubes, with their high heat generation and frequent burnout problems.

Like the navigational tables that bedeviled Babbage, the critical task given Aiken in his wartime role was the construction of naval artillery tables. A battleship turret, with 16-inch guns that can lob one-ton shells twenty miles, had better have some numerical help in accounting for winds and air temperature and pressure in order to get any kind of accuracy. The IBM Automatic Sequence Controlled Calculator, first tested in 1943, went into service in 1944 when it was delivered to the new Harvard Computation Laboratory. Howard Aiken, inspired to carry the art of computer architecture forward but not to keep the restriction to IBM parts, renamed it the Harvard-IBM Automatic Sequence Controlled Calculator, Mark I. Tom Watson was not pleased by Aiken's giving Harvard "top billing," but there wasn't much he could do about it.

Although Mark I could read and punch IBM cards, the unit-record format wasn't suitable for publishing books of tables, so the primary output medium was a small number of IBM typewriters. Nor were the cards useful for holding programs, mainly because of a radical invention in programming: the loop. A fairly complex calculation can be built out of repetitions of operations that are the same except for systematic variations in the data being processed, i.e., iterations of a loop of operations. The simplest kind of variation is a stream of input data, like that on a deck of punched cards. Each iteration of the loop performs the same operations on the data from a new card and prints the results on a new line of typewriter paper.

Aiken's solution to storing a loop was to install four program-reading stations similar to Teletype paper-tape readers except much bigger. The stiff paper tape the stations read was 3¼ inches wide, the same stock from which IBM cards were cut. That width accommodated two channels of pin-feed sprocket holes at the edges and twenty-four channels of small holes, barely a millimeter in diameter, in three groups of eight. Some of the stations would perform logical loops because their tapes were cut and glued into physical loops, bringing the same instructions under the sensing fingers repeatedly until some logical condition caused control to be switched to another reading station. My guess is that 1944 also saw the creation of the classical urban legend about *infinite loops*—the one where a programmer is trapped in a shower stall forever because the directions on the shampoo bottle say "Lather. Rinse. Repeat" without offering any escape logic.[9]

Not only did Howard Aiken come to computer hardware development by a path very similar to Charles Babbage's, he also had a parallel experience in getting critical software innovation from a young woman. Grace Murray Hopper, then a Lieutenant Junior Grade in the U.S. Navy, was assigned to the Harvard Lab and made her name as a programmer, eventually pioneering what we now call compiler languages and rising to the rank of Rear Admiral. Like Babbage's associate Ada Lovelace, she had a sense of history that prompted her to seize on an incident with Harvard's Mark II, a relay-logic successor to Mark I. That machine started producing nonsensical results one day, and a technician fixed it by pulling a dead moth, the world's first literal computer bug, from the contact points of a malfunctioning relay. Hopper made sure to preserve for posterity that page of the technician's log book, with the moth taped to it (Figure 7-1).

Back at the "Golf, Cheese and Chess Society" at Bletchley Park, the flourishing Ultra business of decrypting Enigma codes stumbled when challenged by a more advanced "Lorenz" encryption technology introduced by the Wehrmacht in 1943. Thomas Harold "Tommy" Flowers had been thinking about electronic information processing at the UK General Post Office's telecommunications research station since the '30s. Like Atanasoff in Iowa, Flowers had seen the value of operating thermionic valves in cutoff or saturation. Now he saw how to automate Bletchley's tedious manual process of trying coding-wheel combinations by building a programmable computer out of a thousand or so valves. He had to overcome entrenched

Figure 7-1. First computer bug, preserved by Grace Murray Hopper.[10]

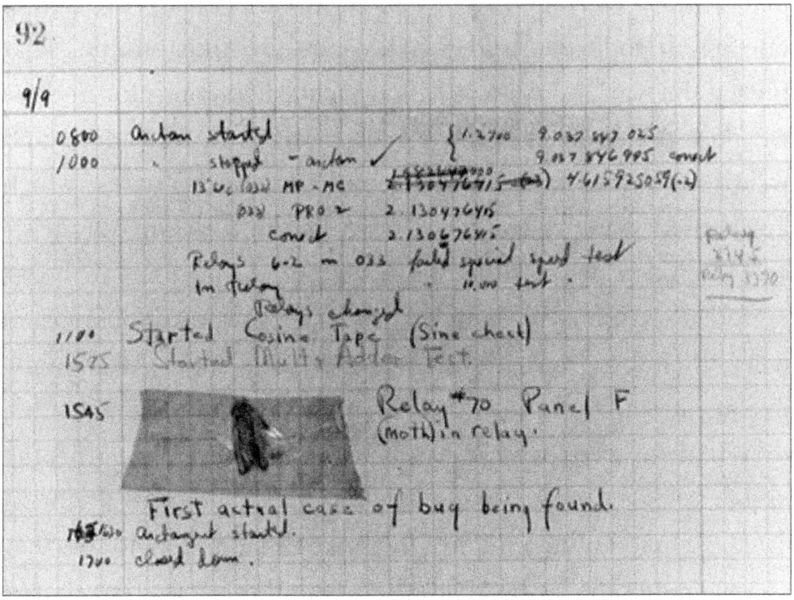

opposition to new technology, just as MIT's Eldon Hall did when introducing integrated-circuit chips into Apollo computer development in 1961. Fortunately, Flowers' long experience in the British telephone system overrode the objections and, with Turing and the rest of his team, he quickly put together two generations of enormous machines, which were promptly dubbed "Colossus" by the Bletchley people. Of this series, Mark 2 went into operation on June 1, 1944, just in time to provide General Eisenhower and his D-Day planners with decrypts of Hitler's refusal to take General Erwin Rommel's advice about reinforcing the defenses at Normandy.

Competition for Aiken's work at Harvard was taking place at University of Pennsylvania, where John Presper Eckert and John Mauchly developed the hard-wired vacuum-tube computer, ENIAC, for the U.S. Army. Even the data memory was made of vacuum tubes, TV-type picture tubes where each pixel's worth of screen stored an electrical charge representing one bit. It took two and a half years to bring on-line, so it missed the war and went on to perform calculations for nuclear weapons design in 1946. Programming ENIAC was a long and wearisome process of plugging and unplugging wires, which aggravated an unwelcome surprise for the brilliant physicists and engineers who wrote the programs. Long used to being regarded as infallible in their fields, they were flabbergasted when their programs didn't work the first time. After many furious attempts to pin the fault on burned-out vacuum tubes, they had to accept the inevitability of software bugs and the embarrassing number of revisions it took to resolve them. In 1948, John von Neumann, the mathematician and nuclear engineer, modified ENIAC to use a stored program that shared the machine's memory interchangeably with data. That upgrade established the "von Neumann architecture" as a revolutionary improvement in getting programs into the machines.

After the war, Howard Aiken continued to develop machines at Harvard with their programs stored in a medium separate from the data—the "Harvard architecture." Mark II, a major upgrade to Mark I, dispensed with the IBM number wheels and used complex relay logic for greater speed to perform "floating point" calculations (automatically keeping track of the decimal point). Mark II also included hardware dedicated to figuring square root, logarithms and antilogs, and trigonometry functions. It was sent to the Navy's Dahlgren Proving Ground to perform simulations and test analysis for naval weapons systems.

Mark III, also for Dahlgren, pioneered the use of magnetic drums—cylinders coated with the same sort of magnetizable material as magnetic tapes. While one drum held up to four thousand instructions, making this Harvard's first stored-program computer, separate drums held data, even segregating constants from variables.[11] For this model, the Dahlgren officials specified much greater speed than could be achieved by the relays in the first two Marks. About five thousand vacuum tubes performed its processing logic, leading a finally converted Aiken to call it the world's fastest electronic computer. This machine gained a pinnacle of public recognition the other Harvard computers did not: it appeared on the cover of *TIME*, where in January 1950 it certainly caught my teenaged eye, giving me my first hint of how cool computers can be. Artzybasheff's cover illustration showed a room-size computer whose central tower sported a Navy officer's cap and a quizzical face studying a long strip of paper held in its bony hand.[12] After Mark III was retired years later, somebody who had hoped to preserve at least some of it for a museum discovered that the Navy had cut it up and dumped it into a Baltimore landfill.

The climax of Aiken's Harvard computer designs, put to work for the Air Force in 1952, was Mark IV. It added ten reel-to-reel magnetic tape drives and two hundred words of ferrite core data memory (at 16 digits per word) to the hardware recipe. A single magnetic drum held a stored program of ten thousand instruction words and four thousand data words, but in separate domains because the instructions were only 20 bits long and it took 66 bits to store a data word, so the Harvard Architecture still ruled. Its "packaging" was a sizeable glass-walled room, complete with a "No Smoking Inside the Computer" sign on the door. Implementing a Mark IV program involved writing a magnetic tape using a separate floor-to-ceiling machine, the only piece of computing gear I ever saw that looked like the standard 1950s cartoonist's image of a "giant brain."[13]

World War II also spawned a major computer development at MIT, called Whirlwind. Its original goal was to control flight simulators for a variety of carrier-borne Navy aircraft, which would make it the first general-purpose digital *control* computer. Design began in 1945, and construction took from 1948 to 1951, too long for the Navy but of interest to the Air Force in ground-controlled interception of enemy planes. The art of controlling aircraft—even simulated aircraft—put MIT on the road to real-time control computers for missiles and spacecraft. Doc Draper and his colleagues worked with Whirlwind and learned much about digital control systems.

Wartime advances in solid-state physics brought about the next giant leap in electronic technology, the transistor. Invented in 1947 by William Shockley with John Bardeen and Walter Brattain, it was a functional equivalent to the vacuum tube triode that began as De Forest's *Audion* tube four decades earlier. Because the transistor was made of semiconductor metals, it didn't need a heated cathode or an evacuated glass bottle. Like the triode, it featured linear amplification but could also be operated in cutoff or saturation for digital purposes. After years of experimentation with different types of transistor, a digital application came first. Philco produced military transistorized computers in 1955 (later marketed as civilian *Transac* systems), a year before introducing transistor radios as a consumer product. Meanwhile, MIT developed the TX-0 computer in the same technology. Doc Draper and his colleagues immediately saw the advantages of the TX-0's transistor logic as a robust low-power technology for airborne electronics.

An urgent need soon arose for digital electronics of that

quality, as part of inertial guidance for long-range missiles. Land-based missiles could use a fairly simple system because the launch site's known location could be programmed in. The Navy required a much more advanced missile guidance system for the submarine-launched Fleet Ballistic Missile system (the Polaris missiles mentioned in the Prologue). Each nuclear-powered submarine's position at missile launch time had to be calculated with more accuracy than could be achieved with radio navigation. The Navy went to Doc Draper's Lab for the Ship's Inertial Navigation System (SINS) as well as the Polaris missile guidance and became quite satisfied with the results. Still, there was some reluctance in high places to let a computer do anything on a ship. Admiral Hyman Rickover, the "father" of nuclear-powered subs, was an immovable object on this point until an inspired staff officer had a brainstorm. "Look, Admiral," he said, "these aren't really computers; they're just sequencers." The good admiral understood sequencers, and was content.

The 1950s also brought about a flourishing of programming languages, at both the assembler and compiler levels. A particular product of computer programming—whether a complete program or a reusable module—is referred to as *code*, not from any resemblance to a secret spy code but because it's a technical encoding, a compact static representation of the dynamic operations the computer is to do.

Assembler language is classed as low-level *source code* because each line of written code corresponds, except for a few special cases, to a single machine instruction or data word, making assembler languages different for each computer architecture.

The only sense in which it's a language at all is the use of mnemonic abbreviations for the operations (e.g. AD instead of binary 110 for addition in the Apollo Guidance Computer) and symbolic names for data items in memory. Assembler source language *implies* where words of instructions and data are to be stored in memory, but the machine can't use it in that form. All those words must be explicitly allocated to memory locations by an assembler utility program that converts the symbolic source code to binary *object code*.

The earliest assembler was written for Cambridge University's EDSAC (Electronic Delay Storage Automatic Calculator), a project led by Professor Maurice Wilkes, which went into service in 1949. The utility was called *initial orders* and provided for mnemonic names of just one letter each. IBM's early scientific computers, the 701 (1952) and 704 (1954), were delivered without any software at all, so it was up to early adopters General Electric and United Aircraft to write their own assemblers.

High-level source code, in the form of algebraic statements, requires a much smarter conversion program, a *compiler*, to make them into assembly-level instruction code. Compiler language has two advantages. It speeds up program development by people whose skill is engineering science rather than computer science. And it greatly speeds up the process of *porting* a program to a computer of a different design than the one it first ran on, provided that a separate compiler exists to support that machine. The disadvantage is that the object code is generally twice as big or more than what a skilled assembly-level programmer would produce, and correspondingly slower. That made a big difference when most computer memories were of small capacity.

Two independent and nearly simultaneous inventions of compilers and their languages occurred in 1952–1953. At MIT,

Doc Draper's people included J. Halcombe "Hal" Laning, Jr., who created a compiler system for the Institute's Whirlwind computer. He called it *George* because it did all the low-level routine work of program preparation. "Let *George* do it" was Hal's motto.

When the ENIAC pioneers were able to strike out on their own, they founded the Eckert-Mauchly Computer Corporation to develop the Univac. It was originally for the Census Bureau, which needed a "universal" computer to handle both scientific and bookkeeping operations efficiently. With a financial rescue from Remington Rand and a change of name to Univac Division, they delivered their first machine in 1951. Grace Hopper, finding Harvard barren ground for programming language development, joined them in 1949 and created high-level source code languages in an algebraic format, coining the term "compiler" for the translating utility program.

The first of these was, logically enough, named "A" and went through several variations starting with A-0 in 1952. Like Ada Lovelace a century earlier, her vision of how multipurpose a computer could be was nearly unique. She had a frustrating time persuading people that her A-0 compiler worked. Many sources, including histories of Yale University and the U.S. Navy, quote her memorable comment: "Nobody believed that I had a running compiler and nobody would touch it. They told me computers could only do arithmetic." By 1954, Hopper headed her own department that turned out compiler languages with more expressive names, including *FLOW-MATIC*. She later evolved that language into *COBOL* (COmmon Business-Oriented Language), still in wide use today despite the somewhat quaint phrasing of much of its grammar.[14]

IBM, a little late getting to the commercial-computer starting gate, put a major effort into high-level languages. In 1954, a team led by John Backus developed *FORTRAN*, with a bias toward algebraic expressions and scientific calculation. Like *COBOL*, it continues in widespread use today despite looking very old-fashioned by comparison to newer languages like PL/I and Java.

With a variety of hardware architectures, high-level languages oriented toward scientific and engineering calculations, and low-level languages usable to build large and complex real-time control programs, computer science had achieved enough maturity to be woven into the braid.

OF A SYSTEMS ENGINEER: 1956–1961

In time for my senior year, 1956–1957, a miracle happened. Remington Rand Univac donated a Univac I to Howard Aiken's Harvard Computation Laboratory, transforming it in a flash from a nest of frazzled graduate students into a digital playpen accessible to undergraduates. The introductory course started with a few lessons in implementing digital logic with relays, taught by Professor Aiken himself.

We who thus received the spark of digital life from Aiken's chalky finger claim a sort of apostolic succession. Among the teaching fellows were Al Hopkins, Ray Alonso, Jim Lincoln and more, the high priests of the "Comp Lab." We learned how to program the electromechanical but still-operating Mark I—in writing only, as that sedate machine had insufficient time to accommodate us. Then we had similar programming practice with the Mark IV, which had been the state of the art within Harvard until that year.

I don't know what became of most of Mark IV, but years

FIGURE 8-1. One word—16 digits and a sign—from Harvard Mark IV's high-speed data memory[15]

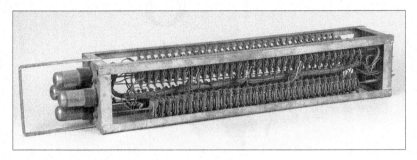

later Al gave me a part of it, a sturdy metal frame 4½ inches square by 30 inches long, packed with 32 sets of four ferrite cores the size of tires on a toy car. Each core was wound with dozens of turns of copper wire. The module had connection pins at one end and was crowned at the other end by four vacuum tubes protected by a croquet wicket-shaped handle. It was one word—16 decimal digits and sign—of that machine's 200-word high-speed memory. In other words, a few million of them, operating a million times faster, would be equivalent to the RAM in a smartphone. A few years ago, I gave it to the Collection of Historical Scientific Instruments (Putnam Gallery) in Harvard's History of Science Department (Figure 8-1).

Having mastered the Old Testament, as it were, we advanced to the "New Testament" of Univac, where each of the 1,000 words of memory was 12 characters long, accommodating one data item or two instructions. Like Mark IV, its central processor occupied a small room accessible by a glass door with a sign: "No Smoking Inside the Computer." Given this magnificent expansion in resources, we were actually allowed to run something. After first meticulously handwriting or typing my program in the machine's native alphanumeric language—not even using an assembler utility—I sat at a glorified typewriter to transcribe it to a magnetic tape. Then I lugged the tape, which weighed ten pounds or so with its metal backing, upstairs to the computer. When it was my turn, I mounted it on one of the ten tape drives and sat at the console to run it, occasionally going into a super-slow mode to catch bugs. Finally, I dismounted the output tape and schlepped it downstairs to the high-speed printer that drummed out the results at two hundred lines a minute, sounding like a machine gun. No OSHA-required ear protectors in those days!

There were similarly hands-on exercises with an Ease analog computer (which one programmed by wiring up the biggest plugboard I ever saw) and a curious hybrid called a digital differential analyzer. The latter's reliability can be guessed from its Northrop nameplate, which sported the typo "NORTHPOP." It would work as long as Al Hopkins was sitting there staring at its oscilloscope screen. Should he but turn away to sneeze, it stopped at once. All this took place in a single semester, and if it seems these moments were the everlasting jewels of my young life, that's exactly what they were. Learning to make these huge complicated machines do exactly what I wanted made me feel powerful and triumphant, as if I were training lions and tigers to do circus tricks. Not many people are lucky enough to have so clear a revelation of what they were born to do.

———⟨∞⟩———

Right after graduation, I got a job with a seminar at Harvard's Graduate School of Public Administration. The task was to program the Univac to simulate fifty years of operation of a water resources system for hydro power, irrigation, and flood control, using historical streamflows for a like period from the Snake and Columbia rivers.

There was a distraction in November 1957 when the USSR launched Sputnik I into orbit. Like everybody else, I gazed up at the chilly evening sky, occasionally catching a glimpse of a fast-moving spark of light as Sputnik caught the last rays of the setting sun. It was clear to me, as to most Americans, that we couldn't just let the Soviets have that domain all to themselves. The Space Race was on, and I felt the tug of its excitement as much as anyone, but couldn't then see any way to get involved.

Keeping my Univac program simple was almost enough to make it effective, but in fact that was my first experience of an application that burst the seams of its hardware-software platform before development was complete. The solution, early in 1958, was to rewrite the whole thing, from scratch, for the giant mainframe computer at MIT. They had an IBM 704 with 32K words of 36 bits each, 144 Kbytes in modern terms—oh, all right, 0.000144 Gbytes in *really* modern terms. (The prefix K, in computer science, means 1,024 rather than 1,000.)[16] This enormous resource was placed at the disposal of qualifying research projects at universities throughout New England. Its gatekeeper, MIT professor "Fierce" Frank Verzuh, operated the facility in a manner more real-world than academic. That was plenty to terrify a new-minted programmer. So, it was with caution that I approached Dr. Verzuh one day to report that I had caught the 704 in a hardware failure. Even then, the oldest wisdom in the book was that wet-behind-the-ears programmers are forever blaming the machine for problems caused by their own logic errors, but I was right.

Switching to the 704 meant it was no longer practical to just type the numerical object code for direct insertion into the machine's memory. For the first time, I had to use a programming language. What MIT provided for the 704 was

UA-SAP3, a symbolic assembler created by Roy McNutt of United Aircraft. McNutt's modest assessment of his work, on the cover page of its programmers' reference manual, was "The probability of undetected bugs in this program differs from unity by the reciprocal of a googolplex." Unlike the physicists programming ENIAC with delusions of infallibility, he was saying the likelihood of bug-free perfection was comparable to that of winning all the world's lotteries on the same day—but I never caught it doing anything incorrect. Later that year, I was persuaded to give up assembly language, with its wizardly feeling of total control over the machine, and rewrite the program in the new algebraic compiler language, *FORTRAN*.[17]

That version finally matured and produced numerical results that were manually graphed and published in an academic volume with five interdisciplinary authors including an economist, Professor Robert Dorfman.[18] As part of the end-of-project festivities, I led the group on a tour of the MIT computing facility in Building 26, the Karl Taylor Compton Laboratory. Bob Dorfman took one look at that up-to-the-minute confection of tinted glass, brushed aluminum, and heavily glazed tiles, and muttered, "Hmphh. Ivy will never grow on that!" It's a stretch, looking back from a time when a fully capable computer can be clipped to one's belt, to picture the new wing, about 100 feet square, added to Building 26 to house the IBM computer and its cadre of IBM field service engineers. It had three walls all made of green-tinted glass, the better to show off this prodigy, with curtains installed that could block it all off. Like all IBM technical personnel at that time, the service engineers wore dark suits with white shirts and conservative ties—but sometimes, when major repair efforts were needed, they'd have to remove their suit jackets! In such a case, they always drew the curtains first, preserving IBM's image as a flawless environment populated by well-groomed, sedate gentlemen.

In IBM's earliest days, Thomas J. Watson Sr. was frequently short of money for the payroll and had to compensate people in part with stock in the company. Endicott, NY, today has a quantity of *very* comfortable houses those employees were eventually able to build. Once the revenues were flowing, Watson brought forward an all-American extension of the Edwardian times he grew up in. Every IBMer had to look prosperous and behave accordingly. Senior employees (including sales engineers) had to belong to IBM country clubs that sprouted near cities with a major IBM presence, where they gathered around the fireplace to sing songs out of the IBM songbook. I've no idea what standards were set for their golfing skills. Harvard was a jacket-and-tie establishment in those days in classrooms and dining halls, but even to us, IBM's corporate culture was off the charts.

My chance to add Rocket Science to Computer Science suddenly came about through a consulting opportunity. One late spring day in 1959, I got a call from a Dan Goldenberg. "I got your name from Dr. Verzuh, who says you have a talent for making 704s behave themselves," Dan explained. "I'm doing a 'moonlight' contract writing a simple little assembly-language simulator program, and it's driving me nuts. If you can spend some time helping me out, I can pay you $5 an hour." Spending spare time earning about three times what my day job at Harvard paid was really OK, and I snapped it up.

Dan's program was a mathematical model to test the design of a "wind shear probe" and its instrumentation, which would be dropped by parachute from a high-altitude aircraft. The probe would use an altimeter and a simplified inertial measurement system to tabulate the force and direction of winds on its way down, particularly the abrupt changes called wind shears. Those who follow air crashes and near-crashes will recognize wind shears as a significant danger, especially near the ground.

"I've got some test data that gets read in from cards, and I know the results I've calculated are right," he told me. "But it wanders away from my results at sort of random intervals, and then wanders back. It's crazy!" Within a few weeks, including only one all-nighter, I solved Dan's problem by realizing that some apparently harmless extra commas in the test-case input data stream were actually harmful. They introduced extraneous zero values, contaminating the legitimate data. His perfectly correct program, being given garbage in, had been responding in the traditional way, by putting garbage out.

Dan promptly offered me a full-time job in the Digital Computing Group he ran in the MIT Instrumentation Laboratory, applying computer science to a variety of aerospace vehicles. He told me the Laboratory had just delivered to the Navy complete GN&C systems for the new Polaris missiles and the submarines that launched them. The new and more challenging job was an Air Force project to send a probe to Mars. Since the Harvard seminar was winding down, I had no hesitation in accepting, and reported to the Lab in September 1959.

The major part of the Lab occupied the old Whittemore Shoe Polish factory at 68 Albany Street in Cambridge. The Grand Trunk Railroad, a freight-car switching line, ran through the middle of the factory's four interconnected buildings, making the whole structure quiver. Its architecture was strictly late nineteenth-century utilitarian brick with hardwood floors decorated with large yellow arrows pointing the way to the stairwells and the exits, and walls painted a sickly institutional green. The manual elevator was a factory type … a huge box of rusty steel mesh giving a good view of large brown messes on the brick walls of the shaft ("Oh right, that must be shoe polish!"). There were no cubicles, just offices furnished entirely in battleship-gray Steelcase office furniture and occupied by one or two or three engineers according to rank and seniority. In the fourth-floor men's room a few doors from my office, drops of water fell occasionally from the ceiling, which would have concerned me except for the facts that (a) it was the top floor, and (b) it only happened during rain.

Just across the hall from the office I shared with two other engineers was the "machine room," heaven in hot weather because computers got air conditioning—engineers did not. The computer there was an IBM mid-size system called a 650, but with some extra features that only MIT could demand from IBM. The machine room was up a couple of steps because of its elevated floor, under which heavy electrical cables interconnected the bulky battleship-gray computer units. IBM didn't re-invent itself as "Big Blue" until years later.

The 650's Central Processing Unit was a robust steel box about the size of three medium refrigerators in a row, containing a magnetic drum memory that held 2,000 words of 10 decimal digits each—equivalent to between 10,000 and 20,000 bytes depending on how much of the data was alphabetic—and a number of remarkably reliable vacuum tubes to perform the logic. The console panel (on one end) included 10 dials, each labeled 0 thru 9, to accommodate manual input of one word, above which was a one-word display in which each digit was

FIGURE 8-2. IBM 650 Magnetic Drum Memory Computer

This system is configured similarly to what we had.[19]

represented by seven small neon bulbs (Figure 8-2). It was surprising how much you could tell about the progress of your run by watching the lights. Occasionally, I saw a programmer staring at the panel with his arms raised like an orchestra conductor, then lowering them in a Leonard Bernstein downbeat just before the output card punch started producing results.

There was a hard disk drive the size of a wide refrigerator, called a 355 RAMAC (Random Access Method of Accounting and Control). Total data capacity was five million seven-bit characters, or about 4.4 MBytes, barely 2% of a Compact Disc (CD) or the smallest 1GByte size of a USB flash drive. It had fifty disks on its vertical spindle and three arms carrying read/write heads, which retreated into one end of the cabinet to move up or down to a different disk. All this was run by an array of heavy-duty relays that made a magnificent clatter— until one of the relays stuck, creating a deathly silence. After a while, somebody learned which relay was the usual one to stick and penciled an X on its part of the steel cabinet. Whenever the deathly silence fell, whoever was nearest would go over and pound the X mark—and the clatter would resume. We loved to do that, especially when visitors were present.

An independent unit, an IBM "519," could duplicate a deck of punched cards, the primary way to make backup copies of our work. It was programmed using a plugboard on which wires steered incoming columns to either the same or different outgoing columns and could do a few other tricks, but for us, it was just a reproducing punch. I was so unimpressed with the badge labeling it a "Document Originating Machine" that I made a similar badge out of cardboard and stuck it on my wastebasket: "Document Terminating Machine."

Another independent unit, an IBM "407" accounting machine, read cards and printed 150 lines per minute, about one-fifth the speed of a modern inkjet page printer, much noisier, and devoid of such luxuries as a choice of font, point size, or color (Figure 8-3a). It too was programmed by plugging wires—their insulations color-coded by length—into a removable plugboard, so that you could change the machine's function by substituting a differently programmed board. Most of the wires associated particular print positions (of which there were 120) with particular card columns (of which there were 80), but some performed other formatting functions such as interpreting a "2" in card column 8 as a command to do double-spacing. The 407's board was exceptionally large, about two feet square, and the nest of wires was one to two inches thick. There could be swooping diagonals, as in one of our boards that shifted columns 9 to 48 of certain cards over into print positions 81 to 120. The arrays of wires, in their eight different colors, made rhythmic contoured patterns of a

FIGURE 8-3a. IBM 407 Accounting Machine

FIGURE 8-3b. Plugboard for IBM 407[20]

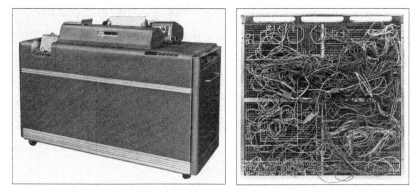

haunting abstract beauty. Such programming was indeed an art, and is now a lost art (Figure 8-3b).

───❄───

Employee orientation at the Lab included getting security clearances. The first level of clearance was *Confidential*, which was perfunctory, followed by *Secret* after a few months. When we newcomers got our clearance badges, the security men told us to wear them at all times inside the buildings and, furthermore, to take them off whenever outside. That last rule didn't make much sense to us, but they pointed out that any restaurant could contain enemy spies peeking at badges to learn who worked at the Lab.

My first supervisor at the Lab was a delightful lanky fellow, Charlie Werner, whose management skills included a wry sense of humor. When he felt something was progressing too slowly, he'd mutter about a universal constant called "the speed of heavy" with a value of $1/c$, the reciprocal of the speed of light. Whenever he caught himself mis-speaking, he had a comic formula: "I got my tongue wrapped around my eyeteeth so I couldn't see what I was saying."

Most of the programming work in our group involved math models testing the latest designs of inertial-navigation instruments that Doc Draper had been developing and refining since the 1930s. We wrote those simulations in a Lab-grown compiler language called *MAC* (MIT Algebraic Compiler). We also programmed trajectory simulations of missiles or spacecraft under development, grinding out numerical-analysis solutions to second-order differential equations.

MAC went miles beyond *FORTRAN* in being useful to Guidance and Navigation engineers. All numbers were kept in scientific notation, a combination of a fraction and a power of ten to keep track of the decimal point automatically. The data types included vectors and matrices to relate the motion-oriented variables to the three axes of inertial space, or to other three-axis coordinate systems. *MAC* source code could also represent ordinary differential equations directly, a feature I never saw in any other programming language. Reading a *MAC* program listing was as easy as reading a math or physics textbook.

Some of the group's programming focused on more computer-science types of tasks, like compiling (translating) *MAC* source language into numerical "object code" that the 650 could run. We wrote those programs in the Lab's own assembler language called *FLAD* (FLoating ADdress), in which each line of source code represented one 650 instruction. The term "floating," in this context, referred to the use of symbolic names for the addresses, leaving it up to *FLAD* to fill in the numerical values in the 650 object code just as *UA-SAP3* did for the 704. As a relatively "deep" computer-science guy, I did most of my 650 work in *FLAD*.[21]

As soon as I was equipped and generally briefed on my new job, Charlie Werner came in to say, "OK, what we need you to do is write a cross-assembler for an unknown number of machines with unknown characteristics." A cross-assembler was no great trick. All it had to do was assemble, on the 650, source code for a very different machine. However, having acquainted myself with a large variety of different computer architectures, I found the part about supporting multiple architectures with "unknown characteristics" a real eyebrow-raiser. Charlie reassured me. "Oh, it won't be quite that bad. Go across the street to Eldon Hall's Digital Development Group and talk to Al Hopkins, Jim Lincoln, and Ray Alonso." That's how I learned that some of the Harvard Computation Lab talent had made the trip downriver to MIT about a year before I did.

They told me that the machines being contemplated were broadly similar, with a fairly small Random-Access Memory (RAM) for variable data and a larger-capacity Read-Only Memory (ROM) for constants and instructions. This ROM technology was a radical innovation, a memory where the program was literally wired in, so that no electro-magnetic disturbance—even a monster solar flare—could erase or change the information. Each instruction word would occupy one addressable location in memory and comprise an operation code and one operand address. These were the "Mars" computers, under development for the unmanned Air Force missions Dan Goldenberg had told me about. They were to be *embedded* control computers permanently hooked up to special inputs like a spacecraft's accelerometers and radio gear to receive digital commands from Earth. They would also be permanently hooked up to special outputs like rocket engine on/off switches and radio gear to send data back to Earth. In 1959, we had no idea they were the immediate ancestors of computers that would guide men to the Moon.

Eldon's group was using another unusual technology called core-transistor logic (CTL), which had the interesting property of being variable in speed. In mission phases where the vehicle is active, each instruction had to be completed in microseconds. During the long months of the interplanetary trip, CTL could cut way down on power consumption by slowing down the processing speed by a factor of a million or more.

The first in the series was called Mod 1A, intended as a proof-of-concept machine rather than an actual vehicle controller. Its memory contained 256 words of 11 bits each, or about 352 bytes in modern terms. Its architecture was minimal, with a repertoire of just three instruction types, compared with forty or more in a regular machine—just barely enough to demonstrate that a CTL machine could work as a computer. Mod 1A was also dubbed the "Christmas Computer" because of an optimistic notion that it and its assembler would be ready to show to an Air Force review team by Christmas 1959. That gave me a name for the cross-assembler that would be my primary labor for the next eight years: "*YUL* system." That wasn't an acronym, just a shortening of "Yule."

My individual efforts would not interpret electrical pulses from accelerometers or turn rockets on and off, nor communicate with Earth. As an assembler utility, the *YUL* system was an essential tool for use by all the Lab engineers whose programs performed those functions. An assembler is somewhat analogous to a publishing house performing copy editing, layout, printing, and bookbinding to bridge the gap between authors' manuscripts and readers' hands.

Converting assembly source code into object code is a

very simple operation compared to the algebraic analysis a compiler has to do. An assembler's first pass through the source code builds a dictionary of the symbolic names created by the programmer, linking each one to a whole number (usually the address of a location in memory). Its second pass through the source language substitutes that number for each occurrence of the symbol. It also uses a built-in dictionary to convert symbolic operation codes to their numerical equivalents, e.g., "AD" to binary 110 for the Apollo Guidance Computer instruction that performs addition. There are a lot more detailed tasks to do, especially catching inconsistencies in the programmer's source language, but that's the essence.[22]

The novel problem I had to address at once was the "unknown number of machines" factor. A cross-assembler program can be a fairly simple thing, but making it support multiple object-machine architectures was unprecedented. Fortunately, the architectures were not so radically different and could be compared to the options available when buying a given make and model of a car. The chassis and the body would be standard, but the powertrain and trim packages could vary. The *YUL* system's "chassis and body" was by far the biggest part. It included the syntax of the source language, the symbol dictionary, the formatting of the object code, and all but a few of the consistency checks. The "options" for different computer architectures included the built-in dictionary to convert symbolic operation codes to numerical form, parameters for the capacity of memory (both RAM and ROM), and rules for special restrictions.

By Thanksgiving, I had amassed about a thousand punched cards of source code, enough to fill half a card box and to produce a listing of some 25 pages ... when disaster struck. I came to work one day and my source code box was missing. After a frantic couple of hours going through desk drawers, obscure corners of the machine room, and everywhere I could think of, I had to sink into my desk chair and face the loss. Sharing the office with two young women, I couldn't let the hurt show too much, but my voice became a croak as it found its way through a wooden throat. My officemates and most of my other colleagues were very sympathetic, but one or two I wasn't so sure of. Was it possible that somebody would want to take me down a peg? Could they want it enough to actually sabotage my project? Some questions are destined never to be answered, and on the whole I'm glad these were among them. With no electromagnetic way to back up my files, I was left with my paper listings and had to punch the thousand cards all over again. That turned out to be quicker and easier than I'd supposed, and I completed the restoration by the end of the month.

Christmas 1959 came and went, but the Mars Mod 1A "Christmas Computer" and the *YUL* system weren't ready. I never personally had to communicate with the Air Force review board, who weren't much surprised nor greatly troubled by the slippage. Being used to much greater overruns from the companies supplying the airframes and avionics for their planes, they weren't expecting any miracles from an academic institution.

By Easter 1960, we'd made good on our new deadline. Source code decks of *YUL* language were getting processed into much smaller load decks of object-code cards, each containing eight numerical words for Mod 1A's ROM. I carried load decks to a separate machine that read them and punched the information into eight-channel punched paper (Teletype) tape, which I then took across the street to load a RAM standing in for the production machine's ROM.

The technicians had cobbled together some demonstration subsystems. One—a small wheel that was painted in quadrants like the spots on a crash test dummy—was rotated at varying speeds. Also, a two-inch pivoted lever represented a rocket engine gimbal to be positioned at various angles. Mod 1A drove them by sending digital pulses to "stepper motors" that turned through a small angle in response to each pulse received.

The Air Force reviewers came, saw, and accepted the key fact: We had fashioned this unfamiliar innovative technology into a minimal but working control computer. They gave us the go-ahead to take the next steps, starting with the upgrade to Mod 1B and incorporating the ultra-durable ROM, which we called a "rope" memory for the stringy appearance of its prototype form.

Mod 1B was a step up in several dimensions. The RAM data memory was 64 eleven-bit words instead of 32, the ROM was 448 eleven-bit words instead of 224, and the instruction repertoire was increased from three to four types by developing an instruction that could add one to a number. For the first time, I had to implement logic in the *YUL* system to notice which object machine was being specified—Mod 1A or Mod 1B—and selecting the appropriate "trim package" to perform model-dependent parts of the assembly. Since the only differences between these two models were larger numbers for the memory sizes and one more operation code in the instruction-type dictionary, my upgrade was complete in a couple of weeks.

Getting ahead of the hardware development gave me time to indulge my curiosity about how the designers in Eldon Hall's group built individual instructions out of simpler logical functions, so I asked Al Hopkins, Jim Lincoln, and Ray Alonso about it. They explained that there were two steps, the first being to organize the action into memory cycles. Most instructions took two memory cycles, one to fetch data from memory or store data into memory, and one to fetch the next instruction from memory.[23]

The second step was laying out sequences of simple actions within each memory cycle to accomplish the rest of each instruction's work. Each action had its turn at using the data transfer "bus" that interconnected all the special-purpose data registers in the Central Processing Unit (CPU). This sort of bus was not an oblong on wheels, though the name comes from the same Latin word *omnibus*, meaning "for everybody" or in this case "for everything." It's the same principle as telephone switching exchanges that organize time-sharing the wires on the poles, making telephone service practical for more than a very few users. A set of twelve wires, one for each bit of a Mod 1 word, carried a whole word of data at a time between any two registers. Using a single, time-shared data bus to interconnect all the CPU registers saved the weight, bulk, power consumption, and cooling requirements of separate point-to-point data paths. Since the data bus was a lot faster than the memory, each memory cycle time was divided into eight "pulse times." In each pulse time, the data bus could be dedicated to reading from a particular source register and writing to a particular destination register.

For a familiar example, I'll flash forward to something that later Mars models had that Mod 1 didn't: an addition instruction. Inside the instruction's data memory cycle, one pulse time used the data bus to copy the contents of the main working register called the "accumulator" (analogous to the number display of a pocket calculator) into one of the input registers for the adder circuitry. Then, a later pulse time used the same bus to copy a data word just obtained from memory into the adder's other input register, starting the addition process. After leaving time for all the carries to settle out, another pulse time used the bus to copy the sum from the adder back into the accumulator.

A computer program is like a book, where each instruction is like a stock phrase having some meaning of its own but not invested with full significance until combined with many others. Similarly, within a single instruction the activity of each pulse time is like one word, and each control pulse is like a single letter in the word.

Regular programming involves laying out sequences of instructions to make a program. This business of laying out sequences of pulse-time actions to make an instruction was called "microprogramming"—and I found *that* arcane exercise to be easily twice as much fun as regular programming. Since we would soon be designing Mars Mod 2, a considerably more elaborate machine that could actually perform GN&C for the Mars mission, the arcane exercise would soon become useful as well as fun.

Al and Ray thought of an ingenious way to familiarize me with the issues. They'd started to design a program to make Mod 1B emulate the instruction repertoire of a much more complex machine, one that had sixteen instruction types including addition. This was a way to try out a variety of instruction repertoires for Mod 2 without having to build actual hardware. It wasn't a complete innovation since such programs, called "interpreters," had existed for other machines. An interpreter had a central logic module to fetch data words from memory and interpret them as the program words of the fictional computer, calling on subroutines to perform the functionality of each interpretive instruction. Al and Ray asked me to write the subroutine for addition, using Mod 1B's minimal repertoire of four instructions. It would be a functional model for the microprogramming of the real addition instruction that Mod 2 would implement. I spent a very happy spring day creating a full page of source code to do that, and refining it by finding ways to save a little time here and a little program memory there. With the low speed and small memory capacity of '50s technology, such things mattered.[24]

What Al and Ray hadn't realized, but which occurred to me while "re-inventing" addition, was a major consequence for the *YUL* system. While this particular interpretive language was created to help design the next computer generation, the same tool could be used to solve another problem. Part of the MIT culture, and the Lab culture in particular, was that the rocket scientists would do all their own programming as a matter of course. However, very few of them had enough computer-science training to be happy or effective in assembly-level coding of embedded control computers with their rather cramped logic design. They would do much better with a logic design that knew what vectors and matrices were, and where they wouldn't have to keep track of all the tricks for using two words at a time to hold data in double precision.

J. Halcombe "Hal" Laning, a founding father of guidance mathematics at the Lab, had outlined an interpretive language to meet these needs. It became clear to me that most or all of the "unknown number of machines" would need an interpretive language as a friendlier dialect for control system engineers to program in. They'd use it wherever it made sense to trade speed of execution for simplicity of programming, in navigation as opposed to flight control, for instance. All other interpretive languages of the day were all-or-nothing affairs, in the sense that the source code for a given programming project was either entirely interpretive or entirely in the machine's "native" instructions. In spacecraft GN&C, the two kinds of program would have to coexist in memory, both in the form of object code. Some words would contain native instructions that the machine could execute directly, and some would look like instructions but actually be data for use by the interpreter program.

Suddenly, *YUL* source language for each type of real machine would have to be a combination of two source languages, one representing the real machine's repertoire and one representing the bigger and fancier repertoire of the corresponding emulated machine. I had to tune the language syntax to allow stretches of interpretive code to coexist with native code, though not quite seamlessly, as certain protocols had to be followed when changing modes. My rules for checking consistency had to expand to enforce those protocols. Of course, each of my "trim packages" had to have a second built-in dictionary and another whole syntax scheme for interpretive code. Clearly, my preliminary "baby" *YUL* system would have to undergo a growth spurt.

Having realized the depth of interdependence between the hardware and software sides required for rocket-science purposes at that time, I had two hats firmly on my head, one labeled "The *YUL* System Company" and one labeled "Apprentice Computer Designer." Heaven and the Lab are the places where such things can happen.

Joining the design table for Mod 2, I found that Al and Ray had sketched plans for a machine with words of 23 bits plus a parity bit for checking, twice the 11-plus-1 length of Mod 1 words. In the instruction words, there was enough space to define 32 instruction types instead of 4. We probably weren't going to implement so many because there might not be physical space or power supply for that much logic circuitry. From our joint knowledge of typical commercial computers of the day, we picked out a useful set of instruction types that weren't too complex logically, enough to determine what special-purpose registers the Mod 2 CPU would need.

After that process, all the immediate design problems to be solved were in electrical engineering, so I turned my focus back to the software side, upgrading *YUL* to handle the mixture of interpretive and native code. The larger memory in Mod 2 made me expand the symbol dictionary to a size that had to use the 650's hard disk. To get good performance in a program that made frequent references to that rather slow disk, I had to develop a kind of search indexing, similar to what we see today when Googling, to ensure that looking up each symbolic name would get the right disk block the first time, every time ... well, almost every time.

⌒⊗⊗⊗⌒

James S. "Jim" Miller had become one of the Lab's bright lights after serving two years in the Air Force at Cape Canaveral, engineering guidance for the Redstone rockets later used to boost Mercury astronauts into suborbital flights. He came to MIT primarily to get a PhD in, well, rocket science. His thesis presented a guidance scheme for a spacecraft that would take a camera into a low orbit around the Moon. It would use a long-lived but tiny engine, just about the lowest-powered rocket imaginable. I was assigned to Jim to shepherd the development of his *MAC* program to test the scheme on the 650. That meant I now had a third hat, labeled "Apprentice Rocket Scientist."

This minimalist spacecraft, weighing about a thousand pounds, would be carried into Earth orbit piggybacked on a regular satellite and released to make its own way to the Moon—very slowly—and insert itself into a low Lunar orbit. The propellant would not be burned as fuel. It was just a tank of liquid hydrogen with a throttle-valve to meter it into an engine-bell chamber where an electric arc would boil it. As hot gas, it would have enough pressure to accelerate the spacecraft, though very gradually. The electric arc would be produced by a Radioisotope Thermoelectric Generator—the same type of energy source left on the Moon by Apollo astronauts a decade later to power the permanent scientific instruments they installed there. The only thing one could call "fuel" was a container of plutonium-238, an isotope with a long radioactive half-life, which would serve as a long-lived battery to power the arc. This engine, designed to produce one quarter of a pound of thrust, was informally designated "Mausfahrt" (German for "Mouse Trip") in comical reference to the German engineers in our space program, as well as to suggest just how small the thrust was. Its developers went so far as to send a deadpan letter to the U.S. Bureau of Standards, asking for a "calibrated mouse."

The designed flight profile, as seen from the celestial North Pole, resembled a very stylized letter 'S' with the Earth in the middle of the large lower loop, the Moon in the middle of the small upper loop, and a huge number of spiraling turns connecting those middles to the loops. The Mausfahrt vehicle, starting from a low stable west-to-east Earth orbit, would turn on its engine while heading east and gradually enlarge that orbit, the engine firing at full throttle (such as it was). Each successive orbit, being larger, would take longer to complete. The initial 90-minute period would grow into multiple hours and days, eventually reaching a place where the weaker Moon's gravity just balances the Earth's gravity, about 71% of the way, 170,000 miles from Earth. There the vehicle would turn 180 degrees, making its engine a retro-rocket, gradually shrinking its Lunar orbit. When it would get down to the intended altitude, the engine would shut off, leaving the vehicle in a stable two-hour Lunar orbit.

My most challenging task in this project was verifying that our digital modeling techniques were adequate to simulate the designed flight profile. The hazards were the numerical instabilities allowed by the barely adequate precision of eight digits that the 650 maintained.[25]

One difficulty with the GN&C of any Lunar spacecraft is that even in its simplest form involving the gravity of only the Earth and the Moon, it's the famously intractable "three-body problem," for which the equations of motion are differential equations that can't be solved by algebraic methods. Where textbook-style calculus cannot provide a solution, a computer can "nickel-and-dime the problem to death." The differential equations that describe the motion are approximated by "difference equations," not so very different from the ones Babbage's difference engine was designed for. They are solved by a finite number of calculations of small straight-line motions, each occurring over a small but definite "time step."

Modeling continuous variables by sequences of straight-line approximations brings about a tradeoff between the fidelity of the math model and the propagation of rounding error. Make the time step too big, and the fidelity of the model suffers because the approximating assumption—that all motions within each time step are linear—is too far from the truth. Make the time step too small, and the rounding errors add up fast enough to destroy too much of your precision. I ultimately found a "Goldilocks time step"—neither too big nor too small—allowing calculations that kept eight digits of precision to produce a believable model of the flight.

I had felt previously that eight-digit precision (one part in a hundred million) was ample, but this exercise made me think sympathetically of the young Howard Aiken in the '30s struggling with his slide rule's three-digit precision, one part in a thousand at best—no wonder he built 24-digit precision into Mark I, knocking the effect of rounding errors into the next county. Grappling with this problem gave me a highly detailed sense of what GN&C computers had to be good at, thus nourishing my Computer Designer hat.

Having thus become familiar with how the Lab's control system engineers used (and abused) *MAC*, I was able in odd moments to help them in an unexpected way. I had an irregular daily rhythm of work, often working at night to avoid the too-many interruptions by colleagues during regular hours. Compiling a large *MAC* program could take some hours, and was often done in the evening to be looked at and hopefully run the next day. From my desk I could hear the 650 punching output cards, and I'd keep a corner of an ear out for that sound. If the first brrump was followed by brrump, brrump, brrump regularly for a while, that was OK ... the compilation was complete and the object code was being punched out. When the punching stopped, I'd go pull out and rubber-band the object code cards and put them in the box with the submitter's source code cards. Then, if I knew other compilations or runs were waiting, I'd get the next run going—a volunteer night operator role. But if the first brrump was followed by an ominous silence, or just a few more brrumps at odd intervals, I knew the compilation had failed and the cards being punched were error diagnostics.

In that case, I'd pick up all the engineer's cards and go print the source code on the 407, then the error cards. Because *MAC* was so easy to read, I could often figure out with a high degree of confidence how to fix the language error. I modified the source code accordingly, always disclosing my intervention by inserting a comment, "This fix supplied by the Uneeda Debugging Service." By taking the cards with the repaired code back to the 650 for another compiling attempt, I was able to save many people a whole day at a time. The slightly taunting name was not quite original with me, just an obvious variation on Cape Cod's Uneeda Termite Service, which supplied termite traps to my parents' vacation house in Dennis, Massachusetts.

***

In the summer of 1960, the Air Force finally sent firm specifications for the weight, power consumption, and physical size allowed for the computer in their Mars probe. Those specs exceeded our expectations, and not in a good way. The instruction repertoire would have to be cut down by more than half, and even the word length with a 24-wire data bus was too much. Mod 2 became a paper monster—a quantity of fat folders in a filing cabinet—and we downshifted to a more modest concept, Mod 3.

So what smaller number of bits would still be a good word length? In any real-time computer system, the key elements connecting physical reality to digital numbers are Analog-to-Digital Converters. In GN&C systems specifically, the measurement of angles had to be accurate to about one hundredth of a degree, or one fiftieth the diameter of the Moon as seen from Earth. Storing angle values as fractions of a circle has the advantage of treating, say, $-270°$, $+90°$, and $+450°$, as all the same value, which for practical purposes they are, and it saves time in calculating trigonometric functions. The number of hundredths of a degree in a circle (36,000) is close to the number (32,768) of combinations of 15 bits. Fortunately, Analog-to-Digital conversion technology for angles was accurate enough to achieve that precision. For a machine that is to "eat its own tail," in Charles Babbage's phrase, an angle value thus expressed seemed a reasonable "portion" size to become our less ambitious word length, so we decided on 15 data bits plus a parity-check bit for Mod 3.

Navigational variables like velocity, position, and time were known to greater accuracy and so required greater precision, about eight decimal digits. Two of our 15-bit words could represent that precision if paired as a "double-precision" item. Our weight-power-size budget allowed for a repertoire of eight instruction types, a bare minimum but just manageable with a little ingenuity. That left us with enough memory addresses to access 4,096 words, almost 8 Kbytes in modern terms. That seemed ample, compared to the sizes of control computers we were used to. We allocated 512 addresses to RAM, and the rest for ROM.

My apprenticeship seemed to be over, so I started acting like a Journeyman Computer Designer and took on the task of specifying Mod 3's instruction repertoire and designing its implementation. The basics, omitting division because Isaac Newton's method using only additions and multiplications approximated it well enough, were straightforward in principle:

✔ Load the accumulator from memory

✔ Store the accumulator contents in memory

✔ Do both of those at once to achieve an exchange

✔ Shift data left or right (one bit at a time)

✔ Add data from memory to the accumulator

✔ Subtract data from memory from the accumulator

✔ Multiply data from memory by the accumulator, preserving a two-word product

✔ Transfer control to an arbitrary location in program memory

✔ Transfer control conditionally based on sign and zero-ness of the accumulator

✔ Edit a word of data to isolate a subset of bits within it ("masking")

✔ Input data from spacecraft subsystems

✔ Output data to spacecraft subsystems

It was all very well to list the basics in this way, but it left some problems unsolved. For starters, this list had twelve items instead of the eight required. Three functions could be achieved without using operation codes, by giving certain RAM addresses special properties for input, output, and shifting, as Al and Ray had done with Mod 1. Ray's approach delegated the initiative for most input operations to the subsystem interfaces, so that they "pushed" data (to borrow the modern Internet term) into the RAM. That was very efficient, but it turned out years later to be vulnerable to a rogue interface, the Rendezvous Radar logic that caused such excitement in Apollo's first lunar landing.

Al built a somewhat obscure trick into one of the CPU central registers to eliminate the need to devote an operation code for masking. All that brought the list down to eight, but it didn't cover two things that had to run especially efficiently in the new design. Within a program loop, we needed a way to make certain instruction words address different memory locations at different times, essentially applying the subscripts that distinguish the X, Y, and Z components of a vector. For example, a vector of three single-precision words might be stored with the X component in location 1234, the Y component in 1235, and the Z component in 1236. Applying subscript values of 2, 1, and 0 to an instruction addressing location 1234 would access each component in turn. The program loop's logic would handle one component per iteration, in the order Z-Y-X. Such looping also needed a conditional transfer of control that could decide by counting when to repeat the loop and when to exit.

I had to reach into every corner of my experience with the Univac and the IBM 704, and of my computer architecture studies. Subscripting, or operand address modification, can be achieved by the brute-force method of picking up an instruction word, adding to it an address modification quantity (i.e., a subscript), and storing that result into a memory location from which it will be executed. Some machines, like Univac, offered no other way, making the processing of a vector, or any array of numbers in a loop, painfully clumsy and slow. Some machines such as the 704 did it the modern way, by devoting a few bits in the instruction word to identifying a special CPU "index register," the current value of which was added to the base address coded in the instruction without any extra steps in the program.

But in a 15-bit architecture, none of the instruction-word bits could be spared to specify such standard indexing. So I borrowed a trick from a now forgotten computer architecture called G-20, from a now forgotten computer company, Bendix.

It was an instruction that fetched a data word from anywhere in memory, added it to the address of the normal next instruction, and executed the result as the next instruction in place of the unmodified next instruction in memory. Suddenly a machine with no index registers could use *any* location in memory as an index register, at minimal cost in running time and program memory. I named that instruction INDEX and for simplicity of design let it do a whole-word addition, so the operation code field (to the left of the address field) could also be affected. That last point came in handy a year later.

IBM's 704 supported loop control by an instruction type that did some serious multitasking. It tested (for zero) one of the index registers used in the loop, subtracted one from it, and transferred control back to the beginning of the loop in the non-zero case. I adapted this approach to the Mod 3 context by providing only one conditional transfer of control, and making it multitask the same way on whatever data the INDEX instruction was using in the loop. I named this Swiss-Army-knife instruction "CCS" for Count, Compare, and Skip. It skipped over one or more instruction words if the data it fetched from memory was zero or negative, and left in the accumulator a number one less than the absolute value of that data. The instructions that might or might not be skipped over were usually unconditional transfers of control, especially one that sent control back to the first instruction in the loop. Programmers who completely understood CCS loved it, and the others hated it with a passion—but they learned.

Introducing the INDEX and CCS instruction types brought the count to nine, so I removed the subtract instruction and packed its sign-changing property into the data fetching instruction by making it always change the sign of what it fetched. That wasn't as bad as it first appeared because addressing ROM with an *exchange* instruction obviously couldn't perform the writing part, and so behaved like a straight data fetch for constants. But I'd created another love-hate situation for those who found it tedious to take two steps to load the accumulator from RAM, one to obtain the negative of the data and then another to change its sign back. My answer was "OK, which other instruction type would you be willing to give up?"

When I wrote up my instruction set design and the microprogram to implement it, I got a reaction from Al Hopkins I wasn't looking for. I'd gone to some effort to make the multiplication instruction develop a double-length product for generality of purpose. If the inputs and the output were considered to be fractions, with their significant bits clustered at the left end of the words, the *upper* half of such a product would be the single-precision answer. If the inputs and output were considered to be integers, with their significant bits clustered at the right end of the words, the *lower* half of the product would be the single-precision answer. The double-length product also made it easy and efficient to multiply double-precision words by performing three regular multiplications and a few additions.

Al felt the multiplication instruction was a frill, since it's not very hard to make a slow multiplication out of add and shift operations. In terms of the Mars mission, he was probably right to estimate that such a slow method would be enough. In any case, he named my design Mod 3C (for Complicated) and wrote up a variation with a masking instruction instead of the multiply, calling it Mod 3S (for Simple). But he agreed to keep both designs in existence, deciding to develop Mod 3S first to be sure of having something to show the Air Force, and then consider upgrading to Mod 3C.

With that, Al and Ray and the rest of the Digital Development team set to work on Mod 3's electronic design. Occasionally they'd call me in to discuss changes to my preliminary microprogram, mostly to refine input, output, and special laboratory interfaces for testing. I got very busy adding two new object-machine modules to the *YUL* system, sharing a Mod 3 "powertrain" option but with slightly different "trim packages" distinguishing 3C from 3S.

———◦∞◦———

While this work was going on in the early spring of 1961, we were transfixed by the April 12 flight of Yuri Gagarin—a Soviet cosmonaut in orbit before any of our Mercury astronauts had so much as a sub-orbital Redstone ride. Suddenly, our Mars probe seemed much less significant, not in the same league at all. We had no hint that in six weeks President Kennedy would sweep it away and put us—the country and the Lab—on the fast track to the Moon.

III

APOLLO: 1961–1975

9

REALPOLITIK AS BACKGROUND FOR THE SPACE RACE: 1945–1961

"These things are so damn dangerous, they're safe," observed a Pentagon sage after V-J Day in 1945. This reference to atomic bombs combined with the means to deliver them summarizes the internal contradictions of the incipient Cold War. If one side had the bomb, the other side had to have it too, as a deterrent. Each side had to spend profligate sums to develop better and more jam-proof means of delivery than the other, in addition to building bigger and more fearsome bombs. Leaders on both sides knew they could never under any circumstances wield such weapons, yet had to hide that knowledge under the deepest of secret coverings. A deterrent that lacked credibility was no deterrent at all. The resulting arrangement, with credible deterrents on both sides, was called Mutual Assured Destruction, all too aptly abbreviated as MAD.

But before there were two superpowers facing off, there was just one nation, the United States of America, ranking as a working superpower after the general ruin of World War II. "Superpower" is a term that gets thrown around a lot without much thought to what it means or why it had to be coined in preference to "great power." My definition involves three factors: an enormous economy, a huge population that can be effectively deployed under arms, and nuclear weapons (since 1945). A superpower is able, and is to some extent obliged, to exert influence over much of the globe. How the second superpower arose, and how the terms of the faceoff developed, created the conditions for a space race.

The Soviet Union seemed an unlikely superpower candidate in 1945. Her vast population was remarkably diverse, and her economy was a backward jumble bleeding everywhere from wounds inflicted by communist ideology. Yet the war had little impact on her natural resources, and she had a large collection of good quality, American Lend-Lease war materiel, shipped in to Archangel around the north end of Scandinavia through waters infested with icebergs and German submarines. The Russian population was united in the pride of having repulsed a major well-equipped invasion for the fourth time in two and a half centuries: Sweden under Charles XII in 1708; France under Napoleon in 1812; the German counter-offensive under Wilhelm II in 1918; and Germany under Hitler in 1941. Militarily, her grievous losses were offset by an influx of nuclear technology secrets leaked by a few Westerners who were much more worried about a continued American monopoly than about what the Soviets might do with "the bomb." And the USSR had her own collection of German rocket scientists from Peenemünde to counterbalance those whisked away to America in Operation Paperclip.

In some ways, Soviet Russia in the mid-twentieth century

was not so different from Czarist Russia in the mid-nineteenth century: a vast nation of people with no freedom but an inexhaustible endurance. There were ample natural resources, a sprinkling of exceptional talent in music, literature, and mathematics ... and a huge inferiority complex. Russian leaders since at least Peter the Great understood that their country was generally disrespected and often invaded as a consequence. With his back covered by China—which was well on its way to becoming a communist and, therefore, friendly country—Stalin took the opportunities in Korea and in central and eastern Europe to build a buffer of client states around the USSR. Any future invader would have to cut through a lot of non-Russians before threatening the homeland.

As a pre-teen in that period, I had a brush with political correctness. My family was visiting my father's mother and stepfather, the latter a successful Wall Street banker with rightist politics to match. One night at dinner, he asked me, "Hugh, what do you think about what's going on in Czechoslovakia?" A tension built in the room, so I knew my answer would have some importance that I didn't understand. I just gave a straight answer, "Uncle Joe [Stalin] seems to be making a lot of unnecessary trouble," and the tension melted away. Eventually I understood that the question was a litmus test on whether my left-leaning mother, the lone Democrat in that Republican household, might be distorting my perceptions of political reality.

Lenin, adapting the Communist Manifesto of Marx and Engels, had created the Soviet drive to attain national relevance as the globally recognized leader of worldwide revolution by the working class. The effort had made a lot of noise but hadn't gotten much traction. Stalin saw a chance to seek postwar relevance in what had been, despite decades of hyperbolic boasting, Russia's most backward dimension—high technology. He was confident of having nuclear weapons soon, and his German rocket scientists would help create missiles to deliver them. The USSR could become, militarily at least, a superpower.

After Stalin's death in 1953, his successors realized that although nuclear-tipped missiles would be very effective weapons if actually used, there seemed to be no way in that situation to still have a world in which to be a leader. Perhaps somebody in the Kremlin also said, "These things are so damn dangerous, they're safe." They must have realized that parading missiles through Red Square and running a few demonstration tests might establish the fact of a deterrent, but wouldn't provide the USSR with any glamorous credentials in world-political leadership. In 1955, Sergei Korolev, building on his prewar role as the USSR's Goddard, saw how to shape his lifelong fascination with Tsiolkovsky's futuristic research and dreams of voyages to Mars into a workable answer.

American initiatives in space in the mid-'50s—mostly a few tentative moves toward participation in the International Geophysical Year (1957–1958)—provided an opening for the USSR. Korolev reasoned that a peaceful Soviet space program, if pushed forward with much greater energy and dedication than America's, could showcase the might of Soviet missile boosters in an ongoing leadership role that didn't involve missiles. The world (even including some in the West) could cheer multiple Soviet achievements without ever quite forgetting how those boosters might be used in anger.

Korolev sold the Sputnik program to First Secretary Nikita Khrushchev in 1957 as an energetic entry to a space race that the USA had so timidly begun. The world political prestige reaped by Sputnik I that November turned out to be everything

Korolev had predicted. Khrushchev embraced it as a way to proclaim to the world that Soviet communism was the wave of the future and the decadent old West was doomed to irreversible decline. He converted space technology from an American monopoly to a full-scale race.

President Dwight Eisenhower, understanding the need to make some response, refurbished the World War I era National Advisory Committee for Aeronautics ("the N.A.C.A.") into the National Aeronautics and Space Administration ("NASA") in 1958. The new agency was defined as goal-oriented instead of research-oriented. NASA awarded and managed contracts to get things done and brought in missile technology people from the Armed Forces, while maintaining the agency's civilian nature. The era of disappointing "snake killers" had already begun months before with the explosion of the Naval Research Laboratory's first Vanguard booster, and continued while NASA learned how they had to exert close supervision on contractors. Most of the failed launch vehicles fell over when rocket engines exploded on liftoff, with the remaining engines sending the horizontal vehicles at high speed through the subtropical vegetation of Cape Canaveral, where snakes were known to be abundant.

Explorer I and a few other satellites, including a grapefruit-sized Vanguard, successfully reached orbit, but the failures in full public view were embarrassing. Scientists who had worked for years on spaceborne experiments began to wonder if their careers would last long enough for them to see their projects actually at work in orbit. Everything we achieved seemed much less than what the Soviets were doing and occurred somewhat later. It's useful to recall that NASA's first manned program, Project Mercury, was started just to get an American into Earth orbit, with no thought of its being the first step toward a manned mission to the Moon.

In 1958, President Eisenhower refused to back a mission to the Moon on the grounds that "We don't have any enemies there." By contrast, the just-inaugurated President Kennedy in 1961 demanded that his aides find "something we can beat the Russians at." His intuition of *realpolitik*, more than any passion for space technology, drove the decision to create Apollo. Thus Kennedy did not start the space race, but he changed it from an open-ended affair (like an arms race) to a contest for a specific goal—a contest the USA could win.

At MIT, my participation in the timid beginnings leapt onto a new platform. Now it was all about building computers that would play a key role in shaping twentieth-century history, giving reality to William James's 1910 forlorn hope, "a moral equivalent to war."

ARCHITECTURE OF THE APOLLO
PROJECT: 1961

During 1961, NASA quickly parceled out responsibility for major components of Apollo to the appropriate centers. These were mostly spread out along the Sun Belt, from launch facilities at Cape Canaveral, Florida, in the east, through booster development at Huntsville, Alabama, to astronaut headquarters and mission control in Houston, Texas, to the spacecraft prime contractor, North American Aviation, in southern California. MIT's New England location, as the home of the prime contractor for Guidance, Navigation, and Control, felt especially distant to NASA's Manned Spacecraft Center people in Houston—a distance partly geographical and partly cultural.

Marshall Space Flight Center (MSFC) in Huntsville acquired the ill-tempered nickname of "Hunsville" because of the concentration there of Wernher von Braun's Peenemünde V-2 team, many of whom had been Nazi party members at least in name. But the value and quality of what they were doing soon put any such reactions to rest, justifying the somewhat irregular laundering of their biographies by Operation Paperclip fifteen years before. Just pushing fifty years old when he'd been made director of the new MSFC in 1960, von Braun was at the peak of his powers. MSFC was effectively a rebirth of the Army's Redstone Arsenal, which had been the center for military rockets. It seemed fitting that our first manned space flights were boosted by an advanced version of the short-range Redstone rocket.

Initially, American boosters, like early Russian boosters, were repurposed missile launchers. Aside from Redstone, used for the suborbital flights of Alan Shepard in May and Gus Grissom in July, there were the intercontinental models Atlas and Titan. Atlas boosted the remaining Mercury flights into orbit, starting with John Glenn's exciting mission where it wasn't clear that his retro-rocket pack had separated correctly to expose the heat shield. The larger Titan was assigned to Mercury Mark II, the program that was soon renamed Gemini for its primary feature of putting two-man crews into orbit.

The first new booster development at MSFC, and the first dedicated to peaceful manned space flight, was the Saturn. Its original concept was a four-stage rocket, with a provision to use just the first and fourth stages for Earth-orbital missions, reserving the four-stage version for flights to and around the Moon. When President Kennedy upgraded the Apollo goal to *landing* on the Moon, analysts figured that a much bigger rocket would be required. Taking educated guesses at what breakthroughs in rocket engine design would be required, they sketched out a design called Nova and estimated it could be ready for use in 1970. That was a clever name because it left an opening for an even larger successor to be called Supernova. At the same time, the Soviets were starting the design of an enormous booster called N-1, for which they finessed the engine breakthrough issue by specifying an array of 24 "normal" rocket engines, later increased to 30 to allow for successful operation even after failures of several engines. For the nearer term, MSFC studied many alternative designs for the Saturn. In the original four-stage model, called C4, the fourth stage, with its single Rocketdyne J-2 engine packing 232,250 pounds of thrust, was the first to go into detailed design and was named S4 or S-IV. That name stuck after MSFC simplified the C4 into a three-stage design by combining the second and third stages into a second stage called S2 with five J-2 engines, and later adopted the name Saturn V for the whole stack.

As director of MSFC, Wernher von Braun had to go to NASA HQ in Washington to present the new second-stage design. A young man in the program management office looked up from a checklist on his clipboard and asked von Braun, "How many nines on the Saturn II stage?" The question sprang from the postwar American fascination with *metrics*, simple-looking numbers that express something significant about a product, in this case the reliability. If a product has three nines, its reliability is 0.999, meaning that you'd expect one failure in a batch of a thousand samples of the product. Or, since only about twenty such boosters are going to be built, the probability of failure in any one would be $\left(\frac{20}{1000} = \frac{1}{50} = 2\%\right)$. In terms of the young man's checklist, that percentage wouldn't be quite small enough to inspire full confidence. Something less than 1% would be better, and much less than 1% would be really satisfying. The questioner wasn't going to be content with anything less than four nines, nor entirely happy with less than five.

"I don't know," von Braun answered, "but when I get back to Marshall I'll find out and call you." What von Braun *did* know was that measuring reliability in this way is realistically applicable only to mass production situations where actual failures in a large population of samples can be counted. There were textbooks full of formulas for calculating the reliability of small sample populations, by combining realistic numbers for components such as nuts, bolts, wires, and welds into an overall system number, and that's what the questioner had been studying in program management courses. Having learned reliability from the real world, von Braun knew that any numerical answer to the question, regarding a stage of the Saturn booster, would be meaningless. Under his direction at Marshall, every component, every process, every subassembly underwent rigorous inspection for quality and margins of safety. The goal was not satisfactory statistics but perfection, as close as human skill and care can get. He was too courteous to dispute with the young man and figured out how to educate him gently.

Back in Huntsville, he made some phone calls to several close colleagues—or maybe he didn't actually make them because he knew it wouldn't yield any information he didn't already have. Then he phoned Washington. The NASA official heard von Braun's answer as "five nines," which he understood to mean the impressive reliability figure of 0.99999.

"That's fine," said the official. "How did you arrive at that figure?"

"Well," answered the director in his German accent, "I called Walter Häusserman in The Astrionics Lab and asked him, 'Are we going to have any problems with this stage?' He answered 'Nein.' Then I posed the same question to Karl

Heimburg in the Test Lab and he also said 'Nein.' I kept at it until I got five neins."

The special irony of this story, from my point of view, is that a Saturn II stage *did* suffer a partial failure years later, during the only Apollo launch that I was at Kennedy Space Center to witness—an unmanned test flight, fortunately.

For the structures of booster stages, MSFC contracted with airplane builders Boeing and Douglas. IBM Federal Systems Division designed a computer and suite of navigational instruments for the Saturn. Their Instrument Unit (IU) occupied otherwise unused space at the payload end of the Douglas S-IV (later S4B) stage. The stage's structure had to be cylindrical to support the spacecraft, but the forward end of the fuel tank inside was dome-shaped, leaving plenty of room for a GN&C system in the form of a ring. The IU was thus in a position to control any combination of booster stages, provided the S4B was on top, next to the payload. To assure reliable operation in a high-vibration environment, there were three copies of IBM's Launch Vehicle Digital Computer (LVDC), with two-out-of-three voting circuits on all the outputs. In the event of a glitch in any of the computers, the voted outputs would maintain continuous control, uninterrupted by any effort to identify the failed LVDC copy.

At MIT, the Lab teamed up with NASA Manned Spacecraft Center people to pick subcontractors: General Motors' AC Spark Plug Division to manufacture the inertial instruments; Raytheon's Sudbury Division to build the Apollo Guidance Computer; and Kollsman Instrument for optical instruments. In all cases, we would carry the design through Class A drawings, which have the force of law, or maybe commandments.

Richard Horace "Dick" Battin, an MIT professor of aeronautics as well as one of Doc Draper's inner circle, formed the Space Guidance Analysis group. Their first task was to determine the outlines of a Lunar mission, trading off speed, energy consumption, and reliability. Limiting the duration of the mission was clearly a priority, eliminating the infinitely patient approach of the Mausfahrt concept. An early principle made the bulk of the trip a free-return trajectory, meaning that the approach to the Moon's neighborhood had to allow for a failure of the main propulsion system. In the worst case, the Moon's gravitational field would whip a passive spacecraft around its far side onto an unpowered path home. That decision, combined with energy minimization by leaving rocket power off throughout the vast majority of the mission, resulted in a finding that the trip would take about three days each way.

At first, NASA made a principle of the complete autonomy of inertial navigation to defeat any attempt by the USSR to jam radio or radar signals between the spacecraft and Earth. Since even the finest gyros would drift enough to become a concern after half a day or so, we had to include celestial navigation instruments in the suite and set up the computer to read their angles and align the gyros on demand. Eventually, NASA accepted the idea that the Soviets, being in a space race with us, would never do unto us what they wouldn't like us to do unto them. That made it possible to assign the ultimate navigation backup duties to ground-based radar, but it didn't eliminate the need for a space sextant because the vehicle's attitude in space was still critical for aiming rocket burns. Radar is good at finding distance and direction, but it can't tell much about its target's orientation.

————— ⨳ —————

North American Aviation (NAA) was naturally pleased to be the spacecraft builder but furious at the fait accompli regarding MIT. As an accomplished builder of airplanes with well-instrumented cockpits, NAA management felt they should have been prime contractor for everything inside the craft. In 1961, there weren't a lot of decisions made about how the complete Moonship would look, but there was a consensus about the shape and general size of the ultimate re-entry part. NASA's brilliant designer Max Faget had convinced everybody of the advantages of the "gumdrop" shape for absorbing the heat of re-entry and maintaining stable flight through the increasing air densities. The Mercury capsule was a somewhat elongated gumdrop because of its small diameter, but the Apollo shape was a better gumdrop because it had to be wide enough for a crew of three.

It certainly wouldn't be practical to send a lone astronaut on a weeklong trip to the Moon. Somebody would have to be in charge while he was in the bathroom, never mind about sleeping time. With a crew of two, the same concern arose for flight phases in which there'd be too much for one man to do. Thus, the minimum size for crew was three. For the high-g phases, acceleration during boost and deceleration during re-entry, each of the crew would have to be supported by a form-fitting couch. To allow all three to see the main control panel, the couches had to be aligned in parallel, with scant walking space between. NAA placed the couches with their headrests near one wall, the one with the access hatch, to optimize the crew's view through windows as well as ease of exit after splashdown. The couches and main panel together took up about two-thirds of the interior volume of the gumdrop, leaving space for a kitchen and workshop in the other third. That area was called the Lower Equipment Bay because it was located "below" the crew's feet while they were in their couches. The smallest gumdrop that could accommodate this configuration was the best size for the Command Module (CM).

A three-man re-entry vehicle could get all the electrical power it needed from batteries, provided they'd been saved for that final phase. Some other module of the spacecraft—the cylindrical Service Module (SM)—would have to generate electricity for the rest of the trip, and the most efficient technology would be fuel cells combining hydrogen and oxygen. Like calculus, fuel cells had been invented almost simultaneously in Britain and Germany—Welsh physicist William Grove published just one step ahead of Christian Friedrich Schönbein in 1839. By the 1960s, they had been refined so that the two gases, injected under pressure into a chamber containing an electrolyte membrane and a catalyst, combine according to the familiar H_2O formula to form nearly pure water, while releasing the energy of the reaction in the form of electricity. The water is drawn off into tanks with the aid of the chamber pressure. Each individual cell generates a voltage of just over half a volt, so they are built into a fuel cell stack with enough series connections to obtain the desired voltage and enough parallel connections to supply the desired current. The only drawback to fuel-cell water—still noticed by astronauts in the International Space Station—is a sprinkling of hydrogen bubbles that don't quite get combined. It has an odd soda-water taste that takes some getting used to.

A CM fastened (until re-entry) to an SM, with electrical and plumbing connections between them, made a viable long-term spacecraft suitable for a trip to and around the Moon and back. The combination was named Command & Service Module (CSM) and included a medium-size rocket engine, called Service Propulsion System (SPS), at the other end of the SM from the CM. All that left a tremendous question unanswered. If we'd committed to put Americans on the Moon and bring them back before the end of the decade, how could we succeed if the Nova booster wasn't going to be ready until 1970? Even in the Moon's one-sixth gravity, a rocket capable of launching a spaceship big enough to bring men and treasure home to Earth would be a large, heavy object. Its Lunar launch pad would be another heavy object, and both those items would have to be landed softly on the Lunar surface, using large (and heavy) amounts of fuel and oxidizer for retro-thrust.

A radical solution existed. Initially, however, it existed only in the minds of a minority band of advocates of the Lunar Orbit Rendezvous (LOR) approach, fortunately led with indefatigable energy by John Houbolt of NASA's Langley Research Center. The idea was to add a third module, a lightweight two-man spacecraft that would separate from the CSM in Lunar orbit and land on the Moon. That part would consist of a sturdy Descent Stage able to withstand a retro-rocket-controlled landing, and on top of it an ultralight Ascent Stage to carry two astronauts and their Lunar souvenirs, which would need only a small rocket to lift off easily from the moon's one-sixth gravity and enter approximately the same orbit as the CSM. Finally, it would rendezvous and dock with the CSM, still a quarter of a million miles from home. Houbolt, never one to submit to protocol when it was getting in the way, had gone over his superiors' heads with this proposal on May 19, 1961 (just a week before President Kennedy put the challenge to Congress), and was politely ignored—for a while. The Soviets made the ignoring more difficult in August, sending Gherman Titov up for a full 24-hour day, 17 orbits. By the end of the year, Houbolt marshaled his arguments into a formal proposal, emphasizing the key point that the LOR approach would make the Saturn V an adequate launch vehicle and eliminate the need to spend billions on the even more gigantic Nova rocket, just getting started on the drawing boards.

The proposal circulated everywhere throughout the project, spurring debate and contingency planning. By mid-1962, he obtained acceptance of his apparently risky approach by convincing everybody that all the most significant risks—landing on the Moon's rough surface and then lifting off without the aid of a heavily manned Launch Control Center—had already been accepted. The only operational element he was adding, rendezvous and docking in Lunar orbit, was an art that could be practiced and perfected in Earth orbital missions. That art soon became the main focus of the Gemini program.

Thus was the Lunar Excursion Module (LEM) born, with its Descent Stage serving as the Lunar launch pad for the Ascent Stage. NASA dropped the word "Excursion" in 1966—hence "LM," but still pronounced "lem." The change was partly because "excursion" seemed too frivolous a word for such serious business, but that was also when exploration analysts started to imagine wheeled vehicles being taken along that would better deserve the word—the first hints of a Lunar Rover. Even with two manned vehicles defined, the total crew of three would still be enough, since two would descend to the surface and explore while the third would ride the Command

Module (CM) in a stable Lunar orbit, not having much to do except monitor subsystems and maintain communications. The adoption of LOR and the definition of the LM finally cleared the room of its elephant—the concept of an impossibly large unified spacecraft that would have had to travel from Earth to Moon, land, stay for exploration time, then lift off enough of a spacecraft to get crew and equipment home. With that daunting prospect out of the way, the engineering floodgates loosed a torrent of design. The LM contract went to Grumman Aircraft Engineering in Bethpage (Long Island), New York. North American Aviation filled out the SM concept to supply the CM with high-gain radio communications and four quads of RCS jets for attitude control, as well as electricity, water, and the SPS rocket engine.

At MSFC, this change lifted a huge burden off the rocket engineers. Instead of having to develop the Saturn and Nova rockets in parallel, they left the Nova concept in its file cabinet and focused on getting the three-stage Saturn V ready by 1968, or possibly even 1967. Developing the Rocketdyne F-1 engines, at 1.5 million pounds thrust each, and making five of them work together in the S1C first stage, would be challenge enough.

With *two* computerized manned spacecraft to develop, MIT's job instantly doubled, and so (MSFC aside) did much of NASA's. Now we had to supply a Primary GN&C System (PGNCS) for the LM as well as the CM. Fortunately, the two systems could be alike in many key respects. The same computer hardware design could serve both, though with different software. The Inertial Measurement Units could be identical, and both systems could communicate with astronauts in a similar way. To avoid ambiguity, we coined the abbreviations LGC for LM Guidance Computer and CMC for

CM [guidance] Computer, reserving "AGC" for the computer type that could be installed in either spacecraft. Having gone to all that trouble, we found that most people went on saying "AGC" instead of "CMC," and I'll do that a lot in this book.

NASA introduced the *block* paradigm to keep this doubling of engineering and programming under control. The first generation of systems—Block I—would be devoted to developing Earth-orbit capability for the CSM. During that time, Grumman would design the LM and prepare it to accommodate Block II systems. Once the Block I engineering was complete, a generation of upgraded systems with Lunar mission capability would go into a Block II CSM in parallel with the LM.[26]

At the heart of the PGNCS in each spacecraft was the AGC, which had to lead the teamwork of all these ingenious devices. And I found myself at the heart of the AGC development— one foot on the hardware side and one on the software side. I could say I was overwhelmed and humbled by this situation, but I'd be lying through my teeth. Right place, right time, right skills ... Lady Luck just doesn't arrange these things any better. Anyway, there wasn't any time for humility. We had to get that thing going!

There was a little time, however, to look forward to 1968 as a year in which U.S. manned spacecraft should be plentiful and triumphant—maybe even achieving the Lunar mission before 1969—and to celebrate the prospect in one of my parody lyrics:

Sing a song of megabucks, a rocket full of π:
Four and twenty astronauts, blasted through the sky.
When the hatch is opened, the taxpayers will cheer—
Now isn't that a helluva thing to do in election year!

Space Race Highlights of 1961

(All manned flights are indicated in bold.)

31 Jan	Mercury-Redstone 2. Suborbital flight. Crew: Ham (chimpanzee).
12 Feb	Venera 1. Venus flyby (no data). Unmanned.
21 Feb	Mercury-Atlas 2. Suborbital flight. Unmanned.
09 Mar	Korabl-Sputnik 4. 1 orbit. Crew: Chernushka (dog).
25 Mar	Korabl-Sputnik 5. 1 orbit. Crew: Zvezdochka (dog).
12 Apr	**Vostok 1. 1 orbit. Crew: Yuri Gagarin.**
25 Apr	Mercury-Atlas 3. Aborted after lift-off. Unmanned.
05 May	**Mercury-Redstone 3. Suborbital flight. Crew: Alan Shepard.**
25 May	President John F. Kennedy announces manned Moon trip within decade.
21 Jul	**Mercury-Redstone 4. Suborbital flight, crew Virgil "Gus" Grissom.**
06 Aug	**Vostok 2. 17 orbits. Crew: Gherman Titov.**
29 Nov	Mercury-Redstone 5. Suborbital flight. Crew: Enos (chimpanzee).

Other flights where a vehicle (often a missile) entered space, mostly suborbital:

USA	291
USSR	179
UK	18
France	18
Italy	8
Japan	8
Australia	1
Total	**523**

Of these, 24 went into Earth orbit. Country names identify where payloads were made. Most boosters were made by USA or USSR.

Astronauts – A New Interface for Our Computers: 1962

In contrast to the relatively familiar celestial mechanics of flying to the Moon, one of our early challenges in Apollo was the presence of a flight crew—astronauts—in "our" spacecraft. While never doubting that their presence was the whole idea of the project, we had to figure out what they were going to do and how they were going to do it. The initial positions on this point were far apart. We'd have been content, for the most part, to have them sit back and leave the driving to the AGC. Their preference was to control everything, just like an airplane.

To illustrate the gap between these opposing views, a Lab artist drew a pair of famous cartoons of the three-man crew in the Command Module (Figures 11-1a and 11-1b).

The "automated" image was partly a sympathetic comment on the astronauts' feelings about having so little control over the computerless Mercury spacecraft, of which three performed orbital flights in 1962: John Glenn in February, Scott Carpenter

FIGURE 11-1a. Astronaut Involvement in a Fully Manual Spacecraft

FIGURE 11-1b. Astronaut Involvement in a Fully Automated Spacecraft [27]

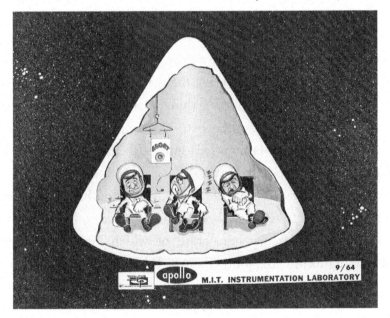

in May, and Wally Schirra in October. The cosmonauts in Vostok 3 and Vostok 4, who orbited simultaneously in August, also had no digital computers, with consequences I discuss in Chapter 15.

I went so far as to make a frivolous suggestion that the ship's complement of three humans and one computer could play bridge in idle moments. To simplify things, the computer would take the dummy role after bidding was completed. The best rejoinder to my notion was a firm reminder that astronauts do not play bridge, but poker. My other disregarded brainstorm was a compact printer that would use edible paper to eliminate waste-paper problems—surely the CIA could have supplied something?

The first principle settled was fly-by-wire, meaning that everything the crew wanted the spacecraft or any of its moving parts to do would be mediated through the AGC. There would be no mechanical cables as a backup.

The simplest and most intuitive controls, derived from the control stick in antique airplanes, were hand controllers similar to joysticks but big enough to wrap a gloved hand around. They became known as "pickle-sticks" for the buttons embedded in them. When moved, they produced streams of digital pulses that incremented numbers in the AGC's memory and triggered interrupt signals to make the computer interpret the numbers and perform whatever combination of rocket firings would execute the astronaut's command.

The crew would have to do autonomous position finding— and refresh the fine alignment of our gyros—several times during each flight. For that, the CM needed a space sextant. On a ship, the navigator wielding the sextant is ideally accompanied by an assistant with a watch. When satisfied with the coincidence between the horizon and the reflected star, the navigator calls "Mark!" and the assistant immediately notes the time to the nearest second. The navigator reads the angle off the sextant's arc, making the raw data complete and ready for workup. In the Apollo CM, the computer would play the role of assistant and more. Instead of speaking, the navigator would press a Mark button, alerting the computer to read the time and the sextant angle electronically, then instantly work up the sight. Because the angle data from the sextant usually had the purpose of refining the gimbal angles of the IMU, those two units were attached to the same rigid frame in the Lower Equipment Bay to ensure that any bending of the spacecraft structure could not vary the relationship between those angles.[28]

To support general data communication, Eldon Hall's group had to design user interface equipment. It had to display data, along with a few single-purpose indicators, and provide a way to enter data, along with a few single-purpose buttons. Since compact graphical displays and the computer speed to run them were a long way in the future, the display had to be numerical and very limited in size. NASA's analysts and the astronaut office agreed that five digits and a sign were enough for display and input of each number, a precision of ten parts per million. The equivalent of five decimal digits is 17 bits, so of the 28 bits the AGC kept for each double-precision navigational variable, the last 10 or 11 bits could be considered as a cushion to soak up rounding errors. We thought six digits would be a mathematically valid precision based on the accuracy of our instruments, but the astronauts would rather have five, so that was that.

Since many of these numbers came in groups of three to express vectors, the display unit had to present three signed five-digit numbers of pure data, plus some short numerical codes to show the current operational modes. Each digit was displayed as seven electroluminescent segments like those in many electronic household clocks. The segments, a restful green to protect night vision, were switched on and off by compact relays blessedly silenced by being sealed in thin glass tubes for contamination proofing.

Input had to be done with a limited number of keys large enough for use by heavily-gloved hands, reinforcing the feeling that short numerical codes would be the best way to identify mission phases and the data being displayed or entered.

The unit combining these functions was named DSKY for Display and Keyboard, with the convenient pronunciation "Disky." One was on the Main Panel facing the three couches, at the right hand of the Commander, who sat in the left seat. Another DSKY was in the Lower Equipment Bay, near the sextant.

The relationship between the astronauts and the AGC was richer and more various, and more in need of efficient and unambiguous communication, than any man-machine interface preceding it in the annals of real-time control. The crew had to exchange data with the AGC about dozens of mission phases, variables, and settings. There were no touch screens nor any feasible way for them to type commands rapidly (with heavily gloved fingers at times). And there was no way for the AGC to understand spoken commands.

The top-level information was clearly the current mission phase. Prelaunch, boost, Earth orbit, trans-Lunar Injection, trans-Lunar coast, mid-course corrections, Lunar orbit insertion, Lunar orbit, descent, Lunar stay, ascent, rendezvous, and so forth, made a list longer than 9 and much less than 100, so a two-digit numerical code looked reasonable. We started calling it "Major Mode" but that was too many letters for the label on the display, so we settled on "PROG" for Program.

Ray Alonso reached into some obscure corner of his broad knowledge and thought about the simplest possible grammar, containing only verbs and nouns. The nouns were straightforward to think about: attitude and instrument angles, velocities, accelerations, times associated with events, even AGC memory addresses. Verbs were easy to start with: display, monitor, enter, update, actions like engine firings. We found that considerably fewer than 100 verbs and 100 nouns would cover the needs. Two-digit verbs and two-digit nouns made up the numerical grammar we offered as a stopgap model until we and the astronauts could think of something better. NASA personnel in general, and astronauts in particular, objected to the academic flavor and perceived complexity of this scheme— at first. As they gradually worked through the topics of the man-machine interface, they found themselves concluding that all *other* schemes were much more complex and error-prone, so the "stopgap" solution became permanent. And not entirely incidentally, "VERB" and "NOUN" made nice readable four-letter labels for their parts of the display.

These decisions filled out the display part of the DSKY. Directly above the three rows of five-digit data displays were a pair of two-digit displays for VERB and NOUN. Above the NOUN part was a two-digit display for PROG, and above the VERB part was a green square labeled "COMP ACTY," again meeting the four-letter-word standard. The square was lit during computer activity, that is, whenever the AGC was working on a job or jobs, and dark when the AGC had nothing substantial to do until the crew commanded something.

William Shakespeare probably would have liked the idea that one of the nastiest speeches by one of his most deep-dyed villains should turn up in the "script" for a machine that would guide men to the Moon. In *Henry VI Part 2, Act IV, Scene 2,* occurs the famous line spoken by Dick the Butcher, a thug in the service of wild revolutionary Jack Cade, "The first thing we do, let's kill all the lawyers," which Cade agrees is a good idea. That quotation sets the stage for further excesses by Cade, a bloodthirsty nemesis for learning of all sorts. In Scene 7, a butthead named Bevis hauls in a captive, Lord Say, an educator who (in actual history) founded a school of grammar. In his indictment of Say, Cade charges, "It will be proved to thy face that thou hast men about thee that usually talk of a noun and a verb, and such abominable words as no Christian ear can endure to hear."

That last quote appears in the introductory comments to a group of AGC routines named "Pinball Game—Buttons and Lights," that control the DSKY. A number of people thought I must have been the one bringing the Shakespeare quotation into the source code—maybe because of my Harvard degrees—but no. It must have been one of Eldon Hall's user-interface specialists, or maybe that polymath, Ray Alonso.

Below the display appeared the keyboard. Its keys were buttons about an inch square, partly for a surer touch in high-vibration periods, and partly to be operable with heavy gloves. They had therefore to be limited to the ten digits, two signs, VERB and NOUN, ENTER and four lesser-used functions—but no decimal point. That rounded out the "pinball game." We called it that, not from any real resemblance to pinball, but because pinball games were the buttons-and-lights experience we'd all had while wasting time at college-town sandwich shops.[29]

FIGURE 11-2. AGC and its Display and Keyboard (DSKY)[30]

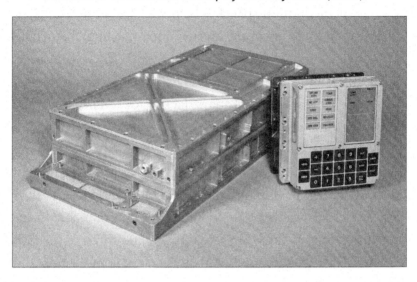

The DSKY's image frequently appears in literature about Apollo because it was the visible face of the AGC, a much more interesting face than the boring oblong metal box identified as the computer by us central processor nerds (Figure 11-2).

In retrospect, it should have been obvious that two-digit codes for programs, nouns, and verbs would have great advantages for conveying detailed information tersely and unambiguously, without an undue burden of learning. Think of the diagnosis codes that doctors put on orders and all the "noun codes" peppered through TV cop shows ("We've got a 179 at 10th Avenue and 42nd Street"). A few codes even lent themselves to abbreviated pronunciation: program 00, pronounced "pooh," named the inactive state, appropriate enough for A. A. Milne's *Bear of Very Little Brain*. Dave Scott, who eventually commanded Apollo 15, summed up the usability of the verb-noun syntax by observing, "… even pilots can understand it."

RAMPING UP THE COMPUTERS: 1962

Eldon Hall's Digital Development Group (DDG) quickly realized that renaming Mars Mod 3C as AGC3 was only the first step toward a real AGC, and the scramble to find upgraded technology was on. The upgraded AGC still had to fit into a volume of one cubic foot, which sounds daunting when considered in an era when computers of similar capabilities took up cubic yards. However, the Lab had plenty of experience in extreme miniaturization, both in the Polaris missile program and in research for the Mars probe. It wasn't even too much of a problem to allocate the volume to one baseplate with cooling and two complete copies of the computer, a requirement that came along a little later to ensure in-flight repairability. The AGC also had to consume less power than one sizeable light bulb of 100 watts.

First, the AGC's program was going to be at least three times the size we'd anticipated, and it all had to fit in the fixed memory (ROM). The volume of data to process would be double what we'd anticipated, and it all had to fit in the erasable memory (RAM). No magnetic media (tapes, drums, or disks) would be small enough, light enough, or reliable enough to put in a spacecraft, so there was no alternative to increasing the capacity of our memories without increasing size or weight. Ray Alonso, having originally teamed up with Hal Laning to find the core rope memory technology for the Mars computers' ROMs, now started working with Jack Poundstone and the other Raytheon engineers who had just become our partners. They soon upgraded the mechanical design of the core rope memory modules so that we could triple the fixed memory rope capacity from 4K words to 12K. On the RAM side, they worked out how to cram twice as many of the tiny ferrite cores and their wiring into the same packaging, doubling the erasable memory from 512 words to 1K.

The enlarged fixed memory had a problem: the address field in the instructions was still only twelve bits, which was capable of addressing 4K words total. Since we had devoted the first quarter of that range to addressing erasable, the number of addresses usable for fixed actually decreased to 3K. Joining the design table, I drew on my experience with commercial computers to support the idea of borrowing the area-code concept from the telephone industry, organizing 10K of fixed memory into banks of 1K words each, electronically selectable by a new central register named BANK. We made the remaining 2K words addressable independently of the bank selection, giving them the oddball name of "fixed-fixed" as a short way to express that property. Fixed-fixed would contain code and constants that would need continuous availability.

Al Hopkins joined Eldon in finding ways to at least double the processing speed of the electronics while substantially increasing its reliability. AGC3's Core-Transistor Logic (CTL) was pretty well maxed out performing 20 KIPS (thousands of instruction executions per second*), but we needed 40 or 50 KIPS. KIPS were still respectable in the 1960s, a time when the MIPS (M for millions) we now enjoy in our phones were only a subject of research. In any case, the ability of CTL to run arbitrarily slowly to save power—an advantage in the Mars mission with its long months of near-idleness—wasn't relevant to the Apollo mission's one-week timeline. Eldon's contacts in the military led him to consider Fairchild's scary new technology called *integrated circuits*, sitting right on the "bleeding edge" of electronics. Such circuits were just starting to be put into missile electronics. Al and Raytheon's Herb Thaler did the calculations to establish approximately how many would be needed, how they could be packaged and interconnected, and how long it would take to redesign the AGC with them.

We're all very blasé now about chips containing millions of transistors and resistors, but back then we'd always worked with individual transistors and resistors as separate parts to be assembled. It was a brave thing to contemplate three transistors and four resistors on a single chip, sitting inside a little top-hat-shaped can with six legs, braver still to bet the whole farm on it. Early adoption of something with virtually no track record in real-world applications seemed in some ways to be an insanely desperate notion. On the other hand, it looked like the only technology that would deliver the required specifications.

There were several things going for the new devices. Their switching time, under a microsecond, was about five times as

---

*In processing speeds, "K" means "about a thousand" rather than representing an exact number.

fast as the core switching in AGC3's CTL. They implemented a simple but powerful Boolean function, a three-input NOR gate, whose output is a one *only* if all three inputs are zeros (A nor B nor C). Aside from being the simplest three-input function to build, NOR is a "universal" function, meaning that all the Boolean functions can be built using reasonable quantities of just this one circuit type. Eldon's group had considerable experience, from Polaris missile logic circuits, with quality assessment of transistors and control of their manufacturing. That experience would transfer neatly to integrated circuits, especially with just one type to worry about.

Eldon, Al, Ray, and Herb took a radical approach to assuring reliability: getting vendors to dedicate a whole production line to circuits for the AGC, with careful inspection by our own experts. DDG engineers Dave Hanley and Jayne Partridge would pull frequent random samples off the line, open the metal cans, and examine the chips under a microscope. Any flaw in size, shape, or placement of the tiny slivers of metal and silicon would result in a meeting with the vendors to scrap compromised chips and solve the problems. Some of the possible problems had intriguing names, like Purple Plague (a contamination/corrosion problem) and Wiggly Leg Disease (a mechanical vulnerability to resonant frequencies excited by electrical signal patterns). They developed this process to address the extraordinary reliability goal for Apollo spacecraft logic circuits: *They shall not fail ... ever.* That's a striking statement even today, but think how extreme it was at a time when many computers were taken down approximately daily so that maintenance engineers could go around replacing burned-out vacuum tubes. Like any goal, there was no way to guarantee it 100%, but our fanatical approach to quality control did ultimately achieve zero failures in flight.

Eldon, his DDG engineers, and the Raytheon engineers put all these preparations together and formed a united front to persuade NASA to accept their recommendation. Adding weight to their arguments was the Kennedy deadline, since nobody could take a line like "Let's watch these things for a couple of years and then decide." Eldon and his "army" admitted that there was some risk in going to such a new technology, but showed that all the alternatives were riskier. Remarkably, NASA soon accepted that view, and the little TO-47 cans, each about the size of the pushbutton at the upper end of a good-quality ballpoint pen, joined the program. During that first year, we consumed about one-third of all the integrated circuits there had ever been.

To ensure sturdy reliable wire connections that would endure the shock and vibration of the aerospace environment, we made most connections by miniaturized welding rather than soldering, adapting the "welded-stick" construction of the Polaris Guidance Computer. In places where welding wasn't feasible, mainly interconnections between modules through a backplane, we adopted a fairly young technology called Wire Wrap, in which the bare end of each wire was wrapped around a square post so tightly that the post's corners cut into the wire. For prototyping, we used a tool like a power drill to make and unmake the wraps. Later, we used a computer-driven machine made by Gardner Denver for production wrapping.

Memory speed was less of a problem than logic speed, and settled in at 12 microseconds for parallel transmission of each 15-bit word and its parity checking bit. On the fixed memory side, that was conservative even though it had to allow for the more complex mode of addressing and longer wire runs to bring the bits out through a larger rope. On the erasable side, it allowed for a suitable pause between the reading and writing parts of the memory cycle time,[31] as required for the efficient input of pulses from controls and instruments. As each pulse arrived, it "stole" one memory cycle from whatever program was running. It accessed whichever erasable location was dedicated to that input, and the AGC would read that word, add or subtract one according to the type of pulse, and write the result back, all in the one memory cycle. To give any instruction type the flexibility to address either fixed or erasable in the simplest possible way, we made those cycles the same duration, and made the data from both kinds arrive at the same microsecond within the cycle.

The faster circuits and faster memory together made a new microprogramming architecture, in which every memory cycle time contained twelve one-microsecond pulse times, each capable of transferring a word of data from one central register to another. That was three times as many as in AGC3. To use this architecture, we had to do all the microprogramming over from scratch. Simple instructions like addition couldn't use all those pulse times because they were limited in speed by memory, one cycle to fetch the data and one to fetch the next instruction—but now those two cycles would take 24 microseconds instead of the AGC3's 40. Multiplication could take advantage of all the pulse times and would take barely one-seventh the time, 96 microseconds instead of 640—and a lot of the value of a control computer is in its multiplication speed.

With the AGC's *programming* architecture thus up for grabs, I put my designer hat on again to sit with Al, Ray, and Herb. For the new model's architecture, which we called AGC4 to keep the model numbers going, we could have just kept the AGC3/Mod 3C instruction repertoire and made it run faster, but there weren't enough programs in existence for that computer to make compatibility much of an issue.

But the slowness of doing division by a software subroutine, thousands of microseconds, was looking like a serious problem. I wrote microcode to perform division as simply as possible, while still making it use a double-length dividend to support division of fractions or integers or double-precision words fairly efficiently. It also developed a remainder, often useful for its own sake when dividing integers, and essential as an intermediate result in a subroutine to divide double-precision numbers. It took a whole memory cycle time's worth of logic to develop each bit of the quotient, but the total for the instruction was only 192 microseconds, just twice the time to multiply. Bringing this microcode to the design table caused something of a sensation. "You did what?" Happily, I was able to show that the amount of logic capacity to be used wasn't excessive because the steps of a division are exactly alike except for the counting logic to make it stop after developing 14 quotient bits.

Al, Ray, and Herb looked at it and scratched their heads and looked again. Herb asked, "What does it do when some dumb program tries to divide by zero?" Most computer designs tested for that condition and set an exception flag for the program to test.

I admitted, "Division by zero will certainly produce useless data, shifting dividend bits off to vanish in the mythical 'bit-bucket,' but it won't stop the machine or trap it in an endless loop or anything dire like that." I paused, then dropped the other shoe. "It's not just about zero. Any case where the divisor's magnitude is equal to or less than the upper half of the dividend will also drop data into the bit-bucket and deliver useless results." Ignoring the frowning faces around the table, I continued, "Remember, the great thing about dividing binary numbers is there's no chance of getting trapped in a loop. For each quotient bit, you subtract exactly once and either keep or discard the result, depending on its sign. Anyway, all our programmers have to do manual scaling of all the numbers all the time, since we can't give them floating point. A divide error looks a little uglier aesthetically than some others, but any bug is a disaster." The frowns started easing off, and I reminded them, "That's why AGC programs have to be rigorously tested by digital simulation—it'll blow the whistle on bad divides, bad adds, bad anything, long before any of the code sees an actual AGC."

Al finally gave judgment. "Well, it might work. But if we're going to have a divide, we're going to have a subtract too, so we can say we've got the big four." I didn't tell him I'd also been studying the binary-number form of Horner's method for square root. That's the one that looks almost like long division, and may still be taught in some schools. I was ready to build a square root instruction that worked almost like division, but figured it might consume too many logic circuits and I should probably shut up while I was ahead. In retrospect, that feels like a mistake. It would have been a very useful and cool feature, and years later it would have been great fun to pressure IBM into including it in the Space Shuttle computers.

Now we had designs for some nice new instructions but had to deal with the limited size of instruction words where there were still only three bits to make eight operation codes. Or were there? I saw a way in which it could depend on how we regarded overflow. In most computer programming, overflow is a Bad Thing, a case of creating a number that just doesn't fit. Anybody who has kept a car going well beyond its design life may have encountered overflow in the odometer, when it runs out of room to show the total number of miles and starts over at zero. In a computer, overflow appears as an extra output from the adder circuit, a carry-out bit that either corrupts the sign bit or has no place to go. But in the AGC4 design, there was a place it could go, temporarily. In memory, only the one bit at the left end gave the sign of the number (0 for plus and 1 for minus), but the accumulator and some other central registers kept two copies of the sign bit. Normally those two bits would be equal; however, in a central register receiving an overflowing result from the adder, the left one would still be the correct sign and the right one would hold the extra carry bit. As the unofficial ambassador of the software people to the hardware people, I was always concerned that double-precision arithmetic should be fast and compact. I created this two-sign-bit scheme in AGC4 for the benefit of double-precision addition, so that a single instruction after the addition of the lower halves would look at the resulting sign bits and set up the carry (or lack thereof) for inclusion in the addition of the upper halves.

One of the things the adder circuit had to do was add a subscript value to an instruction, the essential function of the INDEX instruction type. While we were working with AGC3, we thought of this addition as being concerned only with the 12-bit address field. During the AGC4 design cycle, a sudden inspiration set me to muttering, "Wait a minute! Suppose the data fetched by INDEX includes some bits at the left end—the operation code field—that produces an overflow result when added to the unmodified next instruction's op code field. What comes out of the left part of the adder circuit would look like a four-bit op code instead of the normal three bits, thereby *doubling* the number of possible instruction types. It's like a Shift key doubling the number of different characters selectable by a keyboard."

I took this thought to the design table, where Al said, "What a greasy little trick—how typical of you!" But he was smiling, because it did solve a big problem. However, our budget for logic circuits wouldn't allow us to fill up all the possibilities, so we chose three operations to be *extracodes* accessed in this way: multiplication, subtraction, and division. Multiplication had been part of the original AGC3 set, but we needed to reassign its three-bit op code for a bit-masking instruction that people could use without having to look up the obscure method of masking we'd built into AGC3.

It would have been nice to be able to say that we'd designed a computer with just the right capabilities for its role in the Apollo Command Module but, really, we had no way to be certain. The mission software was just getting started, and almost all of that was still in the form of *MAC* programs to develop the algorithms, revealing very little about how big the program would be and how fast it had to run. We had simply designed all the computer we could fit into the volume and power constraints, as custom-designed to the application as we could make it. If that wasn't going to be enough, we'd have to deal with it later.

The sheer size and complexity of doing Apollo GN&C, triggering this prodigious growth in the spacecraft computer, also required a major upgrade to our mainframe computer. The IBM 650 was not part of a product family, so there could be no significant increase in speed or data capacity with any kind of compatibility. There were many companies building mainframe-type computers for scientific computation, and the one we liked best came from Minneapolis Honeywell. Its architecture was very appealing to serious computer science folks, and the company got credit for having responded capably to a nightmarish accident a decade previously.

In the early '50s, Honeywell had dipped its first toe into the computer field by partnering with Raytheon to produce a monumental vacuum-tube dinosaur of a machine called the Datamatic 1000. In its central registers, the storage of a single bit required a circuit module about the size of a toaster. It featured magnetic tapes three inches wide, spooled on heavy-duty aluminum hubs that could almost be spare wheels for early Volkswagens. They sold only a few, one to the Baltimore & Ohio Railroad, where it occupied a whole floor of their headquarters building. Their on-site Datamatic field service engineer, who was in appearance and manner perfect for the role of a smart but low-ranking U.S. Navy sailor in a World War II movie, came in 1962 to lead the Honeywell field service team at our site. He told us about the day B&O's rooftop water tank burst and sent water coursing down through the huge air-conditioning ducts that cooled the D-1000. Thousands of the computer's toaster-size electronics modules shot sparks as torrents of water shorted all the circuits. Water fountained out of the machine's ventilation holes, loaded with bits of glass from hot vacuum tubes shattered by the sudden cooling. It was a sight to give any engineer the willies. Honeywell stepped up and performed a long cleanup and restoration process, during which time the B&O trains ran "manually."

When Honeywell got ready to go it alone, they focused on designing a machine that worked somewhat like the "multi-core" processor chips becoming predominant today. PC buyers who want to keep up are now moving from dual-core chips to quad-core chips, and there are a few hexa-core and even octa-core processors. The H-800 got its name from being sort of an early octa-core machine, though there was no way it could actually include eight copies of the Arithmetic/Logic Unit (ALU), which came in two parts, one the size of the narrow corridor in a sleeper train car, and one the size of a deep master-bedroom closet for two. The only things there were eight of were cache memories and a few status bits, all of which time-shared the ALU, the 32K-word main memory, and eight magnetic-tape drives. Its word length of 48 bits allowed for powerful instruction types, each doing as much work as two or three 650 instructions, and data words that kept about 50% more precision. Working with that word length would have made the Mausfahrt project a great deal easier. With a state-of-the-art coincident-current core RAM, the H-800 ran 40 to 100 times faster than the 650.

The mainframe selection committee included Dan Goldenberg as head of the Digital Computing Group and Hal Laning as Doc Draper's resident god of computer science. Their first priority after making the selection was awarding a contract to one of Dan's former colleagues, Phil Hankins. Phil's small consulting company, PHI, had written the *MAC* compiler for the 650 and so was perfectly positioned to port it to the H-800. The goal was to make the transition to the new computer seamless for all the engineers writing in *MAC*, and that was achieved, quicker than I would have thought possible. As our assembly language *FLAD* created object code only for the 650, we assembler-level artists just started using *ARGUS*, the assembler supplied with the machine by Honeywell.

Like PHI with *MAC*, I had to port *YUL* to the H-800, modifying it to use high-capacity magnetic tapes for mass storage instead of a disk drive. All programs would continue to originate as decks of punched cards, and the cards would remain on file as an ultimate backup, but the default home for both source code and object code was tape. In addition to the porting, I had to create a tape file management system. Users could provide complete new programs as decks of cards, or they could update a named program by providing just enough cards to define the update. One of the odd bonuses of the mainframe upgrade was the ability to give programs, and the variables within them, eight-letter names instead of just five. Alphanumeric data was stored in six-bit characters, eight to an H-800 word. I was able to give the ported *YUL* system an ample symbol table of eight thousand symbolic names in the memory, with some search indexing to make each lookup find a match for a symbol by examining no more than a dozen entries, usually. The assembly process had three outputs. One was the updated source code on the new file tape. One was the printed assembly listing, showing source code and finished object code together (along with "cusses" about errors). The third was the binary form of the object code, written further down the new file tape, after all the source code files.[32]

Ever mindful of the possibilities of corrupted information on such file tapes, each engineer kept a set of three generations of his or her tape: the current version, its "father" (the immediate backup version), and its "grandfather" version. Naturally, the word "son" got applied to the current tape, leading to quasi-devout references to Father, Son, and Holy Ghost tapes. Maybe that was a truly devout prayer for divine protection of the precious source code within.

The new *YUL* system used two temporary working tapes in addition to the input and output tapes, so one of my challenges was to arrange the activity so that every tape ran at its full speed as much of the time as possible. The H-800 architecture provided an elegant way to achieve that goal by exploiting the parallel processing of the eight cores. I created for each tape its own little "para-program" running in one of the cores, to achieve an effect like what is now called *pipelining* in processor chips. A para-program in charge of reading a tape would always read one record ahead and buffer it in memory until it was needed. A para-program in charge of writing a tape would collect ready-to-write records from buffers in memory. This arrangement decoupled the relatively slow operations of the tapes from the faster internal processing, eliminating all waiting except what the ultimate limits of tape speed imposed. For a hyperactive young artist in a still-new medium, exploiting this feature was pure catnip. Making four of the eight cores play together felt a little bit like composing orchestral music. The mood is captured in a comment I put into my source code to introduce a routine that handed off buffered data records from one core to another: "This is the dance of the index registers, and a right merry whirligig it is too ..."

Besides my work on *YUL* and Phil Hankins' people on *MAC*, my good friend Dick Warren was building a simulator program to enable exhaustive testing of AGC programs on the H-800 long before an AGC even existed. All these efforts reached the stage where they needed some testing about six months before the H-800 was delivered to the Lab. All but the smallest computers then were built in factories more or less on demand, like the way airliners are still built. So another advantage of the H-800 to us was the location of Honeywell's factory in the neighboring town of Brighton. Our machine was made available to us on a sort of beta-test basis while it underwent months of testing. We ran our programs and then had to figure out which malfunctions were in our code and which were faults in a not-fully-checked-out machine.

RAMPING UP EVERYTHING ELSE: 1962

Doc Draper and his lieutenants knew the Lab's real estate was pretty well filled before getting the Apollo contract, since there were ongoing Air Force and Navy projects. The sudden expansion to parallel development for two spacecraft made it even more imperative to acquire an additional building and devote it to Apollo. Transitioning to the new mainframe computer would certainly be simplified by having it delivered to the new building. Staffing up was also a priority, and placing the new people in a new building would save a lot of hassles.

At 75 Cambridge Parkway, down the Charles River not far above the dam with the Science Museum, was a suitably modern ('50s) riverside building, all rigidly rectangular in form. It was occupied in part by Itek Corporation, which had just vacated the first and second floors while staying in the third. The square footage seemed right, the price was OK, and the only major problem was that it more or less floated on landfill. A wide bay of the river had been there a century before, when the name Cambridge Port meant what it said. Vibrations from road and rail traffic could disturb testing of our ultra-sensitive inertial instruments, so we had to make a large square hole in the ground-floor slab and build a pillar down to bedrock to support the test gear in the Hybrid Lab, so named because it integrated the instruments with both analog and digital computers.

There was one logistical problem. Itek was still doing Top Secret work on optics for spy satellites, which made access to certain shared areas such as the lunchroom a little tricky. An arrangement of doors and guards and schedules was worked out so that Itek had their turn at the lunchroom and the staircases, and we had our turn. That only lasted for a few months until Itek moved out altogether, and we expanded (Eldon Hall's Digital Development Group in particular) into the third floor. Parking was also a mite limited: about eighteen slots beside the building (reserved for high-ranking folks), about ten usable curb spaces in front, and not as many as you'd think in back because a branch of the Grand Trunk Railroad ran within inches of the back wall. Everybody else had to forage for curbside spaces throughout the Lechmere area of East Cambridge, fortunately not as aggressively built up as it is now.

Aside from the Hybrid Lab, the other significant upgrade on the first floor was the raised-floor computer room, eighty by thirty feet, for the Honeywell H-800. The free-standing operators' console was in the center, facing most of the CPU, which occupied a fifty-foot-long cabinet along one wall. Left of the console was a ten-foot cabinet housing the floating-point arithmetic processor. Behind the operators stood the line printer with a card reader and punch on one side and two rows of magnetic tape drives on the other. Control and buffering units for the peripherals were peppered around the room. One consequence of the raised floor was that the ceiling clearance, ample in the rest of the building, was reduced to about eight feet. There was a sharply focused nine-inch-wide beam of light running just below the ceiling, the full length of the room, to a photocell array for smoke detection. That was OK as long as you didn't set off the alarm by innocently stretching your arms up, especially if holding a program listing, in the wrong place.

In one corner was the power supply, for which Honeywell had gone to impressive lengths to assure really smooth 5-volt DC power to the myriad of transistors. First there was an electric three-phase AC motor that looked adequate to propel a small locomotive, driving a shaft that turned a DC generator of a similarly magnificent bulk. Any remaining ripples in the voltage were taken out by an L-C filter. The idea of such a filter is that it places electromagnets ("chokes") in series with the supply to attenuate any AC ripples while letting through the DC current, combined with condensers (aka, capacitors) wired in parallel to bleed the AC ripples, but no DC current, to ground. Those of us with electrical engineering training had seen such filters, for which we'd learned to think of capacitors as measured in microfarads (millionths of a farad, often cylinders the size of a Tootsie Roll) and even micro-microfarads (trillionths of a farad, usually like a coated dime or smaller). What we saw in the H-800 filter was an array of 30-odd enormous capacitors the size of Fosters beer cans, each rated at 33,000 microfarads. As Michael Faraday, the Victorian inventor of capacitors, would have been proud to see, we were looking at more than one full farad. No matter how many or few of those thousands of transistors were conducting at any given instant (thereby drawing current that would have lowered the voltage of an unfiltered supply), that voltage wasn't going to budge from the five-volt level all those transistors needed.

Field service engineers were in attendance at all times. Their daily maintenance routine included a curious early-morning exercise that was actually designed to break things. Each of the many hundreds of logic modules was a plug-in unit that was, except for its three-inch thickness, about the size of a hacksaw (complete with handle). In the middle of that thickness was a multilayer circuit board with transistors, resistors, and normal-size capacitors, all connected by soldered joints of which some inevitably were *cold*, i.e., made with an insufficiently hot soldering iron. Cold solder joints are brittle and eventually break. Honeywell's way of coping with this hazard was to run a Honeywell-designed program that exercised all the circuits in the computer while driving the main-bus speaker to belt out an unearthly melody they named *Hecuba*, pronounced "*Heck*-you-ba." While this was playing, a field service engineer would walk along the back of the CPU, rapping each logic module's handle sharply with the handle of a ten-inch screwdriver. When the music stopped, that was the module where a cold solder joint had just let go.

As old and new engineers moved into two-person offices along the exterior walls, I functioned as ambassador from the hardware side to the software side. I got them trained, if not always delighted, as AGC4 programmers. There was still no thought of hiring programming specialists, except for Tom Lawton and Charley Muntz. Up to that time, Hal Laning had been a one-man programming operation creating an *executive* to manage the AGC's multi-tasking of jobs based on their assigned priorities, and an *interpreter* to make the AGC a friendlier environment for control systems engineers programming navigation and guidance equations. They needed not only a set of operations more like what they'd use in *MAC*, vector arithmetic and trigonometry, but also a way to avoid or minimize thinking about temporary storage for intermediate results (neatly dodged in algebra by the use of parentheses).

Enhancing the AGC3 interpreter to work with the AGC4 and its much larger memory was a challenge. Hal teamed up with Ray Alonso and found a parenthesis-free notation for algebra developed by Jan Łukasiewicz in 1924. It exploited a "pushdown stack" for temporary results to avoid having to specify where they should be preserved. Parentheses as such cast no shadow on computer code, but the temporary results they represent would have to have addresses in the code unless those addresses can somehow be implied, which is what this notation does. Not surprisingly, this invention is generally known as "Polish notation," to get out of having to remember the inventor's name.

The idea of a pushdown stack of data registers corresponds to a LIFO (last in first out) rule, and is generally visualized in terms of a common cafeteria fixture to hold plates. A circular well in a counter, with a spring-loaded bottom, positions the top plate just above counter level regardless of how many plates are in the stack. A busboy emerging from the kitchen with a stack of clean plates puts them on this fixture, and gravity literally pushes them down. Each customer takes a plate off the top, allowing the next plate to pop up conveniently for the next customer. That accounts for the terms used for computer operations on a LIFO stack: "PUSH" for placing an intermediate result on the stack, and "POP" for taking one off. Despite the diagrams that often illustrate the topic, data in a computer stack does not move as the plates do. Instead, the much faster operation of incrementing or decrementing an address variable, or *pointer*, re-designates which location in the stack is currently the "top."

Hal then turned these two ideas over to Tom Lawton and Charley Muntz and resumed his post as computer science guru for any of the Lab's projects that needed one. Tom picked up the executive and defined three objects for it to manage: VAC jobs, NOVAC jobs, and tasks. Jobs were substantial software objects to which their programmers assigned priorities. The highest-priority job that wasn't waiting for a timeout or an event such as an astronaut request would run, using all the machine's resources, until it entered a waiting state or a higher-priority job became ready. Tasks were very short program pieces that responded immediately to interrupting events like a button press on a DSKY, and usually raised the priority of the job that was waiting for that event. VAC stood for Vector Accumulator, actually a general work area for use by any job that included interpretive code. NOVAC jobs were those that didn't use the interpreter and so didn't need to be allocated a VAC.

Tom picked up another of Hal's ideas to add a fault-tolerance dimension to the executive. A variety of untoward though not fatal events could make the AGC restart (or re-boot, as we'd say now). It would restart in just a few milliseconds, unlike some modern personal computers, but then what? Erasable memory could, in general, be counted on because of the way ferrite cores held their magnetic states in the absence of power. Also, the memory's surge protection circuits would keep electrical glitches from altering those states. Every major-mode-level program wrote its identifying number in three places in memory. If a restart occurred while a reselection of program was changing those numbers, two of those numbers would be the same and one would be different. That allowed two-out-of-three voting to establish which program was running, and whether it was just getting started or leaving. Each such program had a special restart entry point for the executive to call in that case, so it could figure out how to recover. This restart capability became critical in both Apollo 11 and Apollo 12.

Charley, a boyish newcomer to the field, brought his fresh energy and quick mind to building the interpreter, with occasional support from Hal and me. "First of all," he observed, "we can relieve the users of the whole bank-switching problem by using a whole word for each address. There's even a bit left over." Then he grouped the engineer-friendly operation codes into over a hundred seven-bit codes so he could pack them two to a word, again with one bit left over. "That's a good thing," he said, "if the leftover bit is in the sign bit position, it'll be easy to tell which words contain op codes and which contain addresses." Having thoroughly mastered my obnoxious CCS instruction, he saw at once how to use it to optimize the core of the interpreter logic, picking up each interpretive program word and immediately classifying it as op codes or an address, all while formatting it for efficient use.

I halted his flow of invention for a moment to ask, "I suppose you want me to make the assembler complement each word and add one to it for the object code, just so the CCS will turn it back into the form you want?"

"Of course," he replied. "It won't take you even an hour to do that. What will be more fun is accounting for which op codes take no address, which ones take one address, and which ones either take an address or not, depending on whether they're getting data from the pushdown stack ..."

It *was* fun watching Charley build his castle of logic in the air. He had a gift for making every word of interpretive code, and every part of a word, earn its keep. The interpretive language as he defined it was a little strange to write and to read, with some lines of code containing one or two op codes and no addresses, others containing an address but no op code, and a few containing both an op code and an address. But engineers liked not having to name intermediate results and allocate memory to them, or to keep track of which banks of memory everything was in.[33]

At a time when NASA and CM contractor NAA hadn't yet settled the design of most of the spacecraft's systems, the Space Guidance Analysis group had to turn their attention to the part that was entirely under our control, that is, how the AGC would operate the Inertial Measurement Unit (IMU). Dick Warren's AGC simulator was operational as far as computer emulation went, but there was no way yet to add mathematical models of any subsystems outside our GN&C system. He worked with the SGA people on the first step of mission programming, readying the IMU before launch, and soon produced a *YUL*-language module headed by the comment line, "Post-breakfast erection." When I asked him what on Earth that was all about, he said, "That's exactly right." After enjoying my baffled expression, he explained. "It's literally 'on Earth,' the most important function of the GN&C system while still on Earth."

The official phrase was "Prelaunch Erection of the Stable Member," an apparently manly term for getting the IMU's gyro-stabilized platform properly aligned with the axes of inertial space. With the H-800, it was a new treat to be able to give eight-letter names to everything. "Prelaunch," however, has nine letters and so had to be shortened to "prelunch."

What comes before lunch, Dick reasoned, must therefore be after breakfast. Whatever nonsense went on with the naming, it was a nice starting point for several reasons. It was a high-accuracy upgrade of similar erections we'd done before in weapon systems. It could be done and tested in the Hybrid Lab with high fidelity. A good test was given us for free as the Earth turned under the IMU, requiring the computer/IMU system to perform gyrocompassing by torquing the gimbals to maintain the alignment.

The other subsystem we knew enough about to work with was the space sextant, even though we hadn't settled the design of a spotting scope to find a given star in the first place. One concept was a low-power telescope that would unfold from the outer wall of the spacecraft, with an optical path based on mirrors in the inner angles of the hinges. We called it the "deployable telescope," but modeling it mathematically soon showed us that the hinges and mirrors weren't likely to perform reliably. With no word processors or other office productivity software, we wrote all our technical memos by hand for the secretaries to type, resulting in some proofreading and correction cycles. On this subject, the Hybrid Lab group's secretary misread an engineer's sloppy handwriting and typed a memo about the "deplorable telescope." Everyone agreed she had gotten it exactly right. Soon we made a much more robust design for a Scanning Telescope embedded in the spacecraft wall. In the meantime, SGA people examined the 57 stars commonly used by ships' navigators, and picked a set of 45 that seemed the most recognizable from their constellations. Combining angles and rotations to re-align the IMU platform based on these observations was far from intuitive, and made a really good usability test for the interpretive language.

When the design of the Block I Command Module and its optics subsystem had settled down, Doc had a partial mockup of its Lower Equipment Bay built on the flat roof of our new building, but not configured for a standing astronaut. Instead, he could sit comfortably at the space sextant on fine evenings and indulge his enthusiasm for experimenting with its ability to navigate Spaceship Earth. A widely known photograph shows him doing that and looking very happy (Figure 13-1).

FIGURE 13-1. Doc Draper Navigating Spaceship Earth[34]

Space Race Highlights of 1962

(All manned flights are indicated in bold.)

03 Jan	Mercury Mark II renamed the Gemini Program.
26 Jan	Ranger 3. Missed Moon impact. Unmanned.
20 Feb	**Mercury–Atlas 6. 3 orbits. Crew: John Glenn.**
23 Apr	Ranger 4. Hit back of Moon. Unmanned.
24 May	**Mercury–Atlas 7. 3 orbits. Crew: Scott Carpenter.**
17 Jul	**X-15 rocket airplane. Suborbital flight. Crew: Robert White.**
11 Aug	**Vostok 3. 64 orbits. Crew: Andriyan Nikolayev; failed rendezvous.**
12 Aug	**Vostok 4. 48 orbits. Crew: Pavel Popovich; failed rendezvous.**
27 Aug	Mariner 2. Venus flyby. Unmanned.
03 Oct	**Mercury–Atlas 8. 6 orbits. Crew: Wally Schirra.**
18 Oct	Ranger 5. Missed Moon impact. Unmanned.
01 Nov	Sputnik 23, aka Mars 1. Launched for Mars flyby. Unmanned.

Other flights where a vehicle (often a missile) entered space, mostly suborbital:

USA	417
USSR	206
France	45
UK	22
Canada	5
Japan	4
Australia	2
China	1
East Germany	1
Norway	1
Sweden	1
Total	**705**

Of these, 63 went into Earth orbit. Country names identify where payloads were made. Most boosters were made by USA or USSR.

Anatomy of the Mission: 1961–1963

As the designs for many components of the huge vehicle that would lift off from Cape Canaveral became better defined, we kept our computer-centered view of it all. That wasn't merely techno-chauvinism, though it may have seemed like it. In the Command Module (CM), our Apollo Guidance Computer (AGC) was properly called CMC (CM Computer) but mostly people just called it the AGC. In the Lunar Module (LM), our AGC was more commonly known as the Lunar Guidance Computer (LGC). In the Saturn 4B final booster stage, IBM's Launch Vehicle Digital Computer (LVDC) was in charge of all the Saturn booster stages. In the two spacecraft vehicles, the two AGCs played an impressively central role.

There were many switches and knobs the astronauts would operate—a few settings that would respond directly to radioed commands from the ground—but almost everything that affected the motion of any part of the vehicles was mediated through the computers. Commands from buttons, switches, and hand controllers all set bits for the appropriate computers to process, and the computers would pour out torrents of bits to control all the moving parts: engines, gimbals and other "hinges," indicator needles on displays, and pyrotechnic devices to separate modules. With rare and partial exceptions, the moving parts just did as they were told without any sense of context. One exception was the LM's Rendezvous Radar—once it locked on to return pulses from the Command/Service Module combination (CSM), it automatically slewed its dish antenna to keep pointing directly at the target.

The narrative of the mission from this point of view has six active characters—the three computers listed above and the three members of the crew: Commander, CM Pilot, and LM Pilot. Ground controllers, despite their job title, functioned as advisors to the crew except in very limited special contexts. From our computer-centered point of view, the initiatives taken by the crew were straightforward and predictable to a large degree, the only uncertainty being when each one would occur. The complex and intricate initiatives were actions by the computer programs. On that basis, the anatomy of the mission is primarily a narrative of the actions taken by the three digital actors—AGC, LGC, and LVDC.

Since the actions affected a bewildering array of vehicle modules and subsystems, let's start at launch-pad level and work our way up the diagram.[35]

1. The first stage of a Saturn 5 is the S1C with five enormous F-1 engines, each burning a highly refined kerosene called Rocket Propellant 1 (RP-1) to produce a million and a half pounds of thrust. They were mounted in gimbals so the LVDC could steer by vectoring their thrust.

2. The second stage is the S2 with five J-2 engines, each burning hydrogen to produce 225,000 pounds of thrust. These were

also gimbaled for LVDC steering. A hollow cylindrical structure served as an adapter between these two stages.

3. The third stage is the narrower S4B with one J-2 engine, gimbaled like the others and capable also of being restarted by the LVDC, which resided in the Instrument Unit (IU), a ring-shaped assembly at the top of the S4B. The adapter to the S2 was tapered because of the different diameters.

4. The thoroughly non-aerodynamic LM crouched, hidden, on top of the S4B with its Descent Stage legs demurely folded.

5. With the Ascent Stage factory-installed above the Descent Stage, the overall height of the LM was that of a two-story house. The long, tapered adapter protecting it from the rush of air was a robust structure to support all the other spacecraft modules, also shielding the SPS engine bell (see below).

6. The SM could be thought of as a fourth booster stage, used only in space, and controlled entirely by the AGC. Its main engine, the Service Propulsion System (SPS) was restartable and gimbaled. The SM provided electrical

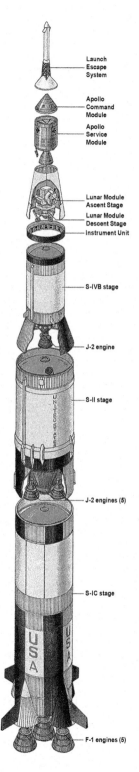

Launch Escape System

Apollo Command Module

Apollo Service Module

Lunar Module Ascent Stage

Lunar Module Descent Stage

Instrument Unit

S-IVB stage

J-2 engine

S-II stage

J-2 engines (5)

S-IC stage

F-1 engines (5)

power, water, communications, and RCS jets for attitude control, as detailed in Chapter 10.

7. At the top of the SM, the CM was securely fastened at its heat-shield base, pointy end up, accommodating the crew in custom-fitted couches.

8. Finally, covering the CM during launch was a conical Boost Protective Cover (BPC) attached to the small Launch Escape Tower (LET), a structure with three rockets that was capable of saving the crew in an emergency by pulling just the CM away from a malfunctioning booster. Fortunately, it never had to. Russian launches of manned vehicles had a similar component, and one of theirs actually had to save a crew.

Here's what the computers and the crew would do with all those modules in a full Lunar landing mission. About 15 seconds before liftoff, the Launch Control Center (LCC) would hand off booster control to the LVDC. If not halted by an emergency hold from the LCC, the LVDC would perform some final checks, then light the S1C's five F-1 engines, give them a few seconds to build up the full 7.5 million pounds of thrust while held down, and then release the four hold-down arms—exactly simultaneously. After liftoff, the LVDC would steer the whole vehicle to build up easterly speed as well as altitude, then control staging to cast off the spent S1C while lighting the S2's five J-2 engines. At that point, the LVDC would signal the LET to unlatch the BPC from the CM and fire a small rocket to take it out of the spacecraft's path. As the easterly speed approached the Earth-orbital requirement of 18,000 miles per hour, the LVDC would cast off the spent S2 and start the S4B's single J-2. When orbit was attained, the LVDC would stop the S4B's engine and await further commands. The AGC had little to do during a "nominal" (normal) boost. It still had to read measurements of the rotations and accelerations from the IMU and display enough data to reassure everybody that the PGNCS was navigating accurately. Everything in the LM was powered down in this phase because the LM's only source of electrical power was its own batteries that had to be reserved for their part of the mission.

If the S1C malfunctioned during the first-stage burn, the LVDC would fire the LET's main rockets, and an explosive guillotine would cut all mechanical and electrical connections between the CM and the SM. The AGC would then have to maneuver the CM-LET combination to a re-entry attitude and release the LET as the IU would have done normally. This maneuver would have to be done promptly but not so abruptly as to injure the crew.

If boost guidance problems arose during the second or third stage, the crew would have an option to make the AGC take over the LVDC's function and solve any problem not caused by a major structural failure. That momentous possibility would be controlled through just a few bits in one of the AGC's output registers.

With the vehicle in parking orbit around the Earth, Mission Control would calculate the free-return trajectory to the Moon and update the LVDC with all the data for the Trans-Lunar Injection (TLI) burn, then advise the crew, "You are Go for TLI." The Commander would use the DSKY to select Program 15 so the AGC could monitor the steering and accelerations of the S4B burn and give the crew the option to stop it.

Once a viable trans-Lunar trajectory was achieved, the S4B would remain attached because the final part of assembling the spacecraft still had to be done. Transposition and Docking, the most elaborate operation so far, would serve also as an ultimate real-world test of many subsystems. The CSM would unlatch from the Lunar Module adapter shroud, use the SM's RCS jets to move out a little way from the S4B/LM assembly, then turn around 180 degrees. The CM at the pointy end of the CSM, now without its BPC, could use the capture probe and latch mechanism for docking with the top of the LM. The CM Pilot, acting through the AGC, would use the hand controllers with the utmost delicacy to nudge the probe in and engage it, then press a pickle-stick button to command twelve latches around the rim to promote the "soft dock" to a "hard dock." Finally, the LM adapter would open up like a four-petaled flower, allowing the CSM to pull the LM out of its "womb" and back away with it. All this would check out the ability of the CSM to maneuver, and rehearse the Lunar Orbit Rendezvous (LOR) and docking by taking the CSM, the CM Pilot, and the AGC through the exact same steps. The AGC would make a considerable adjustment to where it considered the center of mass of the total spacecraft to be, and then adjust the flight path to stand off some from the S4B, now an inert object flying in formation with the spacecraft.

The next order of business would be refining the trans-Lunar trajectory for more accuracy while keeping the free-return property, using the SPS engine for the first time in addition to the RCS jets. Once the ground-based radars verified the free return, the AGC could turn its COMP ACTY light off and take life easy as the crew broke for lunch.

Here would begin three days of mostly idle luxury, interrupted only by a few uses of the sextant to make the AGC fine-align the IMU platform, and occasional determination by Mission Control in Houston as to whether a mid-course correction was required. Often enough, it wouldn't be. I'd like to think of the AGC as smiling a secret smile to itself when a correction was skipped, since it didn't have the sort of display hardware to share it. The crew would keep an eye on all the indicators, but would have time to clown around on TV and admire the extraordinary beauties of space. One of these turned out to be the urine dump at dawn, golden sparkles dissipating slowly into the blackness. But much of that was still far ahead of us as we grappled in 1963 with the parts of the mission.

Crossing from the Earth's sphere of gravitational influence into the Moon's would be a non-event as far as the crew and the accelerometers were concerned. Only the AGC would mark the occasion by following its math model of gravity and switching over from Earth-centered coordinates to Moon-centered. Mission Control's radars would see the deceleration slow to zero, replaced by a gradual acceleration. In our planning at that time, however, we had no assurance that Mission Control would receive unjammed radar signals or be able to communicate that data to the spacecraft.

As the time for Lunar Orbit Insertion (LOI) approached, the AGC would maneuver the spacecraft around to point the SPS engine correctly for the retro thrust. A countdown would appear on the DSKY, but no firing would occur without a press on the PRO (Proceed) key. The AGC would integrate the measured accelerations, watch for pitch and yaw rotations, and tweak the SPS engine gimbals to align the thrust with the ever-changing center of gravity of the vehicle. When the numbers indicated an orbit with a low point (perilune) 60 miles above the Moon, the AGC would shut off the engine. A similar sequence after reaching perilune would circularize the orbit. Like all low Moon orbits, the period was two hours, and the first orbit would soon duck behind the Moon, out of sight of Earth for the first time.

The Commander and the LM Pilot would crawl through the

tunnel into the LM, turn on the battery power, and put subsystems through wake-up checks with the participation of the LGC. They would command the hydraulics at the bottom of the Descent stage to unfold the "lovely legs of the LM" as one astronaut later put it. They in the LM, and the CM Pilot in the CM, would install airlock doors in their respective ends of the tunnel.

The CM Pilot would release the latches to free the LM, allowing him to back the CM off and maneuver around so he could inspect the legs for proper extension. That would be the last reasonably safe opportunity to "chicken out" of landing. Both computers would adjust their center-of-gravity data for independent flight. The Commander and LM Pilot would strap themselves into their stand-up harnesses, with good views through their individual windows (the "eyes" of the LM's "face"), and start the LGC program for Powered Descent Initiation (PDI). The LGC would start the Descent Propulsion System (DPS) engine, the most sophisticated in the vehicle with its steering gimbals and wide range of throttlability. The LGC would roll the LM to a face-down position to allow the crew to recognize carefully memorized Lunar landmarks while most of the deceleration went on. Then it would roll the LM to face-up and pitch it forward to provide a view of the landing area, activating the landing radar to get a direct measurement of altitude. A variety of numbered LGC programs would be available to let the Commander use his hand controllers for various degrees of manual or automatic guidance for the landing. He would have to redesignate the landing spot as the details of rough or smooth terrain came into view. Two large red buttons lurking under a hinged cover would bear the labels ABORT and ABORT STAGE, just in case. The latter would force a separation of the Ascent stage from the Descent stage.

In the CSM with nobody but the CM Pilot for company, the AGC would have little to do, just occasional fine-align work with the sextant, or maneuvering to communicate with Mission Control via the high-gain antenna. Each day would be two hours long, and half of that was on the back side where the CM Pilot couldn't communicate with anybody. Maybe the AGC *should* have been ready to play poker.

While on the Lunar surface, the LGC would have little to do and, as far as we knew in the planning stage, would be turned off to save battery power. We didn't know then how long the stay would be. I remember Dick Battin telling us, "There are no plans for sleeping on the Moon." But that didn't seem like a permanent rule to me nor, I think, to him, since he looked disappointed. Exploring a new world has got to be more than a day trip.

Liftoff from the Moon was designed to be simpler than an on-orbit burn. With no launch control people outside the spacecraft, and with no second chances if anything went wrong, it had to be. The Commander and LM Pilot would stow their souvenirs, dump their life-support backpacks out the hatch, repressurize their Ascent stage, and strap in to their stand-up harnesses. The LM Pilot would make sure the rendezvous radar was ready to work, and the Commander would select the LGC ascent program. Another countdown in the LGC displays, another last-second press on the PRO key, and the LGC would fire up the Ascent Propulsion System (APS) while commanding pyrotechnic guillotines to cut all connections between the two stages. The APS was as simple as the DPS was sophisticated—no gimbals and no throttle, just a cutoff switch. Steering would be up to the autopilot program in the LGC, aided by signals from the rendezvous radar after it locked on to the orbiting CSM.

Once a respectably short distance between the two spacecraft was achieved—that is, a successful rendezvous—the LGC would put the LM in a passive state so the CM Pilot could perform the docking from the CM end, just like the transposition docking so many days before.

Removing the airlocks from the two ends of the tunnel, the crews would reunite and pass their Lunar souvenirs from LM to CM for safe stowage. They would re-install the airlock at the CM end and again release the latches to say farewell to the LM. Backing the CSM off using the SM RCS jets, the crew would take a break and then prepare for Trans-Earth Injection (TEI). That AGC program, having again adjusted its center-of-gravity data, would keep the CSM in Lunar orbit until it reached the point where a nominal trip home would arrive at the right time to re-enter and land at the planned splashdown point. Then it would maneuver around to make the SPS engine point correctly, and display the countdown. At the press of the PRO key, the long burn would begin and the AGC, tuning the attitude as required, would watch the velocity-to-be-gained work down to near zero for cutoff.

The three-day trip home would be a mirror image of the outbound part, with sextant sightings for fine align and possible mid-course corrections. The Lunar-surface crew would be busier than the AGC, regaling the CM Pilot with their adventures and writing their reports.

The entry phase would be a complicated sequence, though only slightly more so than those of previous manned space programs. First the AGC would maneuver the CSM around to point the SPS engine for retro thrust. That burn would remove enough energy to assure capture by Earth's gravity, while aligning the CSM's velocity with the entry corridor. Then the

CM would go on battery power and cast off the SM with a blast of guillotine pyrotechnics, while the SM's RCS jets would back it out of the way.

The AGC would be able to use the few RCS jets on the CM itself for maneuvering, but had no way to control velocity or steering except by tweaking the CM's attitude to adjust the angle of the convex heat shield with respect to the air. No help from outside would be possible because of the radio blackout effect caused by ionization of the superheated air. Finally, the velocity and altitude would get down to where first the drogue and then the main parachutes could be deployed, at which point the AGC's work on that mission would be complete.

Rocket science, navigation science, computer science, and system engineering. Every one of the steps in this plan would be woven from several of those strands, and many would need them all. Everybody involved had to be an expert in one of these sciences (in many cases, not merely an expert but a pioneer) and had to have a good level of competence in the others. NASA had to re-invent the art of project management to get all that mental horsepower to pull together, pull straight, and pull fast.

15

TEAMS, FRIENDS, AND ENEMIES: 1963

In August 1962, before NASA had even thought much about the art of rendezvous and docking, the Soviets scored another first: orbiting two manned spacecraft at the same time. We had no evidence that the Russians had embraced LOR (Lunar Orbit Rendezvous) as completely as we had. In fact, their effort in developing the N-1 mega-booster suggested otherwise. But they read *Aviation Week and Space Technology* faithfully, as we did every week, and must have appreciated the importance of this art. Some sources said that no rendezvous was attempted, but I'm sure that's face-saving revisionism. Why else would anybody orbit two spacecraft? What we understood at the time was that Andriyan Nikolayev in Vostok 3 and Pavel Popovich in Vostok 4 tried very hard to achieve a rendezvous, using the skills and intuitions of their piloting experience, and suffered a frustrating failure.

Those talented cosmonauts succeeded in proving that orbital mechanics is too counter-intuitive to be left to such a manual approach. For one thing, a vehicle in a higher orbit is moving slower than one in a lower orbit, so a pilot in the lower-orbit vehicle can't simply speed up to catch the other. He has to add potential energy to get to the higher altitude while simultaneously shedding kinetic energy to reach the desired speed. It's far from obvious how to implement that energy trade, making it a good thing for a computer to manage with its three-dimensional vector and matrix calculations.

This realization made two things happen. The new Gemini program, the first in which manned spacecraft had a general-purpose control computer on board, made a priority of mastering rendezvous and docking while Apollo spacecraft were under development. And an astronaut turned up at MIT to study in the Aeronautics and Astronautics Department for a PhD in rendezvous technology. Edwin "Buzz" Aldrin became one of Dick Battin's star students, rejoicing then (and still) in the moniker of "Dr. Rendezvous." He became a fixture at the Lab, working with the Space Guidance Analysis group members of the rendezvous team.

In June 1963, the Soviets again put up two manned spacecraft at once: Valery Bykovsky in Vostok 5 and Valentina Tereshkova in Vostok 6, the last of that model. We had no indication that these cosmonauts were attempting rendezvous during the three days they were both in orbit. The Soviets seemed more interested in trumpeting the presence of the first woman in space—then nearly lost her by sending a wrong remote-control command at re-entry time.

Somewhat to our chagrin, NASA accepted North American Aviation's insistence on using their analog Stabilization and Control System (SCS) for autopilot duty in the Block I Command Module. We had concepts for how to do a digital autopilot, but had to admit that the Block I AGC wasn't fast enough to perform that job completely. Our flight control team had to program simplified commands to specify what maneuvers the SCS was to perform.

Controlled re-entry of a Max Faget gumdrop was a new discipline for us, though we could import some experience from Mercury, which had its last hurrah in May, taking Gordon Cooper through 22 orbits. Our entry team also traded insights with the McDonnell-IBM team designing entry techniques for Gemini. Accuracy requirements for landing at the designated splashdown spot were not very stringent, but we took the view that we had to do everything else with pinpoint accuracy—so why not go for it? It was another area in which we didn't want to be bested by the Soviets. Having so little naval resources, they had to achieve good accuracy to land in fairly smooth spots in the steppes of central Asia, using a final rocket stage to assure soft landings.

One surprising result of our research was the need for two phases of initial entry from Lunar mission speeds. A single continuous deceleration would put too great a g-load on the crew for too long. The first phase had to be shallow with a little skip to give the crew some relief before going into the second phase. We had also to learn how to work with an analog device called an Entry Monitor System (EMS), which used SCS signals to move a printed paper scroll. It presented entry parameters in a graphical form for quick analysis by g-loaded astronauts. NASA took some comfort in the ability of the EMS to operate a reasonably accurate entry using the SCS even if the AGC were to fail.

———⊱⊰———

Inertial navigation was a complete solution to flying a vehicle with total autonomy—no dependence on incoming radio waves or even light waves—for the short flights of intercontinental missiles and for airplane flights. Nothing a hostile power could do *electronically* would disturb the paths of such flights, with their durations measured in hours. For space flights lasting days or weeks, however, inertial navigation was less than a complete solution for autonomy, because the stable platform carrying the gyros would drift very slowly from its programmed orientation. Realignment about once a day, or even a little oftener, was required to maintain sufficient accuracy. Ground-based radar could locate a spacecraft well enough, but that wouldn't do any good if the results couldn't be communicated to the AGC. NASA, still concerned then about the possibility of Soviet jamming of such radio signals, specified a full suite of celestial navigation instruments to assure autonomy.

Near the Moon, using the sextant for this purpose was exactly like shipboard use because the edge of a sunlit part of the Moon appears as a sharp line against the black background of space. There's nothing a shipboard navigator appreciates so much as a good sharp horizon. Near the Earth, it's much trickier because our atmosphere, seen from the outside, appears as a sandwich of differently colored layers with somewhat fuzzy boundaries. Mercury astronauts made observations, and Gemini crews had sextants to practice with. An interesting result of this research was that different astronauts had different interpretations of where the true horizon was, but each astronaut was quite consistent from one observation to the next. That made it possible to determine a "personal equation," different for each astronaut, and enter it into the software that worked up the sextant sights. But NASA also identified some special landmarks, such as San Francisco Bay, to use when the horizon proved difficult.

Our celestial navigation team had a member with historical connections. Phil Bowditch was a direct descendant of Nathaniel

Bowditch, who taught this art to common sailors in the early nineteenth century (Chapter 2).

These technical teams, creating complex procedures and software for rendezvous, re-entry, and celestial navigation, had to document their work, not only to support NASA's management functions but also to share with other teams. Documentation, an activity not much loved by busy creative engineers, had to be high-quality technical writing—and there was another issue. NASA was a sometimes uneasy conglomeration of military officers and thoroughly civilian types, so there was bound to be controversy about how much of the Apollo technology should be classified. We wanted to do things openly, partly to show up the Soviet mania for secrecy, but we didn't want to give them too much help either. For a while, the tradition of classifying key software at the Confidential level—carried over from the guidance algorithms for Polaris missiles—held sway. During that time, Raytheon assigned Richard Volpi to document AGC software. Like many Austrians, Richard combined Italian elements—his surname—with Germanic elements—Teutonic thoroughness.

Engineers are forever swapping "war stories," usually not about actual wars, but so called because they can be fully appreciated only by other engineers who have been through similar experiences. Getting to know Volpi, we heard some literal war stories, mostly about his being an on-call Flak officer who had to get up on Viennese rooftops for anti-aircraft duty at any hour of the day or night in World War II. It was a little startling to realize that the targets for his *Fliegerabwehrkanonen* had been Wellingtons, Mosquitos, B-17s, and B-24s.

Richard (properly though not always pronounced Rickard ... but never called Dick, since that's German for Fatso) was a slim, medium-sized man with a gentle voice that nevertheless carried the authority of one who has intensely studied his subject. His Teutonic approach to flowcharting was to draw a rectangle for every single AGC instruction, with suitable arrows connecting to other rectangles. Printed neatly by Raytheon's Technical Publications Department on ledger-size sheets, each page of AGC code became a document the size of a medium blackboard but with less information than the code itself because there was no handy way to incorporate the comments. We could get a clear impression of what a piece of code did by tacking the sheets to a wall, but as each one was stamped CONFIDENTIAL at top and bottom, we weren't allowed to leave them up overnight.

My personal take on all this classification was that we'd rethought so many problems so often, all we had to do to throw the Russians into permanent confusion would be to make sure they got a copy of everything we'd ever written. More serious people did make a point of how wasteful of time it was to follow classification security procedures for so much material. Since much of it described untested approaches, there was little benefit the Soviets could get from a document here and a document there. So the classification roadblock was taken away, another demonstration of how a well-defined goal with a firm deadline can sweep bureaucratic foolishness out of the way.

I guess Raytheon published their wallpaper-style documents in some way or other, but I don't recall ever giving them a moment's attention again. That's a pity, because Richard was intelligent, hard-working, and always a pleasant chap to work with. He just brought the wrong skill set to the task. At some point, we engaged a pair of technical writer contractors, Bernie Savage and Alice Drake, to make more usable documents.

⸺∝⸺

NASA administrator Jim Webb's "instant" contract with MIT was quite broad in scope, embracing all the in-flight GN&C software as well as the hardware. While nobody but IBM was really upset by our developing the computer, more people were concerned about placing so much responsibility for software in the hands of Dick Battin's Space Guidance Analysis group—and some of those people were within NASA. A couple of officials from the agency's headquarters in Washington came to conduct a narrow scrutiny of Dick and his group. Their question was whether some or all of his responsibility should be shifted to another company. Dick was a world-class worry-wart, a very good thing for a software development leader in any case. His general appearance was more subdued than, say, Doc Draper's ebullient confidence. Dick's face in repose gave little hint of the sparkling brilliance his students quickly came to know. In a first impression, he looked a little careworn. Anyone who came looking for a weakness could interpret that expression as indicating a vulnerable personality. But that would be a major mistake, as these visitors soon learned.

As the meeting began, Dick's office window was open to the mild spring air with the scent of boxwood shrubbery drifting in. The visitors sat near the end of the long table and began their cross-examination of a few key engineers and their leader. Dick responded a little warily but with a low-key, unshakable confidence. During a pause in the conversation, a large fly came in through the window. Still groggy from whatever seasonal torpor such insects spend their winters in, the fly cruised down the length of the meeting table toward Dick's desk. Quite casually, Dick picked up a pair of large office scissors, reached up a little, and snipped the fly neatly in half. I wasn't in that meeting, but those who were said the inquisitors never fully recovered the stern composure they'd come in with. And there wasn't any further trouble from that quarter.

Unwilling to risk a failure to repeat his "fly-section," Dick developed another WMD (Weapon of Meeting Destruction), usable when the window was closed. He smoked a pipe and, when a meeting at that long table became a waste of everybody's time, he would lean back and blow a smoke ring, and not just any smoke ring. A genuine Battin ring was accurately circular, perhaps four inches in diameter and over half an inch thick. It would settle slowly onto the table, riding on its own millimeter-thick air cushion, and drift east without losing its shape, finally falling off the far end and disintegrating. All eyes inevitably followed it. Whoever had been saying something not worth saying forgot the topic, and the meeting broke up. Sometimes it took two rings, but never more. Now that's leadership.

The NASA people in Houston, who knew us well by that time, were a lot friendlier than those two headquarters commandos. So far from shrinking our role, they increased it by specifying that the AGC should have connections into the Saturn booster's data network, so that we could guide the booster if IBM's Instrument Unit or its computer were to fail. For some not-so-friendly executives at IBM's Federal Systems Division, that was the last straw. Not only was FSD shut out of the Apollo spacecraft—an injury to an imperial company—but MIT was being positioned to possibly take over FSD's job— an insult. They engaged Bellcomm, an independent consulting company, to perform a study about whether IBM's Launch Vehicle Digital Computer (LVDC) should replace the AGC in the spacecraft.

To nobody's surprise, the study solidly took IBM's side, concluding that the AGC's reliability could never match that of the LVDC. A major part of their argument was based on the LVDC's Triple Modular Redundancy (TMR). It provided "active redundancy" by processing three independent serial streams of data, all identical if everything is working, and voting two-out-of-three to overcome any single failure. Our approach to computer reliability had two parts: the extreme quality control of the integrated circuits, and an in-flight repair capability based on the fact that two whole copies of AGC4—each about the size of a shoebox but double the length—would fit in our space on the instrument shelves. If an AGC were to fail in flight, the crew could pull both copies out and plug the spare into the operational socket. NASA sent us a copy of Bellcomm's report and gave us two weeks to prepare a response to bring to Houston for a head-to-head meeting with Bellcomm and NASA. Such meetings were a favorite NASA method, both effective and efficient, for settling adversarial controversies.

Through their proxy, IBM was mounting an invasion of a sacred part of our space, and we'd have to put on our "Churchill face" to repel it. Eldon Hall felt we knew how to defend the reliability point, having spent considerable time with Houston on its two parts. It was clear to me that Bellcomm hadn't understood much about how and why the two computers greatly differed in architecture. We had designed the AGC4 to be flexible and efficient in a priority-driven multitasking environment, interacting with a variety of spacecraft subsystems as well as the crew and the ground. IBM had optimized the LVDC architecture for the major continuing function in the Saturn booster's flight, a guidance method called "adaptive polynomials." I made up a nasty nickname for the LVDC, "APE," for Adaptive Polynomial Engine—in parody of Charles Babbage's "Analytical Engine" of a century before. After coding up some comparative programs in the systems software area, even I was surprised at how much less memory and time the AGC needed.

Dick Battin's guidance experts performed a similar exercise for powered flight, finding that the AGC produced more precision and better interrupt response and input/output handling. It was about ten times faster than the LVDC while requiring less than half the memory space. Dick, as the designated author of our response, could scarcely believe the strength of our findings. Excellent worry-wart that he was, he kept asking, "Is it really that one-sided?" Everybody on the team assured him, "Yes, Dick, write it. It's real!"

We put together a lengthy memo and slide show to take to the showdown meeting, but we couldn't then fly to Houston's Intercontinental Airport on our way to the Manned Spacecraft Center—because neither of those had yet been built. We flew instead to Hobby Airport, arriving around dinnertime, and checked into an airport motel with (fortunately) Texas-sized rooms. The Bellcomm team, led by a bright though not overwhelming man named Ike Nahama, was staying at the same motel. NASA's temporary Houston footprint was across Interstate 45 from Hobby, in a leased oil-company building, an impressive Frank Lloyd Wright design. The NASA folks were eager to see what we'd done, having been given some idea that it would be "interesting." So after dinner, they came over to the motel to have a preliminary meeting in one of the rooms. Something over a dozen people gathered around two king-size beds, and we spread out our slides and started reading the introduction of our memo. After a very brief outline, our key phrase was, "We are astonished that Bellcomm could have come to this conclusion."

There were a few moments of thunderous silence, followed

by "You are what??" The senior NASA official present said something like, "OK, guys, we'd better hear what this is about." So we walked them through the slides and our thoroughly one-sided measurements, and the Bellcomm people didn't have much in the way of artillery to oppose them. A more "official" meeting may have been held the next day in the NASA offices, or not. I don't remember and it surely didn't matter.

------⚬❈❈⚬------

For much of that year, the real Manned Spacecraft Center campus grew quickly on land in Clear Lake obtained from Rice University in Houston. White stucco buildings with black accents and tinted glass were tastefully arranged on a mega-lawn you could putt on. When MSC opened in September 1963, the center invited all their contractors to send teams for a full-day tour. In the morning, officials walked us around with brochures relating building numbers (MIT style) to their functions. We enjoyed an ample lunch in the cafeteria, then gathered in meeting rooms for more detailed presentations. Every chair in those rooms was a big comfortable reclining swivel chair, several grades better than anything we had in our home offices. The slides for the presentations were in carousel projectors, with fans whirring soothingly in the darkened rooms as young NASA engineers gave the presentations in soft Southern voices. It had been a really good lunch, and those chairs were *awfully* comfortable ... zzzzzzzz.

Let that be a lesson for anyone organizing a facility tour: Devote the morning to slide shows with coffee, do a nice lunch, and *then* walk the troops around to get them past the biorhythmic nadir!

The high point of the tour—then as now—was the Mission

Control Center (MCC), familiar to space fans worldwide from countless hours of TV coverage. The Philco consoles—from the Flight Director's station at the back to the "trench" consoles in the front row next to the gigantic wall screens—were marvels of modern interface technology. The display screens showed close-packed rows of text (no graphics) and were flanked by arrays of dedicated rectangular alert/alarm lights.

GUIDO (the guidance officer) might, for instance, have a screen showing actual and desired velocities for the spacecraft. When he wanted a print-out of a screen, he pressed a button that lit an indicator in the vast computer room, where an operator spotted it and used a keyboard to order a print of that screen. The page printer, of Thermo-Fax technology, cranked out a low-resolution sheet. The operator rolled up the finished page and loaded it into a pneumatic tube capsule, which was then pushed by compressed air through the tube system so it fell into a bin at the requesting controller's console. A technology that went live in businesses offices in 1836—a year before Queen Victoria's reign began—thus contributed to Mission Control, and its heyday is not over yet. Many banks' drive-thru teller stations use such tubes and capsules today.

The computer room was equipped with five 7094s, IBM's first transistorized mainframes. They were architecturally only a minor upgrade of the 704 mainframes I'd used in the '50s, though much faster. This complex was the brain of a global "nervous system," the biggest and most elaborate real-time data system until the Internet, which to some extent it resembled. Radar-equipped tracking stations around the world handled Houston's voice and data communications to and from the spacecraft, as well as capturing video feeds for distribution worldwide. The radars tracked spacecraft positions and velocities with impressive accuracy. The timely creation of this data network gave Houston's controllers virtually hands-on access to the spacecraft systems continuously, even when the bulk of Planet Earth sat between Houston and the spacecraft. Designing and building that ultra-reliable system was the pinnacle of IBM Federal Systems Division's achievements, in my view. It was a prime example of the oft-quoted saying that Apollo was achieved by reaching forward to pluck pieces out of the twenty-first century and splicing them into the middle of the twentieth.

A few weeks afterward, I was upstairs in the Digital Development lab, working with Al Hopkins and Ray Alonso on refinements to AGC4's input-output architecture. The PA system did something it had never done before, coming up with a feed from some radio station: "The President has been shot while riding in a motorcade in Dallas, Texas. There is blood on his head." The reporter continued saying what reporters must say in such cases, nothing really worth saying, but something, anything, to fill the air time. Eventually, he passed on the finding from the hospital, "The President is dead." There was a click, and one of the guards relayed a message from the Lab's leadership to the effect that anybody who needed to leave early would be allowed to do so. Nobody moved and nobody spoke for several minutes.

Somebody said, "Go home early? What would be the point of that? What we're doing is Jack Kennedy's project—let's keep it going." With a sigh of relief at being able to respond in a way that seemed fitting and appropriate, we did. There was time and space for tears and spiritual darkness later, at home. Over the next days, there was a lot more time spent in front of TV sets, trying to rebuild a shattered world out of Lyndon Johnson's swearing-in on the airplane, of rotundas and caissons and a riderless horse with boots reversed in the stirrups. There was a pop song including the phrase "I loved that man, and I loved his wife," that spoke for many of us.

The decision to rename Cape Canaveral as Cape Kennedy didn't have a great effect on us one way or the other. It was a gesture, in a season that required gestures, but meaning was to be found in doing Kennedy's project—our project. A decade later, when gesture season had passed, I for one had no problem with reserving the name *Kennedy Space Center* for NASA's launch facility, while restoring the name Cape Canaveral to a geographical feature vital to charts and other navigational publications. For centuries, wary mariners all around the North Atlantic have known that name as a major bump in the Florida coast, whether they're working with or against the indomitable Gulf Stream.

Space Race Highlights of 1963

(All manned flights are indicated in bold.)

28 Mar	Saturn 1. Suborbital. Unmanned (first test).
02 Apr	Luna 4. Missed Moon impact. Unmanned.
15 May	**Mercury-Atlas 9. 22 orbits. Crew: Gordon Cooper.**
14 Jun	**Vostok 5. 82 orbits. Crew: Valery Bykovsky.**
16 Jun	**Vostok 6. 48 orbits. Crew: Valentina Tereshkova (first woman).**
19 Jun	Sputnik 23, aka Mars 1. Closest approach to Mars. Unmanned.
17 Jul	**X-15 rocket airplane. Suborbital flight. Crew: Joseph Walker.**
19 Jul	**X-15 rocket airplane. Suborbital flight. Crew: Joseph Walker.**
26 Jul	Syncom 2. Unmanned (first geosynchronous satellite).
11 Nov	Kosmos 21. Failed Venus flyby. Unmanned.

Other flights where a vehicle (often a missile) entered space, mostly suborbital:

USA	383
USSR	143
France	21
UK	14
Canada	9
Japan	2
Australia	2
China	1
West Germany	1
Italy	2
Sweden	3
Total	**581**

Of these, 47 went into Earth orbit. Country names identify where payloads were made. Most boosters were made by USA or USSR.

SPLIT DIGITAL PERSONALITIES: 1964

"Multitasking"—as we understand the term in the twenty-first century—falls short of describing the heavy-duty juggling we did in the peak years of Apollo development. Creating just the hardware of an embedded control computer plays out in three different arenas: designing on paper, debugging a "breadboard" prototype, and packaging for real. They can't be strung out as succeeding steps. It's quite typical for packaging to impact the beginning of the process as well as the end, forcing educated guesses as to what's required for the function and what will fit within the constraints on size, weight, and power.

During 1964, the Digital Development Group was: meticulously checking out the logic for the Block I AGC; working with Raytheon's rope-memory weaving operation to double the ROM density and raise Block I's fixed-memory word count from 12K to 24K; working with other parts of Raytheon's Sudbury division to design the dual-computer "repairable" packaging; and doing the paper design of the Block II AGC— the part I was personally involved in. It's similar to engineers at a car company, where some are working on the 2017 model year even before the others finish tooling up to get the 2016 models ready for production. But we had far fewer people.

Early in the history of electronics, somebody was the first to make a preliminary version of a circuit by screwing components down to the surface of an actual wooden breadboard, laid out to allow access by voltmeters and other instruments to all the parts. Somehow the name stuck, and such preliminary versions have been called "breadboards" ever since, even though wood is seldom involved. For all three generations of the AGC, we built frameworks similar to movable blackboards, but with sheet steel panels where the blackboard would be. We drilled thousands of holes in the panels and fitted insulated chip sockets into many of them. The front side of these panels looked fairly tidy, with the chip modules sticking out and a few indicator lamps installed for testing. The back side was not so tidy. It had all the connector pins with a "spaghetti mural" of wires strung from one to another, and labels written on adhesive tape. One panel carried the erasable and fixed memories. The erasable memory was implemented as a standard coincident-current ferrite core RAM, the same technology used in the actual AGC. The fixed memory was implemented by a similar RAM easily loaded from a paper tape, standing in for the actual AGC's rope memory. Another panel embodied the input-output facilities with an indicator lamp for each output bit and a toggle switch for each input bit.

The most memorable NASA visitor who came to see how we were doing was Wernher von Braun, director of the Marshall Space Flight Center (MSFC). He was making a swing through all the project's development centers, but he had a particular interest in ours as a result of our battle the previous year for the AGC's survival in the project (chapter 15). The IBM Federal Systems Division people who had been working with von Braun for years, on the Saturn booster's Launch Vehicle Digital Computer (LVDC), launched their attack on the AGC through their proxy, Bellcomm. We suspected that IBM/Bellcomm had presented their argument to von Braun as a way for him and his MSFC to gain influence within NASA at the expense of Houston's MSC. His natural integrity and long experience dealing with political dirty tricks (starting in Nazi Germany, remember) must have immunized him, we hoped, against being swayed by such underhanded gambits. Our best approach was to give him a good demonstration showing the Block I AGC in its breadboard form doing things the LVDC wasn't particularly good at, like nimble multi-tasking.

With no printer, much less a display screen, for output, we had to come up with something jazzier than a bunch of blinking neon bulbs. Well, actually, it *was* possible to have a display screen of a very limited sort, a standard Tektronix laboratory oscilloscope. Most of it worked the same way as an old picture-tube TV, with a thinly focused beam of electrons painting the image by being steered to particular spots on the back surface of the glass screen. The electrons excited a little dot-shaped part of the phosphor on that surface to produce a glow that, though temporary, would persist for a longer or shorter period depending on the intensity of the beam. Steering the beam to a particular spot was a matter of applying an "X voltage" to a pair of vertical metal paddles at the sides of the tube, to move the beam right or left, and a "Y voltage" to horizontal paddles above and below the tube, to move the beam up or down.

The type of oscilloscope most familiar to people is the hospital device that shows a patient's heart rhythm as a green line on a dark screen, the source of our ominous word, "flatline." What a regular TV tube and this type of oscilloscope have in common is an X voltage that only does one thing: increases linearly from zero to full-scale, representing the passage of time by moving the beam from left to right. It then goes instantly back to zero to start the next scan—the "horizontal sweep." In that mode, only the Y voltage represents measurement of a real-world variable. But a laboratory scope can be rigged so that both the X and Y voltages are real-world variable inputs. In our demo, those were a pair of digital-to-analog D/A converter circuits that took in a number in binary notation and put out a voltage proportional to the value of that number. Thus the two numbers could place a glowing spot anywhere in the square area of the screen, in any one of over sixteen million positions.

We wired a couple of the AGC's output registers to the D/A converters to provide X-Y coordinates for the spot. Al Hopkins cobbled up an AGC program that simulated a bouncing ball in an imaginary "squash court" with a drain hole, using just the vertical sides and the bottom of the scope's square display area as the walls and floor. The program was a math model of a ball with a randomized initial horizontal velocity starting from the upper left corner of the display area. The ball's motion was influenced by a settable acceleration of gravity (g), and bounced off the walls and floor with a settable elasticity (e). Al's program recalculated the position of the ball a hundred times per second, depositing the resulting X and Y coordinate values in the output registers to locate the spot. That's all the detail there was in representing the ball, just a single pixel.

When the ball hit the spot in the floor where the virtual drain hole was defined, it vanished. The "squash court" outline had nothing to do with the program, however ... it was rendered on the scope's glass screen with orange crayon!

We labeled two rows of toggle switches, one for each of two AGC input registers, "Gravity" and "Elasticity" to allow von Braun to vary g and e. Al's control program ran five instances of the math model program, starting about one second apart. Each had its own values of g and e, obtained from whatever was in the input toggle switches at the instant of launch. The persistence of the phosphor excitation made the screen show five balls all moving smoothly. When one vanished down the drain hole, it became the next to launch at the next whole second. Because the D/A converters changed the X and Y voltages instantaneously, there were no dim lines connecting one ball to the next (unlike a heart monitor, which shows relatively gradual changes in skin voltage).

What our creation demonstrated was that the computer accommodated a tiny but effective Operating System running a parallel operation of five instances of the math model program. It also showed that the computer was fast enough to solve five differential equations a hundred times per second. Much as I'd have liked to be, I personally was not involved in this micro-project. I was just one of the group standing around to see whether it would work when needed, and how von Braun would like it. That session was my only claim to have "met" the great man; we weren't actually introduced.

The guest of honor watched it working, then tried various switch settings to set gravity and the elasticity to high and low values, and clearly enjoyed our little video game. His assessment was, "Ach, dot shows der computer iss on de ball!"

I could hear one thought humming through all the MIT brains in the room: *"Danke schön,* Wernher. That is exactly what it shows!"

Grumman's design for the LM and its subsystems was advancing rapidly, presenting challenges to NASA and to us. Grumman project leader Tom Kelly's book *Moon Lander* recounts his experiences with unflinching honesty. When Grumman engineers were doing serious reliability analysis on LM subsystems, they forgot to keep a similarly critical eye on their external sources, in particular a General Electric study. That's how they got bamboozled into passing on reliability data for missile guidance systems, published by GE, as an indication that the Lab's PGNCS was only about 1% as reliable as the missile systems. One of the Grumman analysts was a former Honeywell engineer who bitterly resented MIT getting the contract instead of Honeywell. Kelly suspected him of seeking revenge by twisting and inflating the significance of the GE report, effectively stampeding the other analysts. Grumman's "thermonuclear" report on this issue provoked NASA's Apollo spacecraft program manager Joe Shea into calling a ferocious meeting that could not end until one side or the other backed down in, well, shame.

Grumman led off, presenting data that Shea immediately challenged as being incomplete. Then the Lab's Dave Hoag methodically detailed how the wrong choices of data radically changed the picture. He demolished Grumman's conclusion. The result was a total victory for the Lab, not a happy victory because we were supposed to be, and sought to be, allies with Grumman. Kelly and his people were subjected by NASA to exacting and humiliating supervision. The festering tension between Grumman and MIT must have had a lot to do with Grumman's engineering decision to leave unchanged the issue we later raised about synchronizing AC power supplies. That issue, whose gradual emergence is traced in chapters 22–24, left open a vulnerability in the interface between the LM's PGNCS and its Rendezvous Radar that caused so much excitement in the Apollo 11 Lunar landing five years later.

Most of the challenges in working with Grumman on the LM were technical rather than political. Such a lightweight vehicle, especially the Ascent stage by itself after Lunar liftoff, was an extraordinarily active spacecraft. It responded quickly to even a minimum impulse from an RCS jet, and was sensitive to bodily motions by the crew. NASA's original preference for a separate Stabilization and Control System (SCS), outside the AGC as in the CM, had to give way to a software approach called a Digital Autopilot (DAP). That raised the requirements for computing speed, which were already under pressure from the slow performance of interpretive code. The requirement outlines for a Block II AGC became clear: Double the speed and increase memory size significantly, while minimizing technology risks. The first place to look for speed was in newer integrated circuit chips.

Independently of the Apollo project (though clearly encouraged by our adoption), the technology of integrated circuits raced ahead in the '60s. Fairchild had doubled the number of three-input NOR gates per package, so the little top-hat shape of the six-legged TO-47 can gave way to a ten-legged "flat pack," a slim brick shape roughly the size of the handle of a trouser fly zipper. Later, these got the more dignified name of *surface mount* because the pins, of which five sprouted from each of the long sides, stayed in the same geometrical plane as the chip package and could be welded to contacts on the surface of the multilayer printed-circuit board. This welding technique was reliable, and pressing the belly of the chip package tight to the board improved its heat dissipation, not to mention slimming down the module thickness. The smaller size not only allowed more logic elements in the same volume, but approximately doubled the number of gates for the same power consumption and heat dissipation load. The wires connecting the pins internally to pads on the chip were much shorter and thus less vulnerable to Wiggly Leg Disease. This impressive combination of advantages was not enough for the naysayers from Bellcomm (again!) who insisted the flat packages could not be sealed reliably. We had to point out to NASA that we could detect defective seals by inspection, and in any case missile electronics had built a successful track record with flat packs.

———— ∞∞∞ ————

With my *YUL* system fully operational for the Block I AGC, I was again able to join the Digital Development Group's architecture design table, though more often a follow-up artist than a leader this time. Speed of data processing was our top priority.

The bigger supply of logic gates let Al Hopkins speed up addition by a device called "implicit-carry," in which more complex logic allowed us to process all the bit-to-bit carries simultaneously rather than one by one from right to left. Now, unlike the "ripple-carry" adder of Block I, we could write into both adder inputs during one pulse time and read out the sum in the next pulse time, one microsecond later. The faster adder was crucial to speeding up multiplication and division, and simplifying double-precision addition.

Al had several other long-held inspirations just waiting for this chance to spring into life. One was to unwind the overflow-based association of INDEX with extracode generation. Instead, he substituted a one-memory-cycle instruction, EXTEND, which would function more purely as a "Shift key" to double the number of operation codes.[36]

Al's next inspiration was one I kicked myself for not having thought of first. Some instructions, like TS (Transfer [accumulator] to Storage) could never usefully address fixed memory. Since only 10 bits of the 12-bit address field were used to address erasable memory (1,024 combinations out of 4,096), the leftmost two address bits were irrelevant in such instructions. Al's idea was to interpret those two bits as part of the op code. He thus packed four erasable-only op codes into the logical space previously occupied by one. I named these "quarter-codes." Then he realized that a few instructions restricted to fixed memory could become "three-quarter codes" addressing the other 3,072 combinations. A three-quarter code shared a top-level code with one quarter-code.

The brightest genius-halo floating over Al Hopkins's head was his way of speeding up multiplication. After consultation with Raytheon's Herb Thaler about manufacturability, Al created two new control pulses, named expressively—if a little enigmatically—ZIP and ZAP. Each invoked what you might call nano-programming to make each use of the adder accomplish the function of two consecutive multiplier bits. The bottom line was a multiplication by a 14-bit multiplier in only eight additions or subtractions. The first occurred after determining the sign of the product in the first cycle, as soon as the multiplicand arrived from memory. Five and a half of them occurred in the next cycle time, and one and a half in the last cycle while the next instruction was being fetched. With the one-cycle EXTEND, a Block II multiplication took only four memory cycle times, or 47 microseconds—two and a half times faster than the Block I AGC, or thirteen times faster than AGC3.[37]

The best I could do to match this feat was to speed up division by a slightly greater factor, to six memory cycle times plus one for EXTEND, or 82 microseconds. It was just a matter of using all the 12 pulse times of every cycle to execute 14 instances of the shift-and-subtract step. With no leap of creativity, I just didn't earn as many points for artistry.

In the input-output area, we now had enough gates to build channel registers for each of the spacecrafts' subsystems, and to create programmer-friendly I/O instructions to read and write them. It was fairly simple to define a set of channels that would accommodate either the CM or LM environment. Knowing that nine-bit addresses would be more than ample to address the channels, Ray Alonso and I worked out a set of seven instructions all sharing one top-level op code. We built the Boolean functions AND, OR, and even XOR (exclusive OR) into most of these to shorten and speed up I/O programming. Similarly to quarter-codes, these "eighth-codes" used the left three bits of the 12-bit address field to distinguish which channel operation to perform.

Having been impressed by Ed Smally's self-check program in Block I, I used the last slot in the eighth-codes to provide programmed access to the three-memory-cycle program interrupt sequence. The idea was to give Ed a way to self-check the interrupt logic without having to cause a real interrupt. This instruction, called EDRUPT, was so special-purpose that we didn't include it in most documents, to the eventual chagrin of the many AGC-cloning hobbyists who sprang up in later decades.

When all the extracode logic and quartering and "eighthing" was done, we'd given Block II a repertoire of 34 instructions. That compares with 11 in Block I (AGC4), and just 8 in AGC3. The programmer community was still about evenly split between those who found the unusual architecture a royal pain and those who grasped and enjoyed what we, the design gang, felt was a triumph of creativity.

Had we then achieved our goal of making Block II run most programs about twice as fast as Block I? Since we'd increased our memories' data capacities without upgrading their speed, much of the answer depended on reducing the memory cycles used. To gain confidence in having come close, we used our sudden wealth of op codes to create a very basic set of double-precision operations including a combination add-and-store. Implementing instructions for double-precision multiplication and division would have blown the logic budget. I worked out a software subroutine to perform double-precision division with a probable error of no more than one in the last (28th) bit position. That was acceptable because all the calculations that needed double precision used a fixed-point notation treating the number as a fraction, meaning the rightmost bit was generally approximate to begin with. My method involved just two single-precision divisions and a single-precision multiplication, plus about a dozen instructions to shuffle the pieces around. That came in handy years later when IBM presented their Space Shuttle computer design to us.

———— ✸✸✸ ————

Increasing the size of fixed memory was quite straightforward, up to a point. With the Raytheon rope-weaving people, we revisited the way we'd doubled the Block I size from 12K words to 24K just by stuffing more wires through the same transformer cores. Fortunately, we found there was enough room to have tripled the 12K, so we set our Block II fixed memory size at 36K words. Less fortunately, we realized our bank-switching scheme maxed out at the 32K mark. That was because we could express in one word a *complete [fixed] address* as five bits of bank number to identify one of 32 banks, and ten bits to address one of the 1K words in the selected bank. With mission software sizes snapping hungrily at our heels, just forgetting about those last 4K words was not an option.

Our awkward compromise was to keep the five-bit bank number and the complete-address standard, while defining a "super-bank bit" in I/O Channel 07. We designated four bank numbers as selecting either banks 24–27 or banks 32–35 depending on this bit. Somebody talked us into a more dignified name, "Fixed Extension bit," in place of "Super-bank bit" for documentation purposes, but I ignored it for *YUL* source-language purposes. In telephony terms, if bank numbers were like area codes, this powerful bit was like a country code.

For erasable memory, smaller ferrite cores were available so we could double the capacity from 1K words to 2K. But we couldn't allocate any more addresses, so we had to introduce the bank-switching system into erasable. We chose to make three eighths of erasable unswitched (using three quarters of the address range), for which we coined the oxymoronic but understandable name "fixed-erasable." That left the other five eighths to be switchable as five banks of 256 words each, answering to the remaining quarter of the address range. Our old fixed bank register "BANK" had to be renamed "FB" to distinguish it from a new register "EB" for switching erasable banks.[38]

Had we then done enough, by speeding up operation and expanding the memories, to make the Block II AGC meet the LM's needs? We sure hoped so, but the truthful answer was that we had just done as much of both kinds of improvement as we possibly could—while still meeting the schedule. Fortunately, software can be squeezed into smaller memory allocations by feats of cleverness at the expense of transparency and ease of testing, and many software modules can be re-examined for degree of indispensability, to see whether throwing them off the bus might be a good trade.

HIGH-LEVEL EFFORT ON LOW-LEVEL
SOFTWARE: 1963–1964

One of the stars of the Space Guidance Analysis group was Bill Widnall, a highly talented engineer with patrician good looks who could play himself in an Apollo movie to the satisfaction of any director. He and his wife Sheila, who was not only a professor of Aeronautics and Astronautics at MIT but later served as Secretary of the Air Force, made a formidable combination. Bill became a heavy user of the matrix algebra functionalities we provided in the AGC interpretive language to keep velocities and forces resolved into the appropriate sets of X-Y-Z axes of three-dimensional space. The most elaborate of these was multiplying a matrix (a square array of nine numbers) by a vector (a linear array of three numbers), yielding another vector. It comprised three occurrences of a vector *dot product* (three multiplications and two additions), consuming 9 milliseconds in all. One of the standard uses of this operation was multiplying one matrix by another, which is three times all that again, for a total of 27 multiplications and 18 additions in 27 milliseconds. To put that time interval into perspective, it's a little less than the time a single movie frame stays on the screen and a little more than the corresponding time for a modern high-frame-rate movie. It's also the time interval in which a Moon-bound spacecraft at escape velocity advances about a thousand feet.

I came back to work after supper one evening and noticed Bill's office light on, so I stopped by. "Hey Bill," I said, "Why the midnight oil?" He frowned at the papers on his desk and asked, "Couldn't you have made the AGC about three times faster? I've got to make this simple little equation fit into a quarter of the navigation cycle, and it's just taking too darn long."

Bill's equation didn't look either simple or little to me, with matrices tumbling over each other to bend vectors into the required shape. Then I saw that his program code was performing the matrix operations left to right, as he'd written them in his formulas, even though the Associative Law of algebra would allow more of a right-to-left sequence. "How bad would it be for retained precision if you performed those multiplications right-to-left?"

Bill ran a thoughtful finger over his formulas. "Oh, I see. That would change some of the matrix-times-matrix multiplications into matrix-times-vector ... holy cow! That is three times faster if we can get away with it." He leaned back, seeming to scan data on the inside of his eyelids. "Well, most of my numbers only need about six digits out of the eight available. Changing the sequence shouldn't hurt too much."

I agreed that his conclusion followed from his premise. "Have you got enough test data sets to demonstrate that point?"

He pulled a listing from a far corner of his desk. "Absolutely, over a hundred. I'll just tweak up my *MAC* program to do them all both ways and make a histogram of the discrepancies."

We moved the multiplications around over the course of half an hour, making and catching mistakes. Bill did a sharp intake of breath. "You know, when I look at it this way, that cosine matrix is transposed all the time, so it only has to come in once instead of twice. That ought to help." He wrote the revised formulas on a fresh sheet of paper and looked it over closely for a minute. "OK, let's try it this way, while I've got it all clear in my head." I mentally added up the running times as he wrote it out in interpretive code, and smiled secretly to myself at the result.

He went off to punch up the cards, promising to keep me posted, and I went back to my desk. After a couple of hours, he popped into my office with a grin, saying, "Well, the method comparison results match to seven digits, and we only needed six. And as for the timing ... how did you do that? I ran my little unit test program that way, and it's within a millisecond of being three times faster. Thank you very much!"

That was typical of the informal interdisciplinary exchanges that took place all the time. There wasn't any system for routing queries to other departments because there didn't need to be. People cared about and trusted each other, and a lot of problems were reduced from days to hours as a result.

What might one call a collection of programs, routines, subroutines, procedures, major modes, jobs and tasks, that all have to exert the utmost courtesy in sharing the resources of a single spacecraft computer? The physical form of fixed memory (Chapter 12) gave us our answer: a *rope*. With no tapes, disks, or any form of backing store, every scrap of coded logic had to be built into one rope memory, 24K words in a Block I AGC, for each Apollo mission. Ropes had names (up to eight characters) and early ones were named in honor of Apollo's role in ancient mythology, as driver of the phaeton carrying the Sun across the sky. They were ECLIPSE (begun on the day of a solar eclipse that occurred six years to the day before the first Moon landing), SUNRISE, CORONA, SOLARIUM, and SUNSPOT.

While the AGC programming teams began as a couple of dozen engineers collected in one corner of the first floor, they eventually grew to several dozen scattered over three floors. There were individual specialists, teams dedicated to particular disciplines or flight phases, and some semi-formal groups. At the end of the day (and far into the night), each rope had to have one engineer take responsibility for making it all play together. That person, though invariably male, was dubbed the "Rope Mother."

Although Rope Mothers were in a formal sense assigned their roles by a higher-ranking leader, their environment was effectively as if they had been democratically chosen. The other developers generally held Rope Mothers in high esteem, while simultaneously sympathizing with them as being the occupants of very hot seats. Those who were not Rope Mothers had a somewhat different outlook, that of pursuing an "ultimate" design for their respective functional units, the design that would perform its full bag of tricks all the way to the Moon and back.

Rope Mothers had to focus on what was just enough for the requirements of a particular flight, without putting any serious crimps in the learning process and development path for the subsequent flights. The role demanded an impossible combination of steadfast integrity and creative flexibility. There were disappointments, compromises, bruised egos, exhaustions and recuperations. But our spirits never wavered from our mantra: *We Can Do This.* Just as an effective Cub Scout Pack is enabled by its Den Mother, so the pack of engineers stuffing code into the narrow temporal and spatial dimensions of an AGC was enabled by its Rope Mother.

The first Rope Mother was Albrecht "Alex" Kosmala. His rope CORONA was designed for AS-202, the first unmanned flight of the Block I Command Module to carry a computer. The 200-class number showed that it would use a two-stage booster, a Saturn-1B topped by the generic upper stage Saturn-4B. Thus, it could fly years before the big Saturn 5 was ready and, for that reason, imposed an intense schedule pressure. Despite his Finnish-Polish name, Alex was brought up in England and spoke and wrote pure BBC, for example "manoeuvre," pronounced *man-you-veh*, for a change in spacecraft attitude. A wiry fellow with an ascetic head of very short crew-cut blond hair, wearing a slightly worried look in most circumstances, he had a keen sense of theater and applied Henry V's famous line "We few, we happy few, we band of brothers" as a metaphor of our devoted community.

Like the Rope Mothers, all of us engineers kept our noses pressed pretty close to the proverbial grindstone during this time. There wasn't much attention left over for the wider world, but we kept a wary eye on the presidential race between incumbent Lyndon Johnson—a reliable friend of space exploration— and challenger Barry Goldwater, seeming to be no friend of government work except for weapons. And we did keep track of the space race. The Mercury program had been concluded one flight earlier than planned. Partly, that was a consequence of its operational success, and partly an expression of NASA's eagerness to get going on the Gemini program with its development of skills crucial to Apollo. But all of 1964 passed without a single American going into space, and the first manned Gemini flight seemed to be a long time coming.

The Soviets scored a major advance in October. They launched the first manned Voskhod spacecraft, carrying three cosmonauts on a 16-orbit mission. It could not have been accidental that they chose to match the size of an Apollo crew. One response to this feat, appearing in the "Talk of the Town" feature in the *New Yorker* magazine, was a deadpan imagination of plans for the next Soviet spacecraft to carry the entire Leningrad Symphony Orchestra into orbit to play the *1812 Overture*. Rocket firings were to play the cannon part.

Space Race Highlights of 1964

(All manned flights are indicated in bold.)

29 Jan	Saturn 1. Orbital boost. Unmanned.
30 Jan	Ranger 6. Moon impact. Unmanned.
08 Apr	Gemini 1. Orbital boost. Unmanned.
28 May	Apollo A-101. Orbital boost. Unmanned boilerplate CM.
28 Jul	Ranger 7. Moon impact. Unmanned.
18 Sep	Apollo A-102. Orbital boost. Unmanned boilerplate CM.
12 Oct	**Voskhod 1. 16 orbits. Crew: Vladimir Komarov, Konstantin Feoktistov, Boris Yegorov.**
28 Nov	Mariner 4. Launch for Mars flyby. Unmanned.
30 Nov	Zond 2. Launch for Mars flyby. Unmanned.
All Year	**No Americans in space.**

Other flights where a vehicle (often a missile) entered space, mostly suborbital:

USA	487
USSR	154
France	49
Australia	16
Canada	15
UK	14
Japan	8
European Union	5
Italy	4
China	3
Norway	3
Total	**758**

Of these, 74 went into Earth orbit. Country names identify where payloads were made. Most boosters were made by USA or USSR.

18

REAL AND MECHANICAL PEOPLE: 1963–1965

Unlike the hordes of programmers around the world that collaborate on software products today with little or no awareness of what the others are doing, programmers in the Lab had to coordinate with each other frequently to make everything fit together. After we built and tested each little module of software, we couldn't just hand the object code over to an operating system, saying, in effect, "Here, keep this on a disk somewhere and when I call for it to be run, find someplace in the computer's memory to copy it into and run it there." With all of the software kept in ROM, there wasn't any "somewhere" on a disk; there was just a *permanent* "someplace" in memory— specifically an as-yet-unallocated part of the ROM—that we had to find manually. Since the bank-switching scheme meant that not all of ROM was available at every instant, we had to either find our new module a home in just one of those banks, or divide it into sub-modules that knew which banks to find each other in. On top of that, we had to try and eliminate unused—i.e., wasted—space in each bank of ROM. It was a little like the walls built by the ancient Incas in Peru, where stones fit so snugly into notches cut in other stones that you can't stick a knife between them.

Every time an upgrade was ready to be integrated into a mission-program Rope, the whole program had to be assembled and printed prior to testing. With no way to display the output of the *YUL* assembler on screens, those paper listings were the only medium to examine. As more and more people built their parts of Block I AGC flight programs, the number of lines of source code approached the number of words (24K) in fixed memory. The listings became quite large, hundreds of pages of 11 × 15 inch paper in a fanfold configuration.

Line printers did not have single-page handling like modern "page printers." They used a pin-feed mechanism on both ends of the 15-inch dimension to pull up a continuous stream of fanfold paper for printing, then pass it over the top of the platen to drop down into what (with luck) became a neat fanfolded stack. Pre-punched holes in the corners of each page could be threaded onto the posts of a heavy-duty binder to make a sturdy book-like package weighing several pounds.

Because AGC program listings had to be distributed to numbers of people, there was a way of making four copies at a time with special carbon paper. The printing was done on a "Dagwood sandwich" whose layers were paper-carbon-paper-carbon-paper-carbon-paper. One reason line printers were so noisy is that they were designed to make the print wheels hit the paper hard enough to make a good impression on the fourth copy.

The computer operator took the printed sandwich to an eight-foot-long machine called a decollater—pronounced "*deck*-a-later"—that had four stackers separated by three steel partitions, above each of which was a motorized spindle to take up the carbon paper. The operator had to hand-feed several feet of the sandwich to get copies of the first couple of pages into each stacker, and wind enough carbon paper around each spindle so it wouldn't slip off. He then started the motor and stood back a bit, as sooty bits of carbon tended to fly off. When the sandwich had all run through and become four neat (with luck) fanfold stacks, he pulled off the three grubby rolls of carbon, threw them out, and went to wash up before distributing the copies.

Individual engineers kept their research programs and data on magnetic tapes, nearly half a mile long, bearing their names compressed to eight characters, such as BATTIN and JIMILLER, each with its first and second backup. A separate tape for each AGC programmer was not a possibility because each program had so many contributors, so I created a family of tapes named YULPROGS. With several AGC programs under development for different flights, its capacity was eventually exceeded, so I parceled out the programs among three tape families, naming them for the Space Guidance Analysis secretaries. Nancy Stone compressed neatly into NANSTONE, Andrea Kramer into ANDREA.K, and Lynn Ward into LYNNWARD.

These were all intelligent and articulate young women, but I particularly noticed Lynn because she was a little larger than life. She was tall and trim, about 5'11" with wide square shoulders such as the '40s clothing designers drew. She had curly blonde hair and a southern accent matched by an outgoing manner with a huge smile. In season, there was a good tan on those shoulders, and she dressed so that we could admire them. She was grumbled at by other women in the Lab for straying so far from the demure ideal, a reaction that bothered her as a serious injustice.

Her "nametape" figured in a curious episode one day, when I stopped in at the computer room to see when I could get some mainframe time for testing. Benny, the operator on duty, was threading that tape onto one of the reel-to-reel drives. As I approached him, he turned and said, "What a sly dirty old man you turned out to be."

I was every bit as puzzled as he wanted me to be. "Well, I'm not really that old, for starters. And I can't imagine what sort of sly dirt you've discovered."

"Look at the console," he said. There I saw that *YUL* was running and had just typed out its request for the program file tape: "MOUNT LYNNWARD." Innocent that I was, I'd had no idea of how that automated phrase would look to a receptive mind.

I chuckled and said, "All right, Benny. Just don't take it the wrong way, OK?" Shaking my head, I went back to my desk, leaving Benny to his fantasies.

Although rocket science was an overwhelmingly male pursuit in those years, there were notable exceptions. In 1963, Valentina Tereshkova in Vostok 6 was definitely Right Stuff when she had to work quickly with a ground control error sending her into a higher orbit when it was time to re-enter. And on the academic side, our own Sheila Widnall was outstanding, always ready to apply the highest mathematical models, and making it clear to her students in aeronautics/astronautics courses that she expected them to do the same.

But software, true to its beginnings with Ada Lovelace

(working with Charles Babbage in the 1840s) and Grace Hopper (working with Howard Aiken in the 1940s), was already an equal-opportunity game. Staffing up as the deadline pressure for Block I flights climbed, we hired several programming generalists of both genders, starting with Tom Lawton and Charley Muntz. Margaret Hamilton was our Good Witch of the Northeast, not to be confused with the same-named actress playing the Wicked Witch of the West in *The Wizard of Oz*. Her star quality quickly became apparent when she joined the Apollo mission software effort. Slim, with very long straight brown hair, her physical presence was striking. In repose, she wore a half-smile that readily broadened to full scale in almost any conversation. Complementing this was a brilliant and imaginative mind, and a temperament that defined serenity.

Many women in the '60s wrestled with the changing ideas of femininity, some old-fashioned, some revolutionary, some both by turns. Margaret, managing to rise above all that, had a manner that said, "It's all right, this is how I was going to be anyway." If I dwell on her, it is not merely to express my own admiration (ample as that is), but to suggest how she was perceived by most of the other engineers. She was the Goddess of Software, a presence that went beyond competence and general compatibility to something grander—an eminence, perhaps. A great deal of the mission software progressed from a morass of stressful challenges to a successful integrated system with the aid of Margaret's wise and kindly direction.

Although Margaret was freshly divorced when she joined us, I didn't see all that male admiration triggering any great amount of courtship—for a while. Most of us were simply too busy, married to our work. But a couple of years later, when we had improved our software procedures and lowered the pressure a little, there was a party at one engineer's suburban house, attended by around three dozen of us. The big room had a nice oriental rug, and I became aware of two figures sitting on that rug in the middle of the room. One was Margaret; the other was Daniel J. Lickly, a notably wise and kindly fellow, also recently divorced. Oblivious to the party, they were consumed with the fascination in each other's eyes. "Ah … Margaret has made her choice," I thought, " … and Dan has made his." They were married not long after.

Whenever there was a break from leadership duties, Margaret made a specialty of analyzing how errors in software were made. Much of the low-hanging fruit in that area was just stupid things done by bright people who were momentarily distracted. There were typos and inconsistencies that *YUL* caught in the process of assembly, or logical blunders that appalled their authors ("How could I … !") once they saw the problem. Then there were subtler logical bugs like dealing with less than all the possible cases, mathematical problems propagating errors (in the sense of inexactnesses) or needlessly sacrificing precision, and following erroneous specifications.

The most vexing cases were bugs that occurred once, fouled up a test run, and vanished into thin air. No amount of re-running the test, to subject them to analysis and resolution, could make them happen again. With her customary serenity, Margaret named these bugs "FLTs," for Funny Little Things. That may sound cavalier, as if we didn't somehow care enough to find and fix the problems, but every software project has some FLTs, and one mustn't devote more effort to reproducing them than their severity calls for.

After Apollo was over, Margaret and a female colleague left to found a software company—Higher Order Software—

exploiting her ideas about ways to prevent bugs. Being mid-century male chauvinist pigs, we guys naturally referred to her establishment as "The House of Ill Compute."

———— ∞∞ ————

Along with the design of the Block II AGC hardware, we applied lessons from Block I programming experience to create the Block II AGC interpretive language as a significant upgrade of the Block I model. In making it meet the needs of people like Bill Widnall and Margaret Hamilton, I felt I was again functioning as a bridge between the hardware and software sides. That's a funny thing to say when talking about an interpreter, which is after all a piece of software, but from the point of view of its users, the interpreter *was* hardware. The difference was, the users could come to Charley Muntz or me during the design cycle to plead for additional features, and we were generally able to oblige.

One example of a user request was adding logic to handle data items whose word length was exactly one bit, that is, flagbits. In a complex spacecraft there are lots of on/off or true/false variables, such as CM-docked-with-LM or landing-radar-enabled. So we added sixty flagbit variables and a variety of operations like "Branch if flagbit x is on and change its value."

The interpreter itself was a fairly simple program, despite its many parts. All it had to do with each operand address it picked up was to perform whatever memory bank-switching it implied and put the operand data in a standard place in unswitched memory, and all it did with interpretive operation codes was to call the right subroutines. Aside from straightforward detection of numerical overflow events, it had no diagnostic functions for erroneous programming. With so little room in the AGC, we left it up to the digital simulator to catch the bugs. Less simple was the effect on the *YUL* system, which had to incorporate all the rules for the use of each op code and present clear and unambiguous "cusses" for any violation.

Because *YUL* was my individual product, I ran short of time dealing with those complexities and began to fall behind. Help was at hand, fortunately, in the form of an outstanding newcomer. Clifford F. Ide was a big Colorado guy who could step into almost any Western movie and fit right in, especially the somewhat cowboy-style voice and idiom. He was smarter than 99% of almost any group, and I liked him at once. We shared an office on the ground floor in Dick Battin's corner of the building, and it didn't take long to grasp what Cliff's style was going to be. He wrote code as fast as he could think, which was impressively swift, and the result was pretty solid. I'd call it a pedestrian style, by contrast to the conceptual elegances I liked to build into mine, but maybe "power-walking" would be the better term. Just one thing bothered me: He wouldn't write a word of comments in his code. Cliff's mighty mental horsepower had never been harnessed to the wagon of vocabulary, still less that of systematic exposition.

But setting that peccadillo aside, Cliff was a happy colleague for me. I got to know him and his wife Pauline and their kids, though they never did succeed in getting me to go clog dancing with them. They suffered a terrible tragedy, losing a teenage daughter to an accident, which may be part of the reason they moved back West after a fairly short time at the Lab. Aside from losing touch with a good friend, I had reason to regret his departure when I couldn't break loose enough time to convert *YUL*'s tedious magnetic-tape sorting (putting the object code in sequence by ascending addresses) to use the Honeywell's massive disk file unit that arrived as part of the mainframe upgrade about then. Cliff would have made that thing sing.

———— ∞∞∞ ————

As we staffed up and began to make long test runs for several different Apollo missions in parallel, we filled more and more of the Honeywell 800's time and could foresee our demand soon exceeding more than twice the machine's capacity. Worrying about this prospect in conversations with Honeywell people, we got a pleasant surprise: they were just getting ready to make an announcement. Their newer model, the H-1800, was fully compatible and at least three times as fast in most operations, simply because its memory cycle time was 2 microseconds instead of 6, and even faster than that for heavy-duty number-crunching. Its time-shared Arithmetic/Logic Unit (ALU) was not only large but exotic. The sub-unit that performed floating-point (scientific notation) calculations was blazing fast, because it was made of "tunnel diodes" that exploited a quantum-mechanical phenomenon much faster than regular transistor switching. That was the first I'd ever heard of such a technology, and I certainly haven't met it since, though I imagine supercomputers may include such things.

Regarding compatibility, Honeywell was as good as their word. They spent a frenetic weekend taking out the H-800 boxes and installing the H-1800 boxes. On Monday morning, everything ran. The new machine came with a disk drive, what today we'd call a hard drive since the media were not removable. And what a hard drive!

Instead of the fifty horizontal platters on a vertical shaft on the old IBM 650's RAMAC, it had twelve aluminum platters about the size of manhole covers, though only five-eighths inches thick, on a massive horizontal shaft. The disks rotated at a stately 1,000 RPM, with a total capacity of over 50 Mbytes on their twenty-four recording surfaces. Instead of the RAMAC's three access arms that darted in and out of the stack of platters, the Honeywell drive had a comb of twenty-four arms, one permanently dedicated to each disk surface. A powerful hydraulic stepping motor drove this comb to place all the twenty-four read/write heads at the same track level, creating small floorquakes that were felt all over the room. The heads were mounted on curved surfaces, roughly the size and shape of old-fashioned nonpareil candies but very much smoother, to assure a thin air cushion between head and disk. There was logic to pull the comb all the way out of the disk array when shutting down the unit, and startup logic to prevent the comb from entering the array until full rotational speed was attained.

Every morning, our resident Honeywell field service engineers had to open the unit, service the hydraulics, and tighten everything up again with a precisely calibrated torque wrench. They told me one day how installers had neglected to fasten another customer's disk unit to the elevated floor. In operation, certain rhythms of hydraulic stepper usage hit a resonant frequency. Those vibrations made the unit walk across the floor like a spastic elephant until the cabling stopped it.

Keeping our system programs, like the *YUL* system and the *MAC* compiler, on the disk along with everybody's *MAC* programs gave us another significant time saving. To handle low-level tasks with card records, which didn't need the processing power of the H-1800 but took some of its time, we installed a Honeywell 200 as an auxiliary computer and got that time back. The H-200 could talk with the H-1800 at high speed over a dedicated channel. It had a faster and more capacious punched card reader, a fast punch, and a high-capacity (over 2 Mbytes) magnetic drum storage, in addition to the printer and a pair of tape drives. It could, for instance, print a long file from the H-1800 while copying a considerable card file to the drum for later transmission to the H-1800.[39]

———&&&———

The space race finally began to show some balance in 1965. There was just one manned Soviet flight, though an impressive one. Voskhod 2 carried two cosmonauts, instead of the three that were crammed into Voskhod 1, because Alexey Leonov carried special gear that enabled him to perform the first walk in space. Regarding the Moon itself, we sent Ranger 8 and Ranger 9, which successfully returned detailed images while crashing on target, thus making up for the failed Lunar-impact missions of Rangers 6 and 7 the year before. The much more aggressive Soviets found that their Lunar reach exceeded their Lunar grasp. Their unmanned spacecraft Luna 5, Luna 7, and Luna 8 were all intended to land on the Moon and return data, but all crashed.

The American effort got up to speed with no less than five manned Gemini missions. Gemini 3 was a quick, three-orbit flight just to show that the spacecraft could take two men into orbit and bring them safely back. In the event, it also showed the effects of smuggling an unauthorized sandwich into zero-gravity. The regular bread and other ingredients, from a fast-food joint in Cocoa Beach, Florida, generated hundreds of crumbs floating everywhere in that two-man "telephone booth," enough to create a real nuisance. Command Pilot Gus Grissom, miffed by the fact that his junior Pilot John Young was the only one supplied with food designed for space, was the culprit.

Gemini 4's duration of 62 orbits set a record, and Ed White performed the first American spacewalk while command pilot Jim McDivitt held the fort. Like Leonov before him, he had the devil's own time squeezing himself and his space suit back into the vehicle. Gemini 5's week in orbit, 120 orbits, kept Gordon Cooper and Pete Conrad cooped up but thriving for a period that would be typical of Apollo missions.

Gemini 7 almost doubled that again, to 206 orbits with plenty of opportunities to try out what were politely called "waste management systems." That led Frank Borman and Jim Lovell to characterize most of their mission as "two weeks in a men's room." Things got more interesting when Gemini 6A, the rescheduled Gemini 6 after a booster glitch that was caught before launch, brought Wally Schirra and Tom Stafford to within a few feet of Gemini 7 for a computer-guided successful rendezvous. The two spacecraft were close enough to show each other dueling placards: "Beat Army" in the window of all-Navy Gemini 6A, and "Beat Navy" in West Pointer Frank Borman's window of Gemini 7. The rendezvous was their Christmas present to the country—the first time we had beaten the Soviets to a solid achievement in manned space flight. It certainly cheered our Lab rendezvous experts to see how accurately computer-aided control did the trick.

The Gemini flights affected our work at the Lab by underscoring something we'd first seen in the Mercury program. A lot of humidity builds up over time in a manned spacecraft, compounded by its being salty sweat and, therefore, electrically conductive. All thought of building the AGC with a plug-in spare vanished in favor of moisture-proofing the electronics. We adapted our Block II packaging concept, two well-sealed flattish halves the size of dress-shirt packages, to contain the

Block I logic. With a dazzling disregard for consistency, we called that configuration "Block 100," and made it ready for Block I CM flights.

NASA/Marshall tested the early first-stage Saturn boosters throughout the year, lofting three *boilerplates* into orbit. A boilerplate version of a spacecraft, here just the Apollo Command Module, was an inert object the same size and weight as the real vehicle, with no electronics. It remained attached to the Saturn 4B booster stage, thus becoming a large and useless satellite. That meant we didn't have to do anything about those missions except read the reports in *Aviation Week and Space Technology*.

We did, however, have to prepare for the more advanced unmanned missions that would be tests of the spacecraft as well as the booster. Those Block I flights needed a smattering of functions that would be performed by astronauts in a normal flight, but couldn't be emulated by uplinked DSKY keystrokes. They were performed by a Mission Control Programer (MCP) in the CM that required some AGC code additional to what was needed in a manned flight. This unit was—let's face it—a *kludge*, in the classical sense of a large ugly object that had to be thrown together to fill some quick-and-dirty need; indeed, its very name included a non-standard spelling. It was full of relay logic and elementary timers to do things a well-trained astronaut would do; for example, sensing whether aerodynamic deceleration at the beginning of entry was recognized by the PGNCS in a timely fashion. More critically, it had to turn on the Service Propulsion System's heavy-duty gimbal motors one at a time, inserting a pause to make sure the current-draw surges on startup didn't coincide and overload the electrical power supply.

We always referred to the MCP as the "Mechanical Man"—

and there's an even better reason for that designation. It was installed in the CM where the couches and crew would normally be, resting on the shock-absorber struts that normally supported the couches. Some extra mass was built into it, to match that of the missing couches and crew. Thus, its electrical/logical functions were augmented by the purely mechanical function of stress-testing those struts. The Mechanical Man was necessarily built from off-the-shelf relays and other standard parts. To assure reliable operation of such run-of-the-mill components, its design included fault-tolerant configurations like the Triple Modular Redundancy logic in the Launch Vehicle Digital Computer. Foreshadowing the more elaborate fault tolerance designed a decade later for the Space Shuttle, the Mechanical Man successfully maintained full functionality through several component failures.

Space Race Highlights of 1965

(All manned flights are indicated in bold.)

16 Feb	Apollo BP-16. Orbital boost. Unmanned boilerplate CM.
20 Feb	Ranger 8. Moon impact. Unmanned.
18 Mar	**Voskhod 2. 17 orbits. Crew: Pavel Belyayev, Alexey Leonov.**
23 Mar	**Gemini 3. 3 orbits. Crew: Gus Grissom, John Young.**
24 Mar	Ranger 9. Moon impact. Unmanned.
12 May	Luna 5. Moon lander, but crashed. Unmanned.
25 May	Apollo BP-26. Orbital boost. Unmanned boilerplate CM.
03 Jun	**Gemini 4. 62 orbits. Crew: Jim McDivitt, Ed White. First US spacewalk.**
30 Jul	Apollo BP-9A. Orbital boost. Unmanned boilerplate CM.
21 Aug	**Gemini 5. 120 orbits. Crew: Gordon Cooper, Pete Conrad. Longest manned spaceflight to date.**
07 Oct	Luna 7. Moon lander, but crashed. Unmanned.
03 Dec	Luna 8. Moon lander, but crashed. Unmanned.
04 Dec	**Gemini 7. 206 orbits. Crew: Frank Borman, Jim Lovell. Longest manned spaceflight to date.**
15 Dec	**Gemini 6A. 16 orbits. Crew: Wally Schirra, Tom Stafford. First rendezvous.**

Other flights where a vehicle (often a missile) entered space, mostly suborbital:

USA	555
USSR	150
Canada	78
France	39
Australia	28
Japan	21
UK	18
European Union	9
Argentina	3
Sweden	2
Norway	2
India	2
Total	**907**

Of these, 96 went into Earth orbit. Country names identify where payloads were made. Most boosters were made by USA or USSR.

COOL TOOLS AND HOT PRESSURE
1965–1966

As the prospect of a rapid succession of Apollo missions came into focus, the Lab had to apply a higher, un-academic level of discipline to hardware development, software development, and project management. In each area, we brought in sophisticated tools to help achieve the robust quality required to take men to the Moon.

The final packaging design for the Block II AGC took the form of two slabs the size of dress-shirt boxes. One contained all the central processing logic, and the other contained the two memories and the hybrid circuitry to operate them. The memory slab had a well at one end where we could plug in up to six rope modules. Each module was about the size and shape of a video cassette cartridge and held 6K words. In accordance with the humidity lessons from Gemini, these were screwed into place and sealed before flight. It couldn't be too long before, because we had to complete stringent testing of the software woven into those ropes. Until we inserted the ropes, there was no difference between an AGC in the Command module and an LGC in the Lunar Module, so any AGC could be exhaustively tested with a special test program rope before even being assigned to a spacecraft.

The two slabs had a multi-pin connector between them, placed so we could seal the slabs together, all around the edges, after plugging them together. But within each slab was a space called a backplane because it was the back of the surface the individual logic modules plugged into. The backplane space was a forest of thousands of inch-high square posts in neat rows and columns, one hundred per square inch, each carrying a digital signal from or to a logic module. For corrosion-proof high conductivity, our posts were beryllium copper plated with gold. We had a specialist who programmed a computer-driven machine to perform wire-wrap connections among the posts.

Robert F. Morse was tall and athletic, with an eye for quality, a man of uncompromising standards. He could be counted on to produce quality software. Bob created a database which related every inter-module signal defined and named by Eldon Hall's Digital Development Group to its particular backplane post, and identified the other post or posts to which it had to be connected. For testing his database, he had to make up a five-character signal name that he knew would never coincide with that of an actual signal, so he called his test signal *4NIC8*. To see why that wouldn't have been a real signal name in our polite community, pronounce it as you would if you saw it in a text message. Just another way Bob was ahead of his time.

More liberally educated than many MIT staffers, Bob recalled the mythological oracle of Apollo at Delphi, naming his database Delphi. Unlike most databases that display their data for human inspection, Bob's program mediated between this file and a Gardner Denver Wire Wrap machine that did the actual wiring. Delphi figured out the optimal way to lay out the wires, making sure to place no more than three wraps on any one post, and punched a teletype-style eight-channel "paper" tape (actually Mylar for durability) for the Gardner Denver machine to read. Every wire run had to follow a path of up to three cardinal-direction segments, that is, no diagonal paths. Delphi specified the locations of the two posts and exactly how long each wire run had to be, plus the required locations of one or two "dressing fingers" to make the wire turn right-angle corners.

With the backplane secured to a motorized bed, the machine pulled insulated wire off a spool and cut a length, two inches longer than specified, then stripped an inch of the yellow insulation off each end. It fed one end into its wrap tool, slewed and rotated the workpiece bed to bring the designated post under the tool, sensed how many wires were already wrapped there so as to back off accordingly, and wrapped the stripped end around the post seven times, so tightly that the corners of the square post cut into the wire and assured a contamination-free contact. The wrap tool let go of the completed first end and picked up the other end of the wire, slewing the bed to pull the wire gently in the specified direction. If a zig or a zig-zag was needed, the machine maneuvered one or two dressing fingers into place and made the required right-angle turns. Finally, it positioned the workpiece bed to bring the destination post under the tool and repeated the wrapping action to complete the connection.

That procedure, repeated every six seconds for a few thousand times as dictated by Bob's data on the Mylar tape, produced a fully wired backplane. The next step was 100%

continuity testing to verify that every post had an ultra-low-resistance connection to all the correct posts, and no connection at all to any of the other posts. For a population of ten thousand posts, the number of continuity tests required was over fifty million, definitely a good thing to do at computer speeds.[40]

Once a completely assembled AGC passed all its acceptance tests, we poured Room-Temperature-Vulcanizing (RTV) potting compound into the 1.1-inch-deep tray in which the forest of posts resided, burying them in solid insulation. When it cured, we fastened and sealed a sheet of aluminum snugly over each of the two RTV-filled trays. That was our belt-suspenders-and-cummerbund road to reliability: each wire wrap was itself a gas-tight cold weld; the RTV blocked any wandering fluids and inconvenient gases from getting anywhere near the wrapped posts; and the metal skin kept any of those bad things from touching the RTV.

───⬡───

As deadlines—more politely known as "estimated dates"—for many parts of flight software began to pile up, the Lab's project leaders had to keep adding programmers. Starting from our original culture that control system engineers would pick up the art of programming without much effort, we weren't well prepared for the opposite situation. New people who were general-purpose programmers had to be made into control system engineers, which we knew would be harder, but we didn't really know how to do that. The project-management art of creating software specifications wasn't highly developed anywhere that we knew of, and we had to pick it up as best we could. We became another good example of Fred Brooks's trenchant observation in *The Mythical Man-Month*, "Adding people to a late project makes it later." That wisdom, even if accepted philosophically, is hard to apply because if you have a late project, you must be seen as Doing Something about it, and adding people is usually the only available Something.

The influx of so many new people who weren't rocket scientists, and who had to learn the complexities of the Block II AGC without having any experience with Block I, affected my ability to get things done. No longer could I train programmers in one-on-one sessions using a two-page list of AGC instruction types—there had to be something closer to a real manual. Besides, NASA officials were upset about the lack of a programming manual and a computer specification as they understood such things.

In the 1950s and '60s, every general-market computer came with a programmer's reference manual. Since every computer had a novel architecture to be explained and puffed, such manuals tended to be a hundred or so pages long, loaded with beautiful glossy pictures of the computer and all its ancillary units and a few perfectly scrumptious models who looked as if they almost knew how to operate the machinery. The manuals also contained documentation of the assembler with extensive examples of code showing how to make the most of the architecture. We didn't have time or inclination to publish anything of the sort. When it came time to document the programmers' view of the Block II AGC, there was a large cadre of engineers who already knew the rules of the *YUL* system.

Using our established technology by which I scribbled and a secretary typed, I wrote "AGC4 Memo #9" to document how to use the expanded memory and the expanded instruction set. I distributed it starting in 1965, as the engineers got ready to shift from their *MAC* studies and simulations to Block II AGC coding. It had a chapter on all the instructions, another on the unprogrammed sequences that stole memory cycles as needed for input/output operations, and one on the address formats recognized by *YUL*.

All that took twenty-seven pages of typed text, with some tables and a few very simple schematic diagrams producible with a typewriter and a ruler and pen. In the months after it was issued, I decided to round out the document by including what we had for a computer specification. It began with a list of the individual control pulses that were the bricks of which instructions were built and microprogram listings showing how the instructions were in fact built. Then there was a nice schematic our drafting department had drawn up to show the entire scheme of memory types and the addresses to access them, so I re-issued Memo #9 as fifty-one pages in mid-1966. The name "AGC4" in its title showed that it belonged to the existing series of "AGC4 memos." It wasn't very logical on a Block II document since AGC4 was the name of the Block I AGC. The extreme informality of this rather key document, and its consequent invisibility to the NASA review committee, is what caused people to refer to it as "infamous."[41]

There were some software tools to help project managers. Anybody who has had occasion to use Microsoft's Project software may be aware of its roots half a century ago as PERT, for Project Evaluation & Review Technique. That was the tool the Lab's Peter Peck used to help our leadership maintain some idea of where we stood relative to NASA's schedule. PERT was no less primitive than other software tools of the period, and Peter's combination of intelligence and sunny disposition was essential to making it achieve anything at all—no wonder he acquired the nickname of Peter PERT. Picture this summery scene: an original Volkswagen Beetle with a distinctly heavy-set man crammed into the driver's seat wearing a short-sleeved shirt. He fit there OK if his whole left arm was out the window. Now, picture the black ice on the streets and the snow swirling down, and that arm still out the window, still short-sleeved. Peter's unfailing good nature shone through, evidently enough to keep him warm at heart, where it counted.

PERT and its successors made graphical representations of the predicted duration of various tasks in a project. The results were printed in ordinary characters on a line printer, a primitive presentation compared to the graphical media of later decades. The software accounted for which tasks could be done in parallel and which ones had to await the completion of which other tasks, or had to await the availability of certain key people. The longest-duration chain of tasks was called a Critical Path (in fact, a successor to PERT was named CPM, for Critical Path Method), calling the leadership's attention to places where modification of the task structure would best pay off.

Artisans of all sorts are often frustrated by the amount of time it takes to get something done right, and engineers are no exception. A visit from the man who asks how long it will take to finish is inherently stressful, so Peter's benign manner in this role was another important instance of caring and trusting. By contrast, consider the famous two-liner in the story of the Sistine Chapel's ceiling:

"*When will it be done?*" growled the Pope.

"*When it's finished,*" snapped Michelangelo.

While much of my attention was focused on helping people get up to speed with the Block II architecture, a considerable group at the Lab, mostly old hands like Tom Lawton and Charley Muntz, was racing to bring the second Block I flight "rope" (the first for a manned flight) to a well-tested readiness. It was called SUNSPOT, and Alex Kosmala became its Rope Mother since he'd done well with the unmanned AS-202, which had taken the Lab's Primary Guidance Navigation and Control System into space for the first time. As 1966 wound down, the schedule stress mounted, forcing both MIT and NASA engineers to accept "pretty-well-tested" as a compromise criterion.

Out in Downey, California, North American Aviation was in a similar situation with Engineering Change Orders, stimulated by the AS-202 flight experience, for the Block I Command Module. More and more wires had to be stuffed behind sheet-metal panels that were already bulging. They tested everything in normal atmosphere, and passed the updated CM to NASA for limited testing in the pure-oxygen atmosphere to be used in flight AS-204, early in 1967.

In Houston, the designated crew for the first Block I flight consisted of Gus Grissom, Ed White, and space-rookie Roger Chaffee. Gus, veteran of both Mercury and Gemini missions, had also been busy working on Block II problems, primarily the design of the Lunar Module. One of the bigger new tasks facing them was becoming proficient at fine-aligning the IMU's stable platform using the space sextant. First as a joke, then to make conversation about the stars they were sighting more efficient in a noisy environment, Grissom invented new names for three stars on their list that didn't have convenient well-known names like Sirius and Rigel. Gamma Cassiopeiae he named *Navi*, his own middle name spelled backwards. Gamma Velorum became *Regor*, spelling Chaffee's first name backwards. Spelling any part of Ed White's name backward presented more of a problem in making anything pronounceable yet unique, until he realized that his crewmate's full name was Edward White II, so Iota Ursae Majoris was re-christened *Dnoces*, reversing Second.

Throughout 1966, the Soviets had been keeping the pressure on in their own way, starting with the first soft landing of a spacecraft on the Moon, which was also the first at any place other than Earth. They also sent three successful Lunar orbiters that returned detailed photos, including the Earth's first images of the Moon's far side. The Soviets closed out the year with another soft Lunar landing. We countered with one soft landing (Surveyor 1) and two Lunar orbiters, but most of Houston's attention was on the final five Gemini flights. Those included the first docking in space (the second American "first" in the race), eight Extra-Vehicular Activities (EVA) and two more dockings. For the first time since Yuri Gagarin's flight in 1961, a whole year went by without a single Soviet cosmonaut in space.

Three of Marshall's Saturn boosters made successful launches, and both sides made forward-looking unmanned missions. We orbited a prototype of the Manned Orbiting Laboratory, the first gesture toward a Space Station. The Soviets made their first test of a Soyuz spacecraft, showing their three-man high-endurance vehicle. The name "Soyuz"— meaning "Union" as in Soviet Union—was also a persistent reminder that it would be adept at making "unions" in space; that is, rendezvous and docking. Our lead in that art would not go unchallenged very long.

Space Race Highlights of 1966

(All manned flights are indicated in bold.)

31 Jan   Luna 9. Moon lander: first soft landing on Moon. Unmanned.

26 Feb   Apollo (AS-201). Suborbital boost. Crew: Mechanical Man (MCP).

16 Mar   Gemini 8. 1 day. Crew: Neil Armstrong, Dave Scott. First docking.

31 Mar   Luna 10. First Moon orbiter. First images of Moon's back side. Unmanned.

30 May   Surveyor 1. Moon lander: first U.S. soft landing on Moon. Unmanned.

03 Jun   Gemini 9A. 3 days. Crew: Tom Stafford, Gene Cernan. 1 EVA.

05 Jul   Apollo 2 (AS-203). Suborbital boost by Saturn 1B & 4B. No spacecraft.

18 Jul   Gemini 10. 3 days. Crew: John Young, Michael Collins. Docking, EVA.

10 Aug   Lunar Orbiter 1. Photography. Unmanned.

24 Aug   Luna 11. Moon orbiter. Photography. Unmanned.

25 Aug   Apollo 3 (AS-202). Suborbital boost. Crew: MCP. First flight of PGNCS.

12 Sep   Gemini 11. 3 days. Crew: Pete Conrad, Richard Gordon. Docking, EVA.

20 Sep   Surveyor 2. Moon lander, but crashed on Moon. Unmanned.

22 Oct   Luna 12. Moon orbiter. Photography. Unmanned.

01 Nov   X-15 Flight 174. Crew: Bill Dana.

03 Nov   Gemini 2A. Suborbital test of Manned Orbiting Laboratory. Unmanned.

06 Nov   Lunar Orbiter 2. Photography. Unmanned.

11 Nov   Gemini 12. 4 days. Crew: Jim Lovell, Buzz Aldrin.

28 Nov   Kosmos 133. First test of Soyuz spacecraft. Unmanned.

21 Dec   Luna 13. Moon lander, soft landing on Moon. Unmanned.

Detailed data on other flights is not available for 1966.

20

DISASTER AND AGONIZING
REAPPRAISAL: 1967

To make room for the army of programmers working at the Lab, offices on the second floor of our building got converted into a greater number of spaces, the forerunners of today's cubicles. As 1967 began, I occupied one such space near the center of that floor, occasionally missing my former view of the Charles River and Boston.

At the Kennedy Space Center, the first manned flight of an Apollo spacecraft was scheduled for 21 February, and NASA workers made preparations for crew drills in the actual vehicle. There was some concern over what the atmosphere in the Command Module (CM) should be for these exercises. While in space, the CM would have a pure-oxygen atmosphere at three pounds per square inch, the same as the partial pressure due to oxygen at sea level. North American Aviation (NAA) had designed its structure and skin to accommodate an inside pressure over three pounds greater than the outside, somewhat like a jetliner. But having only a three-pound atmosphere inside, while on the ground with fifteen pounds outside, would be likely to damage the vehicle by working *against* its pressure design. NASA and NAA decided to eliminate any pressure-differential problems by giving the CM a pure-oxygen atmosphere of 16.7 pounds during ground operations, ensuring *some* overpressure inside but not too much.

The mission was known as SA-204 to the Marshall Center people (giving Saturn the top billing) and as AS-204 to the Houston people (giving Apollo the top billing). Gus Grissom and his crewmates preferred simply Apollo 1. On the afternoon of 27 January, 1967, the crew was driven out to Launch Complex 34 and took the elevator in the 380-foot Launch Umbilical Tower with its cantilevered Service Arms reaching out to the booster and spacecraft. They rose past the cluster of eight rockets and tanks making up the Saturn 1B first stage, then past the smoothly unified Saturn 4B second stage and the empty tapered Lunar Module adapter shroud, and finally past the Service Module bristling with RCS jets, to the CM Service Arm level. A short walk along that arm brought them to a rigorously clean chamber enclosing the hatch side of the CM itself. This was the "white room," manned by technicians responsible for every detail of the CM's configuration before launch. That day's exercise was a dress rehearsal for both the astronauts and the white-room crew. As Commander, Gus climbed first into the spacecraft and settled into the left-hand seat. Pilot Roger Chaffee strapped into the right-hand seat, handy to the voice communications gear. Finally, Senior Pilot Ed White climbed in and turned his lanky powerful frame around to secure the robust pressure hatch and secure its latches with some help from the white-room crew, then wriggled into the center seat. Signaling the white-room people to start the pumps that replaced humid Florida air with dry oxygen, they turned on their various devices and commenced the day's scripted drill.

Nobody knows exactly what happened. Most likely, Gus put his left foot in its bulky Apollo space boot in a place where there'd been room for it in the CM mockup used in training. But it may have bumped hard into a small metal panel with recently added wiring poking out of one edge. That bump made a spark, and the normally safe insulation material flared up in the pressurized oxygen atmosphere. Somehow, the flame reached one of the many lightweight plastic parts in the main panel and touched it off.

The white-room crew jumped when Roger's voice came over the intercom, "Fire in the spacecraft!" Horrified, they realized that they had no quick way to open the pressure hatch because its latches were inside. At that point, the fire was rapidly converting oxygen molecules into larger, and much hotter, carbon dioxide molecules, raising the overpressure far past its design limits. The spacecraft's skin ruptured and threw a huge sheet of flame out into the white room, making rescue efforts impossible until that fire could be brought under control. When they finally pried the hatch open, it was clear that Ed had exerted all of his unusual strength, aided by Gus, to get the latches undone in time, but their efforts were in vain.

Most of my colleagues had gone out to supper or gone home. But Tom Lawton, ashen-faced, looked in from the narrow corridor to ask, "Did you hear about the fire?" He gave me what few details he had and added, "Poor Gus, the hard-luck guy. He barely escaped drowning in the Atlantic when his Mercury capsule blew its hatch after splashdown, then got into all kinds of trouble with the Agency over that unauthorized sandwich in Gemini, and now … God help us." We silently tried to imagine what the would-be rescuers saw: the darkened interior of the spacecraft lit only by the white room's emergency lighting coming in the windows, all the gray panels with their white lettering turned black and caked with soot, and the three charred bodies that had been our friends and colleagues.

It was a long silence.

Finally I looked up at Tom and asked, "Will this be the end of Apollo?" He frowned, searching for a way to be sure of what we knew was the only possible answer. "And hand the keys to world domination to the Russians?" He shook his head slowly. We—the Lab and the nation—couldn't just walk away. We had to go forward, but how?

How could such a thing happen, in a project where so many people were checking everything so carefully? Months of investigation, complicated by anxious intervention by congressmen, uncovered a picture of schedule pressures overriding craftsmanship in far too many ways. It was the dark side of President Kennedy's challenging deadline, which had in other ways done the project so much good. Somebody at NAA must have urged an in-depth review of spaces where new wiring couldn't be fitted in compliance with mil-spec standards, but wasn't heard. Nobody, apparently, had thought to question the combination of light plastic parts and Velcro fasteners with a pure oxygen atmosphere. Nobody took the time to consider whether normal air would have served just as well as pure oxygen for ground work. And nobody had taken a systematic look at rapid escape.

NASA and NAA leaders set the deadlines aside and took some time to make more sense of the safety and quality issues. No Americans would be scheduled for space for the rest of

1967. Block I vehicles and equipment could continue in use for unmanned missions, but manned Apollo flights would be strictly Block II. It was far enough along that applying the lessons there would be simpler and ultimately faster than upgrading both blocks. In any case, the Lunar Module (LM) was an all-Block II vehicle.

Some of the lessons would require heavier materials, which would have to be compensated for with smarter designs. The CM's hatch for Block II acquired a quick way to open it from outside. The AGC took over some of the functions of the CM's Stabilization and Control System by adding a Digital Autopilot (DAP) function similar to what we were developing for the LM. With some experience of booster performance in hand, modest increases in weight could be tolerated for greater safety.

While these deliberations were going on, one event showed that the Russians, for all their 1966 achievements in Moon science, also had problems that could slow them down. On 23 April, their new spacecraft Soyuz had its first manned flight, achieving orbit, but on return to Earth the following day it crashed, killing Vladimir Komarov. He was the only human to venture into space in 1967.

There had been another event, though not a recent one, that helped us back away from our fatally excessive haste. Nobody could mention it in public, because that would have given away too much about how we found it out. In 1960, American intelligence assets discovered a catastrophic explosion deep in the USSR, where an R-16, the biggest booster rocket in history, was under development for a missile system to deliver a thermonuclear warhead of an overwhelming weight. Several illustrious Russian rocket scientists were killed in the explosion, which turned a large launch complex into a larger crater laced with deadly fumes of hypergolic fuel. The Soviet authorities covered it up, gradually leaking stories of how one or another of the victims had died in air crashes. The surviving Russian rocket scientists approached the development of monster rockets with considerably more caution. But they still tried, after Kennedy's announcement of Apollo, to build a booster that could send a single manned vehicle to the Moon that was capable of returning to Earth. By the time they decided it wasn't feasible, and consequently followed the U.S. lead in adopting the Lunar Orbit Rendezvous approach, it was too late. All the Apollo contractors had too much of a head start.

At the Lab, we were shocked and saddened by the Apollo 1 disaster but knew that nothing we could have designed into the AGC or the GN&C system would have prevented or mitigated it. Looking forward again, we were relieved to be able to cut back our Block I work to just the unmanned flight tests of the Saturn 5, and eager to apply our DAP techniques to both Block II spacecraft. But, in rigorous system testing of those Block I programs and in porting that code to Block II, we found a disturbing number of flaws that could have created embarrassing problems in Apollo 1 if it had flown. They wouldn't, in all probability, have endangered the crew, but might well have defeated some flight objectives and possibly led to an early termination.

As test pilots have always known, even an ill wind that blows death to brave men can bring better chances to others. The loss of Gus Grissom, Ed White, and Roger Chaffee gave NASA and the contractors not only the rededication but the time to assure more safety for those who followed.

PICKING UP AND DUSTING OFF: 1967

After the Apollo 1 fire, NASA improved quality control by assigning larger roles to other companies, including General Electric for systems analysis and ground support. GE was not new to the project. They'd been in the 1961 race for the spacecraft contract, submitting a design called the D-2, which NASA dismissed in favor of their in-house design by Max Faget. Sergei Korolev in the USSR was not so negative. He picked up many features of the D-2 for incorporation into the Soyuz spacecraft.

GE's engineers assigned to the new system analysis tasks needed increased understanding of the Apollo Guidance Computer (AGC). They asked the Lab's project leaders for a one-week tutorial, offering to pay consultant rates. The Lab's not-for-profit status made it impractical to respond as an organization, so the leaders asked me if I'd be interested in picking up this opportunity as an individual contractor. Well, yes, I would. The fact that consultant rates were approximately double my salary earnings was a nice bonus.

After putting together a lesson plan and settling the financial details with a GE manager by phone, I flew from Boston to Houston in one of Eastern Airlines' well-filled Boeing 727s that we called "cattle cars." Having heard for years that GE people referred to their employer as "Generous Electric," I tried to rent a Shelby-Cobra version of a Mustang for the trip, but had to settle for a regular car.

Fortunately, my GE students were veterans of GE's line of real-time computers and had faced many system-software problems similar to those of the AGC. I was able to take that group through my lesson plan quickly enough to leave the Friday open, so their manager offered to take me through all the Manned Spacecraft Center (MSC) facilities tourists and visitors never see.

The Command Module training mockup/simulator consisted of a full-size replica of the CM. To provide realistic views out all the windows, it was surrounded by so many bulky projectors, perched at odd angles, that people called it "The Train Wreck." I wonder if architect Frank Gehry was inspired by this sight. I enjoyed a few minutes in that unit, marveling at the window views and playing "drunken astronaut," operating the commander's hand controller to drive the simulated attitude into the dreaded "gimbal lock" condition where attitude reference is lost because two of the gimbal axes are too closely aligned. It was comforting to find out that wasn't easy to do. Then there was a close-up look at the astronauts' centrifuge, but no ride to try out excessive g-forces.

The high point was an extensive tour of the Thermal-Vacuum Chamber, a gargantuan fixture that appears in a forgettable movie called *Future World*, though not identified as part of MSC. We started in a smaller preliminary chamber where we viewed from a high observation deck what looked like a pressure cooker on the floor beside a table. There was an overhead crane to lift the lid off and put it on the table. The "cooker" was about 40 feet in diameter and 60 feet high, and the "table" was 40 feet square and 50 feet high. That was for smaller spacecraft.

The main part, "Chamber A," was a silo 60 feet in diameter by 120 feet high to its domed top. Its floor-level circular door was 40 feet in diameter, reinforced to withstand outside atmospheric pressure on its 181,000 square inches for a total force of 2.7 million pounds. That's the door appearing in the movie, swinging shut behind a squad of uniformed Delos Theme Park staff. Inside, there were two full-height columns on opposite sides. Liquid-nitrogen plumbing filled one column to serve as the cold of space. The other column was composed of huge heat lamps to serve as the heat and light of the Sun.

The interior volume was sized to accommodate the complete Apollo spacecraft stack: the Service Module at the bottom but propped up to make room for its SPS engine bell, the Command Module attached to the top of the SM, and the Lunar Module upside down on top of the CM. The pumps took eight hours to reduce the pressure inside those 300,000-plus cubic feet to one-millionth of normal atmospheric pressure. Those were the three primary functions of the chamber, to expose the spacecraft to the vacuum of space, a "heat soak" on the solar side, and a "cold soak" on the opposite side. The spacecraft stack was mounted on a giant turntable to test the effectiveness of "barbecue mode," used in the long stretches of coasting through space to even out the heating and cooling.

There were observation catwalks at various heights in the chamber, and we missed none of them, quite content to be visiting at normal temperature and pressure. Then we toured the outside of the domed top, clambering through criss-crossed steel girders bent to shape, reminding me of a pie with a lattice crust. When I thanked my host for a day of wonders, I added a mischievous appreciation of such a close-up look at "the expensive toys." That turned out to be a mistake. He must have had some bad experiences with cynical reporters, because he got a hurt look on his face and said, "Please don't ever call them that!" I flew home regretting my faux pas but quite happy with the consulting fee in my pocket.

―――― ∞∞ ――――

As we got various parts of the AGC software under better control, we would get requests from astronauts and others for little extra features here and there. One good example is "MINKEY" (for "Minimum Key-pushing"), wanted by some of the less keyboard-agile astronauts to reduce the number of DSKY button-pushes required for common tasks. In essence, this was exactly the function now performed by macros in Word and other modern software. By itself, MINKEY was no great challenge; all it needed was some additional code to switch in and out of MINKEY mode, and a few tables, plus a little code to interpret them.

The problem was that there were many people in many groups around the Lab saying "Sure, we can do that" to many requesters. The individuals whose job was to keep the size of the program, and its running time, under control got very frustrated about this. After all, they too were Lab engineers, as full of the can-do spirit as any of the rest. The solution was to bring in an adviser, a man with a lot of experience dealing with such problems at our sister outfit, MIT Lincoln Labs, where he had been Acting Director.

C. Robert Wieser, our instructor in the use of the word "no," appeared to some of us as a threat to our freedom of action, though he was in fact a perfectly civil and affable fellow. I thought his surname might get mispronounced by some of our less literate engineers, so I made up a (presumably) helpful limerick:

A stern old adviser named Wieser
Popped a young engineer on the beezer
When that august adviser
Was addressed "Dr. Wiser."
What a stern old adviser is Wieser!

Soon enough he established himself as a valued friend to the Lab, and the explosion of requests for "just one more thing" simmered down.

No such simple application of discipline was going to relieve the ever-increasing load on our mainframe(s), even though we'd changed that singular to a plural the year before by acquiring a second H-1800. Both our twin mainframes were bulging at the seams, struggling to run simulations of AGC programs for several missions at once. We looked hard at Honeywell's concept for the next step up, which they called the 8200, combining the functionality of a sped-up 1800 with that of a high-level Series 200 machine. I was on a small team that visited them and two competitors. Sperry Rand Univac made their 1109 the capstone of their scientific series, which began years previously with the 1101 and 1103 and evolved into the widely used 1108. Burroughs offered their 5000, a radically advanced architecture that delighted me but appalled the other team members.

Visiting Univac's Washington office, we met with a sales executive—a small man with uptight everything, even illustrating the fanciful trope of "clenched hair"—who sat in an enormous executive chair that towered a foot above his head. He spent almost all of our time regaling us with tales of his adventures fishing, or maybe it was golf (who cared?). Occasionally, he'd lean toward an improbably large bank of office intercom switches to flick a switch and bark orders. In our efforts to get him to tell us a little about the computer, we stayed so long that we were in danger of missing our flight home. Mr. Uptight arranged for the company limo to take us to National Airport and drive right out onto the taxiway so we could walk a dozen yards or so in the rain and climb the air-stair up to the propeller-driven Convair, still fuming with frustration at our wasted meeting. As soon as we were out in the open air, our sanity was quickly restored by the sight of a brilliant double rainbow stretching from horizon to horizon.

Visiting the Burroughs development center in Paoli, Pennsylvania, we met with a small group whose star member was a Dr. Hammer. He was the company's visionary, the one who had driven the design of a major computer to optimize use of that era's most advanced programming language, *ALGOL*. But the computer world was coalescing around IBM's 360 architecture and the already ancient languages, *FORTRAN* for scientific computing and *COBOL* for business data processing. Dr. Hammer's expression showed a tragic tiredness: the air of someone who knows that his vision is the best way but has become convinced that nobody wants to hear about it.

I had to grant that none of these competitors were quite ready to respond to our urgent needs, and I soon came to feel that our mission was a *pro forma* gesture. NASA had already settled on a complex of IBM 360 Model 75 computers for the Manned Spacecraft Center and were leaning on us to get in line. So it was no great surprise when a large part of the third floor of IL7 grew an elevated floor on which rested an IBM 360 Model 75, with an enormous memory of 256 Kbytes and a laser-type page printer that could do graphics as well as text.

It was swarmed over by software contractors from PHI, reprising their role of porting our software from the IBM 650 to the Honeywell 800 back in 1962. Their primary task was to port our *MAC* compiler to the 360 using a brand-new IBM-sponsored language modestly named *PL/I*, for Programming Language One. Just as the 360 architecture was supposed to embrace all scientific and business applications, *PL/I* was intended to replace both *FORTRAN* and *COBOL*. In that respect, history has shown a substantial disregard of IBM's wishes.[42] Scrambling to keep up with demands for tweaking the *YUL* system, I was not available to port the Honeywell source code for *YUL* to IBM 360 assembler language source code. The 360 version had to have built a respectable track record for reliability by the time the Honeywell 1800s were taken away. So the PHI people did the porting, without a single consultation or question for me, and I've wondered whether to feel insulted or complimented thereby. On the whole, I feel it's a compliment because it suggests my efforts to make the source code readable, with expressive symbolic names and ample comment text, were entirely successful.

There was just one thing I really objected to: they changed the name from *YUL*, with its poetic link to Christmas 1959, to *GAP*, for General Assembly Program. Now that's prosaic and pedestrian, and therefore reprehensible. I don't know whether they attempted to realize the full multi-target capability of *YUL*, which went out of business when the Lab returned both H-1800s to Honeywell. *GAP* also did its work quietly in the sense of nobody having user issues with it. The engineers could concentrate on their engineering and programming, just taking the assembler for granted. That's the way I (and everybody else) wanted it.

Among the unknowns of Lunar Orbit Rendezvous (LOR) was whether the ascending Lunar Module would need any help in getting its radar locked on to the orbiting Command/Service Module. The only case in which this seemed likely to be a problem would be an abort fairly late in the descent phase, when the CSM had had time to get far ahead of the decelerating LM. Such a distance could place the CSM too far to be a visible target for aiming the Rendezvous Radar (RR), the satellite-dish-shaped affair sprouting from the middle of the LM's "forehead." NASA decided to ask the Lab to address this risk by adding a small software routine, which they named Routine 29 (R29), to make the LGC hunt for the CSM automatically when the LM Pilot couldn't see the target.

George Cherry, LUMINARY (LM software) Project Director, walked into my cubicle and sat down with a broad grin on his face. "Hey, Hugh, you've always wanted to do a little GN&C-type programming, right?" I was too amazed to speak, and he went on, "Looks like you might have some time to do R29."

"Well, George, I guess I might," I replied through a grin even wider than his. "The first thing would be to learn what the hell R29 is."

He handed me the functional spec for the RR and gave me a quick summary. "The RR is the only subsystem in the LM with any brains of its own. Once it's locked on to a target (which is always the CSM), it can tell when the return signal is starting to drift away from dead center in the dish, and it slews the dish a little to bring the target back to center. The only problem is how it gets locked on in the first place."

I knew that tactical radars had to be able to do that, going back even to the famous SCR-584 that did so much to preserve the Anzio beachhead in World War II by tracking Luftwaffe fighters and giving ack-ack gunners accurate information to lead their targets. And I knew that the two motorized axes to point the LM's RR dish were called Shaft and Trunnion—the latter word borrowed from the heavy pivots sticking out both sides of old cannons. "OK, I know from the interfaces that the LGC can command the shaft and trunnion to point the dish anywhere over a wide range of angles, and I know we can read those angles when something else changes them. I see how the pieces fit together so far, and the LGC should know where the CSM is, and it can point the dish correctly. So what is it that suddenly needs—"

George held up a hand. "I was just coming to that. In a nominal world, all that would work out as you say. But in an abort situation, there's things happening that can throw the LGC's knowledge off a little, or maybe more than a little. We don't really know yet. The LM Pilot has an idiot light to show when lock-on is active, and if he gets tired of waiting for it and can't do the aiming manually, he'll enter the verb and noun to bring up Routine 29. What R29 has to do is wave the dish around in a random but systematic search pattern, and watch for even a feeble return signal. Then you'll know how to narrow the search down, getting better and better returns until it's safe to command the lock-on."

"Golly," I said, "Nothing to it, eh? How much of a memory and runtime budget do I have?"

George's grin widened. "Probably not enough of either, though we're not sure yet. Most people who've looked at it think it's impossible. So we thought of you."

Now that was a compliment, accurately tuned to my favorite kind of programming. I've always loved to squeeze code into improbably tight corners of memory and make it achieve things there isn't really time to do. Feeling a little like the Dan Briggs character in *Mission: Impossible*, I happily accepted the assignment.

The trigonometric functions needed to steer the antenna in its search pattern couldn't be calculated properly in the LGC time available, so I cobbled up "heuristics" to approximate them. I couldn't make a mathematical proof that they'd converge on a good value in every circumstance, but once the bugs were worked out, they ran like the wind and never misbehaved in testing—so my R29 was built into a few of the early flight ropes. It was certainly never needed on a mission, but I was ecstatic to have a little piece of mission code to call my own, my gargoyle on the cathedral.

Despite the ghastly start of 1967, both sides achieved some degree of redemption. On our side, it began by reaching flight readiness with the final Block I AGC rope, called SOLARIUM, to fly on AS-501 and AS-502, the two unmanned trial runs of the three-stage Saturn 5 booster. These two flights were soon renamed Apollo 4 and Apollo 6, respectively, since Apollo 5 was to put an unmanned LM into earth orbit between them. Dan Lickly, the Rope Mother for those flights, was practically a Founding Father of the Lab, only a step behind Eldon Hall in that respect. A medium-large man with a receding hairline, Dan had the mellow air of a man who has unlimited faith in his own abilities and those of the people he's working with—and would do whatever it took to justify that faith. Throughout the project, anyone with a question could go to Dan and get answers, sometimes with a punched card or two from his shirt pocket to get the ball rolling. Under Dan's leadership, SOLARIUM was tested and ready for AS-501, which flew successfully on November 9. It was the second flight for the Lab's PGNCS, and the first flight of Saturn 5.

On the Soviet side, the fatal Soyuz mission was followed by a significant achievement in the interplanetary arena. Venera 4's probe plunged into the hellish atmosphere of Venus as planned, returning unprecedented data for 94 seconds before getting fried.

Space Race Highlights of 1967

(All manned flights are indicated in bold.)

27 Jan   **AS-204 rehearsal. Crew: Gus Grissom, Ed White, Roger Chaffee. All killed in Command Module fire on launch pad.**

08 Feb   Lunar Orbiter 3. Photography. Unmanned.

20 Apr   Surveyor 3. Moon lander. Unmanned.

23 Apr   **Soyuz 1. 1 day. Crew: Vladimir Komarov. Killed in crash landing.**

08 May   Lunar Orbiter 4. Photography. Unmanned.

17 Jul   Surveyor 4. Moon lander. Crashed on Moon. Unmanned.

22 Jul   Explorer 35. Moon orbiter to study Solar radiation at Moon. Unmanned.

05 Aug   Lunar Orbiter 5. Photography. Unmanned.

11 Sep   Surveyor 5. Moon lander. Unmanned.

01 Oct   Orbit decay and Lunar impact of Lunar Orbiter 2.

10 Oct   Orbit decay and Lunar impact of Lunar Orbiter 3.

18 Oct   Venera 4. Soviet probe explored Venus atmosphere. Unmanned.

19 Oct   Mariner 5. Flyby of Venus (within 2500 miles). Unmanned.

31 Oct   Orbit decay and Lunar impact of Lunar Orbiter 4.

09 Nov   Apollo 4 (SA-501). Suborbital boost. Crew: MCP. First test of Saturn 5.

10 Dec   Surveyor 6. Moon lander. Unmanned.

Complete detailed data on other flights is not available for 1967.

AHEAD TO STAY: 1968

NASA launched the first LM flight, called Apollo 5, into Earth orbit on January 22. LM-1 was a complete Lunar Module with two small exceptions. There was no Rendezvous Radar (RR) installed, and it carried the smaller LM version of the MCP ("Mechanical Man") used in the unmanned CM flights. Since the LM version's mass had to represent only two astronauts instead of three, it bore the nickname "Mechanical Boy."

This maiden flight of our Block II Guidance Navigation and Control system worked well up to the point where it tried to start the Descent engine. Unfortunately, ground controllers, reacting to a suspicion about a leaky valve, made a last-minute change in the sequencing. To guard against an explosion hazard, they delayed a valve opening in the engine's fuel system, not realizing that doing so would violate the specification for how quickly the engine should build up thrust. Our Lunar Guidance Computer (LGC) program, with no knowledge of the change, concluded that the engine had failed to start and shut it down.[48] Ground controllers, still unwilling to trust the valve, radioed commands in through the Mechanical Boy and by that means successfully achieved the mission's two main objectives. One was varying the thrust ("throttling") of the Descent Stage engine, the first rocket ever to have that feature. The other was rehearsing an "Abort Stage" event, based on the possibility of a descent to the Moon having to be aborted while the Descent Stage engine was still firing. Lighting off the Ascent Stage engine in this dynamic situation, while firing pyrotechnic guillotines to separate the stages, gave the mission its nickname of "Fire in the Hole."

A little-known result of the preparations for this flight was to cast a long shadow. The Lab's resident engineer at Kennedy Space Center, George Silver, had noticed something strange in pre-flight testing. The LGC wasn't expected to be very busy during a mission where some of the spacecraft's systems weren't yet installed, but it was supposed to generate a steady stream of down-telemetry data. George saw interruptions in his data during tests that suggested an overload of the computer. After a while he could see that the RR interface was stealing many more of the LGC's memory cycles than it was supposed to. Grumman had left the absent RR's electrical signal interface open instead of temporarily installing terminating resistors as best practice requires, with the result that our RR interface unit was trying to make an impossible calculation. Since all manned LM flights would have the RR installed and tested, this phenomenon was deemed not worth holding up Apollo 5 to fix. However, it was our first glimpse of an electronic gremlin that would make life interesting for LM-5 when it became "Eagle" in Apollo 11.

⸺❈⸺

Looking forward to manned LM flights, the Lab got involved in one aspect of astronaut training, spotting the intended Lunar landing point through the "eyes in its face," the two triangular windows. Both windows were double-glazed, two glass panes sandwiching an inch or so of vacuum, originally just for thermal insulation. However, Grumman built into the left (Commander's) window an elegant way to show the Commander exactly where the LGC would land if not directed otherwise. Its Landing Point Designator (LPD) consisted only of some thin lines scratched in the glass, labeled with numbers, similar to the lines and numbers on the glass body of an old-style mercury thermometer. What made it able to "designate" was the fact that this *graticule* was etched on both layers of the Commander's window, the outer one at a somewhat larger scale than the inner one. When the Commander skooched his head up or down to make a particular line on the outer pane coincide with the same-numbered line on the inner pane, his line of sight to the Lunar surface was down by a known number of degrees from the horizontal. The LGC, knowing what that angle would be for the current intended landing point, displayed the number that the Commander should line up in the inner and outer graticules to be looking right at the point. When the Commander used his hand controller to "redesignate," the LGC would calculate the surface distance being requested and display whatever new number would direct the Commander's eyes to the new point. It's a little like a sailor using a sextant to measure the height of a known light above the water in order to calculate his distance offshore, but completely hands-free and with no moving parts—except the Commander's head.

While NASA/MSC's sophisticated mechanical model of Lunar surfaces was under a long process of development, it was up to us to train astronauts how to use the LPD, the hand controller, and the relevant LGC program. We had to create pictures of how a particular area of the Lunar surface would look through the Commander's window. With no display screen technology available to us, we got a flatbed plotter that accommodated paper up to thirty inches square, driving a single pen along the X axis on a bridge that was driven along the Y axis. We could command pen-up and move the pen to a specified X-Y position without drawing, and we could then command pen-down and draw by moving the pen to another X-Y position. This primitive graphics tool allowed the Lab's Allan Klumpp to program the H-1800 to draw perspective pictures of parts of the Lunar surface based on photographs returned by our Surveyor landers. Each picture included how the LPD graticules would look at various stages of the landing.

Allan's program presented a very simplified perspective view of the surface, really not much more than the ridges around crater rims and outlines of the outer slopes. These were line drawings with no more detail than, say, a *Dilbert* strip today. By making a series of these drawings, using simulated LM positions a few seconds apart, Allan made primitive hard-copy "movies" helpful in training astronauts.

Allan was so identified with Lunar landing that a riddle made the rounds:

What sound does the LM make when it touches down?

"KLUMPP!"

The response is entertaining but especially silly when you consider that on the airless Moon, there is no sound at all.

Once the flight software started to stabilize, it became possible for some of us to be on call to manage problems by exception, rather than keeping our noses pressed continuously to the grindstone. There was even time for trips to gain wider experience of the project. In some ways, these were R&R trips, rewards for our long and patient efforts of which a large fraction was unpaid overtime. Steve Copps and I were told to go to the Cape to support the launch of Apollo 6 (formerly called SA-502), the second unmanned launch of the huge Saturn 5 to boost a Block I CSM and AGC. It was to be the final flight of any Block I component.

We checked in with the Lab's Kennedy Space Center office and got our assignment. We were to copy down measurements from display screens in the backup control room during the midnight shift before the 7 a.m. launch on April 4. In the meantime, we were to stay out of the way of the people doing the work. OK, we could handle that. As we settled in to our motel, Steve called me to come and see what "Father Cornflower" was doing on the TV. That was President Lyndon Johnson, announcing with obvious pain that he would not consider running for re-election. We felt that his main reason was that the baggage of escalating the Vietnam War was too much of a liability for the party. I suspected that he'd heard enough of the chant, "Hey, hey, LBJ, how many kids did you kill today?"

We treated ourselves to a thorough tour of the Vertical Assembly Building (VAB), in which three of the four high bays were occupied by booster stacks being readied for future missions. An elevator took us to the 42nd floor, above the four nests that swallow the seven upper "sashes" of each door and just under the roof. Seeing a sign by a door strictly forbidding anyone to go out onto the roof, I suggested we check it out, and we did. It's an odd view, establishing that most of Florida is 450 feet below. We could look down a bit at the launch complex connected to the VAB by three miles of the crawler-transporter roadway, the spacecraft superhighway with a speed limit of one mph. Launch Pad 39A supported the whole carefully assembled Apollo 6 stack—Saturn 1C, Saturn 2, Saturn 4B, an empty LM adapter, the SM, and finally the CM with its Launch Escape System. Fixed gantry structures gently embraced all those stages with their extended arms.

Inside again, we decided to take the stairs down to see what there was to see at every level, and we got a surprising bonus. At every working-platform level, the stairs had to be available for emergency use, so we just walked into every forbidden place. These were inter-stage areas with their hatches open so we could see the bafflingly elaborate plumbing serving each rocket engine. Hundreds of red tags dangled from various components to identify what was not yet flight-ready. There were narrow catwalks leading to other bays. Their open-mesh construction made it an uneasy feeling to walk them looking at the solid floor hundreds of feet down, even though the sturdy railings eliminated any actual risk. The tour's final lesson was: If you walk down 42 flights of stairs, your knees aren't going to like it much.

Having napped some in preparation for the night shift, we entered the base a little before 10 p.m. to go to work. The warm clear night gave a stunning view of Apollo 6, from which most of the gantry arms had now been pulled back, brilliantly illuminated by floodlights. It's not often you feel compelled to use the phrase "achingly beautiful," but this was the time. The 363-foot tower in its white paint seemed to glow like a living thing, expressing all the passion and love and care that had gone into making it stand straight and true and ready.

Steve and I paused to gawk at the Launch Control Center's

huge glass wall facing the pad, found our consoles, settled in with clipboards, and started taking down numbers in the long night hours before launch. What, we wondered, could be the use of doing this—if it were important, there would be a computer capturing this data and formatting it to show any significant anomalies on the screen … wouldn't there? We felt confident nobody, under any circumstances, would read what we were writing. In fact, we regarded it as a charade to allow all involved to say we were doing actual work in support of the launch.

In retrospect, perhaps we were too cynical. The computer development for KSC facilities often played second fiddle to what was done for Mission Control at MSC, and perhaps KSC's budget didn't allow for data handling in the style we were used to. Maybe our scrawled numbers would have their forensic uses if the launch went badly wrong.

We did our jobs conscientiously anyway, and went off duty after being relieved about a half hour ahead of the 7 a.m. launch. Out on the LCC's fire escape stairway, we stood as close to the launch—three miles—as any human was allowed, with nothing but humid Florida air between it and us. While the loudspeaker boomed the countdown, we noticed that unlike most fire escape structures, this one had solid waist-high walls, so we could duck behind them if there was an explosion.

At T minus 7 seconds, ignition started, building a volcanic blast turned horizontal by the pad's flame trench, growing to a substantial fraction of a mile. Those were seven long seconds, burning 30 tons of kerosene with 69 tons of liquid oxygen to build up 7.5 million pounds of thrust, all in perfect silence. As the last arms swung away and the hold-down clamps jumped back, the white skyscraper began to climb, still in silence. Only after it cleared the launch tower did the sound reach us, fourteen seconds after ignition. I don't imagine any reproduction system can make that sound. It was a roar punctuated by bangs like an artillery barrage, perhaps as supersonic gas plumes burst. A lot of the "sound" was well below 20 Hz, the general minimum for human hearing, and the only way you could sense it was by noticing your ribs vibrating. I found myself hyperventilating, speechless because nothing in human speech was adequate.

We watched until it was out of sight, which didn't take very long. Steve and I got into our car and headed off-base to the motel to catch up on sleep. I was driving and still so over-stimulated I started reaching for change to pay the toll, until Steve pointed out that what we were approaching was the KSC security gate, not a toll booth. We grabbed a bite of breakfast and tumbled exhausted into our beds, intending to be fresh for the splashdown party in the evening.

All the interesting stuff happened during the day, while we slept. Notwithstanding von Braun's confident collection of "Neins" regarding any fallibility of the S2 stage, one of its five J-2 engines did fail to start due to "pogo-stick" oscillations set up by the enormous force of the S1C engines, and the problem was compounded by a bug in the engine safing logic in the Instrument Unit (IU) and its computer. It misidentified the failed engine and shut down a second J-2 instead of completing shutdown of the failed one. With only three of the five engines working, the second stage burned longer but couldn't achieve orbital velocity, so the single-engine S4B third stage had to make up the difference. That saved the mission from failure but forced some operational workarounds.

Aside from booster testing, the key objective of Apollo 6 was to evaluate the CM's ability to re-enter at the speed it would attain when returning from the Moon, much greater than the

Earth-orbital speed faced by all previous manned spacecraft. To produce this effect, the plan had been to use the S4B to perform a Trans-Lunar Injection (TLI) burn, just as it would in an actual Moon mission. Then the CSM would separate, dodge out of the way of the booster, and fire the Service Propulsion System (SPS) engine to take the outbound Trans-Lunar velocity out again and add the inbound velocity required for a realistically hot entry.

Because of the S2 shutdowns, the S4B stage was nearly exhausted just getting into orbit, and failed to restart when commanded to do the TLI burn. NASA asked the Lab people supporting the flight how much of its job could be done by the AGC guiding the SPS. We replied that the only limitation was imposed by the amount of SPS fuel. Just uplink the appropriate velocity-to-be-gained (V_G) numbers to the AGC and the PGNCS would do the rest.

Happily, there was enough SPS fuel for the AGC to command three good burns. The first burn produced a respectable fraction of the TLI thrust. Then, after maneuvering to the required attitude, the second burn built up an equally respectable fraction of the return-from-the-Moon speed. Finally, the AGC commanded another end-for-end maneuver and a regular deorbit burn, then the rest of the entry sequence, ending in splashdown in the Atlantic, almost ten hours after launch.

We'd never tested this particular sequence in simulations, but from the point of view of the PGNCS, when you've seen one V_G, you've seen 'em all. Just point the spacecraft in the right direction and fire the engine for the proper time. The Lab's approach to flexibility in applying the basics saved as much of the day as could be saved.

Steve and I got up refreshed in time to go to the splashdown celebration, and when we heard about the Lab's heroic role in the day's achievements, got ready to do some first-class partying. Then somebody called for quiet in the crowded room and announced the news that Dr. Martin Luther King had been shot and probably killed. The room went silent with one thought hanging in the air—"Oh Christ, what's going to happen now?" The '60s had seen enough violent reaction to what was wrong with the world. Surely this would top it in some really gruesome way. At least James Earl Ray didn't stand for anything that would attract vengeance, other than his white skin. He was an empty shell of a man, apparently, fit for nothing but to hold a rifle and pull the trigger.

The splashdown party occupied its appointed space and time, but nobody's heart was in it, and it wasn't much of a party. All who had gathered at the Cape for the mission went home sobered and wary. Why, in a world that can prepare to visit another world, must the insanely murderous hatred of The Other still drive men to do what makes them deserve no world at all?

And is evil itself contagious? Only two months later, Bobby Kennedy was cut down by Sirhan Sirhan, a man with no program, no feelings, no heart, and no brain.

Life at home went on, and it was increasingly possible to have a life. Dick Warren recruited me to be his partner in racing a sleek sailboat in Marblehead, a northeastern suburb. The International One-Design class, wooden boats built in Norway in the '30s, had become popular in the Lab. Bill and Sheila Widnall had one, and another partnership was Bob Morse and our East Anglia import, Bob Crisp. Also, I got involved in a unique community theater group in Lexington that performed only world premieres. One of the shows was a new opera written by local talent, and at the cast party I asked the leading lady if she'd like to go sailing. No, she said, but her housemate Vicki probably would. And so she did, having spent teenage summers racing small sailboats in Edgartown, Martha's Vineyard. A long and graceful lady, Vicki gave her height as "five foot thirteen" and worked at Harvard on a study of independent schools—decent of her, I thought, since she'd been raised as a Yale "faculty brat" in New Haven. She had sparkling blue eyes, blonde hair, two golden retrievers she'd rescued in Colorado, a very furry cat, and a way with words ("You've got too many peas on your knife"). One thing led to another and we married three months later, both age 32.

With the transition from Honeywell mainframes to the IBM 360 completed, my *YUL* system finished handing the baton to *GAP* and retired. I had to look outside of Apollo to find an opportunity to do more computer design, and so transferred to Eldon Hall's Digital Development Group. As was usual in the Lab, I remained available for any support I could give to Apollo as it entered its operational phase. The DDG's focus turned to an advanced integrated circuit chip by Fairchild, an 8-bit Arithmetic-Logic Unit—the "3800 ALU." We put together a novel microprocessor that looked like a tiny eight-story building in which each floor was a ceramic substrate holding 3800s and other advanced chips. We called it the cubic inch, even after we realized that each side actually had to be an inch and a quarter. If anyone questioned the name, we explained that of course it was an imperial inch, hoping that people wouldn't remember that the British 25% bonus applies only to liquid measure. But there was a point to the little computing cube: it would make possible distributed processing systems in which the central computer could send high-level commands to local processors installed at such subsystems as engines and radar dishes. While our work on this particular task went nowhere and sat on a shelf, the Space Shuttle's MDM units were essentially the same idea, emerging a few years later.

Other resources within the Lab got a NASA mandate to develop a Strapdown Inertial Reference Unit (SIRU) to exploit the ability of high-speed computers to maintain a continuous math model of how a vehicle is oriented in space, thus doing away with the need for gimbals to support a physically stable platform.[5] DDG's part was to supply the new system's Digital Computer Assembly (DCA), incorporating advances in computer logic since the Block II AGC design. That was my chance to take part in designing a more flexible kind of microprogramming logic, in which the control pulses for each step of an instruction would be read out of a super-fast Read-Only Memory (ROM). In this architecture, designers could modify instruction types or create new ones by a software-like process. The word "firmware" came into use for this melding of software and hardware. It was a beautiful architecture, if we do say so ourselves, but the results of this task also went and sat on a shelf. That was quite a disappointment, and our only relief from it was to see the same approach used years later in such minicomputers as the Data General system lovingly portrayed by Tracy Kidder in *The Soul of a New Machine*.

All that advanced work by DDG, remember, got started months before Apollo achieved even its first manned flight. Complex projects typically have skewed timelines like this, in which the engineers developing the parts you might call infrastructure tend to move on to new projects years before the engineers concerned with operational details of the missions. On the Lab's operational side, the space guidance programmers, working with Jim Miller's digital simulator, wrung the bugs out of Block II AGC software for the CM and passed the object code along to the Hybrid Lab to make sure it worked with the actual instruments. The Rope Mother for the first manned CM flight was a former P-38 fighter pilot, John "Crash" Dunbar. His rope SUNDISK reached flight-ready status, and *GAP*'s manufacturing function completed its first task for a manned mission, punching the Mylar tape for the rope-weaving machine at Raytheon.

This machine wasn't as comprehensive as the Gardner Denver wire wrap machine Bob Morse worked with. Built by the United Shoe Machinery Company to Raytheon's specifications, it held half a rope module with 256 transformer cores. Every time it read a few frames from the tape, it positioned a particular core between two stationary funnels. The operator had a spring-like coil of wire inside a long blunt needle about a millimeter thick. Using one of the funnels as a guide, she poked the needle carefully through the bundle of wires already passing through that core, without scraping any insulation off the dozens already threaded through it, thus adding one more wire to the bundle. Then she pressed a switch to let the machine read more tape and advance another core to the funnel position, then passed the needle through the opposite way. Having passed a particular wire through or around all 256 cores, she then welded its end to the appropriate header pin and welded a new wire (coiled up in its needle) to the next pin, and so on.

I remember meeting three or four of these operators, all white-haired ladies with gentle voices and an infinitely patient dexterity they had developed in decades of working at the Waltham Watch Company factory. They were widely known as the Little Old Ladies, or LOLs, and "adopted" visiting astronauts. Like mothers anywhere, they knew they held young lives in their hands and made sure their work was flawless.

While the completed ropes were undergoing final validation testing, the Soviets scored another first. Zond 5 looped around the Moon and returned on a free-return trajectory, carrying the first Earthly life forms on that path—two Russian tortoises.

On October 11, Wally Schirra, Donn Eisele, and Walt Cunningham became the first Apollo astronauts in space as their Saturn 1B boosted Apollo 7 into Earth orbit for an 11-day mission. Their Block II Command/Service Module and the Block II PGNCS worked well, and their testy exchanges with Mission Control were about their workload in other areas. The Lab's people were a very happy group in what time they could spare from sweating out the development of Lunar Module software. I was certainly glad to see the AGC and the rest of our system just quietly doing the job, and glad of no interruptions of the SIRU/DCA development.

A few days after the Apollo 7 astronauts came home, the Soviets tried a docking in Earth orbit. They sent Georgy Beregovoy up in Soyuz 3. With the help of his onboard computer, he achieved rendezvous with the unmanned Soyuz 2 that had been orbited the day before, but couldn't complete the docking despite repeated attempts.

———∞———

The Zond missions and the expanded testing of the three-person Soyuz spacecraft were clear indications that the Soviets were getting ready to send cosmonauts around the Moon first, if they could. NASA's project schedule problem at the same time was that LM-3 wasn't going to be ready for the first manned

LM flight in its intended place as Apollo 8. NASA saw how to deal with both issues at once, by postponing LM-3's flight to be Apollo 9 and redefining Apollo 8 as a CSM trip to the Moon with some Lunar orbiting. That didn't accelerate or upset our software operations very much because our CM programs had been designed for the Moon trip all along, and only the focus of testing had to be adjusted. Getting a little more time to wring bugs out of the LM software was welcome indeed.

While NASA was scrambling to set up communications and tracking for Apollo 8, the Soviets tried to replicate Zond 5's feat with Zond 6. A cabin seal failed and depressurized the cabin, killing the "biologicals"—presumably more tortoises. Zond 6 obtained good Lunar images and made a good entry on return to Earth, but a parachute malfunction made it crash, destroying everything but one image.

Frank Borman, Jim Lovell, and Bill Anders—the Apollo 8 crew—were ecstatic to see their mission moved up to 1968, giving them the near-certainty of becoming the first humans to approach and orbit the Moon. On December 21, the first Saturn 5 used for a manned flight boosted them into Earth orbit. The "pogo-stick" oscillations that had been identified as the cause of Apollo 6's boost problems (the mission Steve Copps and I had attended) had been brought under control and caused no further trouble. When Mission Control gave the crew that momentous clearance, "You are Go for TLI," IBM's Instrument Unit restarted the S4B, and it delivered the thrust for Trans-Lunar Injection.

Drifting silently away from their home planet at escape velocity, the crew broke the CSM free of the empty LM adapter and turned it around to perform as much of the Transposition and Docking program as possible. The four panels of the adapter opened on their hinges like a flower, revealing a dummy docking target where the LM would have been. From the CM, the crew could see that one of the "petals" opened only partway, which would have threatened the mission if they had a LM to pull past it. Houston engineers made a note to take out the hinges on later flights and let the petals float away.

About 70% of the way to the Moon, the AGC had to make a change in its math model of the spacecraft's motion that had never before been necessary in manned spacecraft. As long as Earth's gravity was the greater influence on the spacecraft, it was simple and efficient to calculate the position and velocity relative to the center of the Earth. But since the main objective of Apollo 8 was to make several orbits of the Moon, it made sense to switch over as soon as the Moon's gravity became dominant, and start calculating the position and velocity relative to the center of the Moon. In our simulated universe, we'd tested the switchover logic and had no particular anxiety about its working with the real Moon, but the media were in a different situation.

At Mission Control in Houston, a prominent display always showed the spacecraft's position in Earth-centered coordinates because that's what NASA used to aim the global network of radars. When the AGC changed internally to Moon-centered coordinates and sent those numbers home by down telemetry, Houston's mainframe computers converted them back to Earth-centered for the display. Because the display showed a little more precision than the numbers' accuracy justified, the displayed numbers appeared to show a small but sudden jump in the spacecraft's position, and reporters watching the displays made their own jump—to the conclusion that an actual jolt had affected the spacecraft. Anybody with a technical background understood at once that the new numbers were just as good an estimate of the exact position as the old numbers were, but reporters (ever alert for anything that looked like a dramatic malfunction) pestered flight controllers to explain how the "jolt" affected the crew.[43]

After nearly three days of coasting, with only one midcourse correction, Houston gave the crew what they wanted above all else: "You are go for LOI." The AGC started a countdown display as the spacecraft went out of sight behind the Moon on its free-return trajectory. With the crew all in their couches riding "backwards," Commander Borman took a deep breath and pressed the PRO key, allowing the AGC to proceed with the burn. The Service Propulsion System engine gave them an impressive jolt as it reduced the vehicle's kinetic energy to achieve Lunar Orbit Insertion. Their altitude settled in at between 193 and 70 miles above the Moon's devastated surface, and for eight two-hour orbits the Apollo 8 astronauts observed and examined and struggled to find the best words to convey unprecedented awe. For one hour out of every two, the Earth was out of sight and they were out of touch with any known form of life. Their photo of Earthrise helped express their feelings of release from that ultimate isolation; it also startled the rest of us into a heightened sense of how isolated our home planet is.

Back home, my whole family had gathered—as whole as it could be without my father, who had died in January—at Cape Cod for Christmas. On Christmas Eve, we stood outside to look up at the crescent Moon, contemplating how it had, for the first time, become an immediate neighborhood for human beings. My bride Vicki stood with my mother, and the six-member Northcott family were there: my sister Pam, her professor husband Kenneth, and their four children, ranging in age from sixteen to eight.

Nephew Mike had a problem. "I can't see it, Uncle Hugh."

"Well, no, if you can't see an airliner at the head of its contrail, when it's only thirty thousand feet away, how could you see something roughly the same size that's thirteen hundred *million* feet away?"

"The Russians have always been a step ahead of us, haven't they?"

"Not any more, they're not." A huge grin.

The ninth orbit was showtime. Coming in from the December chill, we gathered around the fire and the black-and-white TV set. The voices of the crew came through clearly from a quarter million miles away. Lunar Module Pilot Bill Anders led off.

"In the beginning, God created the heaven and the earth; and the earth was without form and void, and darkness was on the face of the deep; and the spirit of God moved upon the face of the waters. And God said, 'Let there be light,' and there was light. And God saw the light, that it was good. And God divided the light from the darkness."

Command Module Pilot Jim Lovell took his turn.

"And God called the light Day, and the darkness He called Night, and the evening and the morning were the first day. And God called the firmament Heaven, and the evening and the morning were the second day."

Commander Frank Borman concluded the reading.

"And God called the dry land Earth, and the gathering together of the waters He called Seas. And God saw that it was good."

The spacecraft coasted on toward the darkness that only the shadow of an airless world can produce. "And now, from the crew of Apollo 8, we close with, good night, good luck, a Merry Christmas, and God bless all of you, all of you on the good Earth."

And to you, Frank and Jim and Bill, I thought. And to *you*, little computer.

Space Race Highlights of 1968

(All manned flights are indicated in bold.)

10 Jan   Surveyor 7. Moon lander. Unmanned.

22 Jan   Apollo 5 (SA-204). 7 orbits. Crew: MCP. First flight of LM.

31 Jan   Orbit decay and Lunar impact of Lunar Orbiter 5.

04 Apr   Apollo 6 (SA-502). Suborbital. Crew: MCP. CM heat shield test.

10 Apr   Luna 14. Moon orbiter. Gravitational and communications research.

18 Sep   Zond 5. Lunar flyby and free return. Crew: Two Russian tortoises.

11 Oct   Apollo 7 (AS-205). 11 days. Crew: Wally Schirra, Donn Eisele, Walt Cunningham. First manned Apollo, first Block II CSM.

25 Oct   Soyuz 2. 3 days. Unmanned. Docking target for Soyuz 3.

26 Oct   Soyuz 3. 4 days. Crew: Georgy Beregovoy. Rendezvous with Soyuz 2 but failed to dock.

14 Nov   Zond 6. Lunar flyby and free return. Depressurized and crashed.

21 Dec   Apollo 8 (AS-503). 10 orbits of Moon. Crew: Frank Borman, Jim Lovell, Bill Anders. First human mission to the Moon.

Complete detailed data on other flights is not available for 1968.

PUTTING IT ALL TOGETHER: 1969

Finally, LM-3 was on the verge of achieving Flight Readiness. In Apollo 9, it would be the first place men in space would go that could not, by itself, get them home. Safe return depended absolutely on rendezvous and docking with the CM, and rendezvous was now known to be dependent on a computer: the LGC nominally, or the Abort Guidance System if necessary. Commander Jim McDivitt (already the AGC/LGC expert in the astronaut corps), CM Pilot Dave Scott (the biggest fan of the DSKY's Verb-Noun syntax), and LM Pilot Rusty Schweickart thus felt the importance of the computer more than previous crews. They were the first to ask for a course of familiarization with the LGC software, and arranged a visit to the Lab to get a two-hour training session. Among those with a broad view of the flight software, I was the one who didn't have to spend every waking moment wringing the bugs out of it, so I became the designated trainer.

The astronauts were already in the second-floor classroom after lunch when I came in bearing a binder containing over

1,700 pages of program listing. That sight made three strong jaws drop a little. I could almost hear the thought, "Uh-oh. We weren't careful what we wished for." The program I used for a textbook was the LGC program for their flight in Earth orbit. Since Dave would be always in the CM, I could have also brought along an even bigger binder containing the listing for the CM's rather different AGC program, but somehow enough seemed to be enough—and more.

Readability of *YUL* program listings was always a priority, and I'd put a lot of effort into providing tools to help readers find their way around listings that grew to nearly 2,000 pages as we filled up the 36K words of fixed memory. There was clearly no chance of taking the crew through a detailed analysis of even a little part of the program, so I spent the time showing them the tools. Mostly, that involved going through the 200-odd pages of index-like material at the back, starting with the symbol table.[44]

The astronauts weren't really disappointed in the way the session turned out. They were content with having been educated about how much there was they didn't need—or want—to know. Having gone through most of their training on the assumption that their flight in the LM would be Apollo 8, these astronauts were the least behind schedule, and the least stressed, of all the people involved. In forcing the reversal of Apollo 8 and 9, the teething problems of LM-3 gave them some extra time to prepare. The switch even gave us in the Lab some extra time to refine the LGC software, saddled as we were with anxiety about whether our math models of the LM subsystems were absolutely current with all the last-minute changes. (There *was* a flaw in our knowledge of the Descent engine, which we overcame by good engineering practice before we learned about the flaw. If we'd slavishly followed the engine's obsolete design document, any of the early LM flights could have been aborted because of unstable throttling of that engine. That in turn could easily have made Apollo miss the 1969 deadline.)[45]

Most of the head-pounding chorus of "You're late, you're late" fell on the Grumman engineers in Bethpage, Long Island. I think that explains in part what happened to our rediscovery at the Cape of an ominous shadow on the LGC-Rendezvous Radar interface. The Lab's George Silver had seen a little of the shadow in the integration testing of LM-1 for Apollo 5 (Chapter 22), where the absence of an RR caused a big waste of the LGC's time due to a wiring error. In LM-3 for this mission, the RR was installed and would be used. It was wired correctly according to Grumman's design, but in Flight Readiness testing at the Cape, George caught it—just once out of many test cycles— committing the same "sin." And it didn't matter whether the RR's radar transmit/receive functions were powered on.

The sin was theft of a sort, legally "stealing" LGC Erasable Memory cycles to increment or decrement data words showing where the RR dish antenna was pointing. Like other ambivalent deeds, it only became a sin when done to excess. Because the RR's internal brains had to enable it to track a target automatically, even a fast-moving one, the LGC's logic allowed a rate of increment/decrement requests that would accommodate the maximum antenna slewing speeds. If it was whipping diagonally, maxing out the rates of both its shaft and trunnion angles, each angle could make 6,400 requests per second, for a total of 12,800 requests. That sounds like a lot but it was only 15% of the LGC's time, and the physical stops would prevent the antenna from moving that fast for more than a couple of seconds. It became a sin when the electrical signals from the RR *falsely* implied the maximum antenna motion, *and* then kept it up indefinitely. In LM-1, failure to replace the missing RR with terminating resistors had produced that effect.

In LM-3, the same effect came out of a fiendishly obscure corner in the RR interface, where electromagnetic devices called resolvers produced analog voltages proportional to the sines and cosines of the RR's shaft and trunnion angles. Being transformer-type devices, they needed AC power supplies, and the aerospace standard for AC frequency was 800 Hz rather than the household standard of 60 Hz. George Silver, an old hand with resolver-based systems, figured out how the two 800 Hz supplies, one from the Lab's Primary GN&C System and one from Grumman's backup Abort Guidance System (AGS), were vulnerable. They would produce the sinful falsehood if there was a critical phase difference between them.

The "alternating current" best understood by non-scientists is the tidal cycle of the sea, which has a period of about twelve and a half hours. It goes through two full cycles about every twenty-five hours, gravitationally dictated by the Moon's motion in its orbit. Massachusetts has a place that perfectly illustrates phase differences between tidal cycles observed at two points: the Cape Cod Canal. At both ends of the canal, the tidal cycle necessarily has the same period, but the time of high tide is very different. At the Buzzards Bay (southwestern) end, the tide turns at the same time as at Newport, Rhode Island. At the Cape Cod Bay (northeastern) end, it turns at the same time as at Boston. Because of the different shapes of the bays, sounds, and gulfs at the two ports, the tide at Boston turns a little over three hours later than at Newport. When the tide is at its highest or lowest level at one end of the canal, it's approximately half-tide at the other end. That's a phase difference of a quarter of a cycle.

The LM's two AC supplies were only partially synchronized. The frequency was synchronized at 800 Hz, but, like those tidal stations along the coast, the phase could differ. In the LM, the phase difference was a function of a perfectly random variable, namely the exact interval between two manual operations, powering up the Abort Guidance System and powering up the Primary GN&C system. George found that whatever the phase difference turned out to be, it stayed constant during each test run, but varied randomly from one run to the next. Of the seventy-some test runs he studied, the only one in which the RR interface hogged too much of the LGC's time showed a phase difference of about 310 microseconds, very close to one-quarter of a cycle. Thus, the problem had a probability between 1% and 2%.[46]

To make things even more obscure, the problem could never happen while the RR mode was set to be under the LGC's control. The critical phase difference would cause the problem only when the LGC was running while the RR mode was set to be under the control of the AGS. I and many engineers in the project had originally expected that to be a rare to impossible situation—either everything would be primary or everything would be in backup mode, right? Well, not quite right as it turned out in later flights, but nothing about the Apollo 9 mission gave us the clue.

George concluded that Grumman's design was defective because it frequency-synchronized the 800 Hz supplies without also phase-synchronizing them. He wrote up an Interim Discrepancy Report (IDR) as his job required. Then, being a typical Lab engineer, he couldn't resist sketching a very simple circuit to perform the phase synchronization and solve the problem once and for all.

The review board processing IDRs showed George's report and circuit to the Grumman electronics engineers. They pointed out they were spending 150% of their time fixing much bigger and more likely problems. Every ounce of electronics and every hour of testing was too precious to justify making any change for so unlikely an event. Years later, we wondered whether 1964's embarrassing battle between MIT and Grumman, over the distorted system reliability estimates, helped to sour their attitude toward our solution.

As if there weren't already enough pressure on getting LM-3 and the rest of Apollo 9 ready, the Soviets jumped in with more firsts. In mid-January they orbited one cosmonaut in Soyuz 4, then the next day orbited three cosmonauts in Soyuz 5. The two vehicles rendezvoused successfully and performed the first-ever docking of two manned spacecraft. Two cosmonauts climbed out of Soyuz 5, space-walked across the docking collars to Soyuz 4 and got in, making the most elaborate Extra-Vehicular Activity (EVA) to date. Soyuz 4, with its crew thus expanded to three, re-entered and landed safely. That was the first time anybody had gone into space in one spacecraft and returned in another. Boris Volynov, left alone in Soyuz 5, re-entered not so safely, as his Service Module failed to separate. That made his vehicle start entering backwards instead of heat-shield first, but his SM finally let go as the temperature climbed, and he got turned around properly. With part of the parachute gear disabled, his retro-thrust landing rockets let Volynov down hard, alive but with a lot of broken teeth.

Early in March, Apollo 9 was ready at last and lifted off, the first time all the Apollo module types went into orbit together. Because of the weight, a Saturn 5 did the launch, the only time the big booster was used for a merely Earth-orbital manned flight. The Transposition and Docking phase went according to plan, the first time a CSM pulled a docked LM out of its adapter atop the S4B stage. Commander Jim McDivitt and LM Pilot Rusty Schweickart crawled through the tunnel to the LM, the first internal crew transfer. They sealed off the tunnel from their end while CM Pilot Dave Scott did the same at the CM end. Jim and Rusty powered up the LM systems, and there was no hint of the time-wasting glitch that George Silver had written up. The IDR review board's decision to ignore that possibility looked wise.

For a few days, all the astronauts went through an exhaustive checklist of all the systems in both vehicles, then performed simultaneous EVAs. Rusty had a bad case of space sickness, raising the horrifying thought of what a load of vomit would do inside a space suit helmet—probably drown him. But he worked through it and put on his new-model Moon suit and went space-walking outside the LM, named *Spider* for this mission. Dave put on his older-model space suit and stood up in *Gumdrop*'s open main hatch to take pictures of Rusty.

With everybody indoors again, they practiced the Lunar-area activities, starting with separation. Right away, that was another first ... humans in a free-flying spacecraft that could never return safely to Earth. Jim and Rusty commanded their LGC to fire *Spider*'s Descent engine to move over a hundred miles from *Gumdrop*, then separated the two LM stages. Leaving the detached Descent stage to drift (its orbit decayed and it burned up in Earth's atmosphere two weeks later), they told the LGC to fire *Spider*'s Ascent engine and steer to a rendezvous with *Gumdrop*. That docking was history's second involving two manned spacecraft.

After Jim and Rusty floated gracefully through the docking

tunnel back into the CM, they reassembled the parachute assembly in its nose. Separation sent *Spider*'s Ascent stage into an Earth orbit that didn't decay for twelve years. Finally, *Gumdrop* cast off the SM and re-entered, concluding a ten-day mission that had performed every spacecraft function possible without actually going to the Moon. And they never asked me any questions about the LGC program.

───── ∞ ─────

With Apollo 8 and 9 both successfully on the books, the Apollo program was back on schedule and ready to put those two flights together. In mid-May, Apollo 10 was the "dress rehearsal" in which Commander Tom Stafford, CM Pilot John Young, and LM Pilot Gene Cernan went to the Moon and did everything except land there. The black-and-white communications caps the astronauts wore inspired the call signs *Snoopy* for the LM and *Charlie Brown* for the CM. On their first pass behind the Moon, Tom and Gene powered up *Snoopy*, again with no hint of a time-wasting glitch.

After separation, the LGC controlled DOI (Descent Orbit Insertion) using the Descent stage engine to lower the LM's perilune to a mere 8.4 miles above the Lunar surface. Only when they reached that low point did Apollo 10 depart from the nominal Lunar landing timeline, and with great reluctance. NASA understood that the temptation to go on and perform an unauthorized landing would be overwhelming. They deliberately assigned LM-4 to the Apollo 10 mission even though it had not undergone the final weight-reduction program that would be essential for LM-5 in Apollo 11. Then, to make LM-4's weight come out right, they filled its Descent engine's fuel tank with only enough fuel to achieve the DOI burn—well short of enough to land. Crew training for this mission made it quite clear that a landing would be impossible for that reason. So at that 8.4-mile low point—the moment the Commander would nominally have commanded Powered Descent—Gene pushed the Abort button, switching control of the LM from the LGC to the Abort Guidance System (AGS). Over the next 22 seconds, the AGS performed some unexpected maneuvering, but then stopped and seemed to have decided to behave. The maneuvering was caused by a wrong setting of the autopilot mode (due to a checklist error), but that wasn't obvious until the next 13 seconds, when the LM spun up into eight rapid adrenaline-pumping rolls, using precious time and fuel. Gene jumped on the Abort Stage button within 5 seconds, to force separation of the Ascent stage from the Descent stage. They switched back to LGC control, and it took Tom 8 more seconds to correct the mode and bring the spacecraft under control. Fortunately, the LGC managed a respectable rendezvous without running out of fuel. After docking, Tom and Gene rejoined John in *Charlie Brown* and took some time to unwind.

Snoopy's abandoned Descent Stage remained in the Descent Orbit with its 8-mile low point (perilune) and crashed within days, dramatically demonstrating how quickly the Moon's irregular gravity degrades a low orbit. Scientists had coined the phrase "bucket of rocks" for the Moon's general makeup as soon as they saw earlier spacecraft pulled off course by *mascons*, the mass concentrations caused by some of those "rocks" being considerably denser than others.

Snoopy's Ascent Stage remained attached for the Trans-Earth Injection burn. Then the astronauts separated it and let it go into orbit around the Sun. There it remains, the only intact LM to receive this treatment. It will fly for as long as the Solar

System lives, a tantalizing puzzle to the astronomers trying to spot it, and perhaps an intriguing artifact for visiting aliens.

Apollo 10 returned home in good form, and the Navy took the crew home to Houston. Like other conscientious travelers, Tom, John, and Gene took a quick look at their offices to see what had piled up while they were away. Their path took them through the "skyscraper" building of MSC, where NASA's "Wild Bill" Tindall was hosting a Data Priority meeting in his inimitable fashion. There was so much laughter, typical of a Tindall-chaired meeting, they couldn't resist peeking in to see what was going on. They knew it would be a real issue that had to be resolved, and the laughter showed that the resolution was being made, most likely in the best possible way.

Howard Wilson Tindall was a paragon of leadership. He had the gift of persuading people to do things they didn't want to do, infecting them with his indomitable good humor. His Data Priority meetings, which began in 1966, were civilly conducted wrestling arenas where difficult decisions about AGC software were fully faced and promptly made. In a community of incorrigibly creative souls, he often had to rally his troops under the banner, "Better is the enemy of good."

Best of all, Bill's writing style matched the disciplined exuberance of his chairmanship. The meetings were memorialized in "Tindallgrams" so readable as to be welcomed even by those whose sacred oxen had just been gored. What he said wasn't what everybody wanted to hear, but it was a decision and it made clear how to proceed. Above all, we could trust that the people at these meetings had settled on something that would work, and that Bill was reporting it accurately and clearly. Combining "the friendliness of a puppy" (in one colleague's phrase) with his technical and organizational skills, he promoted at NASA some of the same cultural paradigms so valuable to the Lab:

- ✔ We're all in this together;
- ✔ We're here to help each other succeed;
- ✔ Tell me how it can be done and not why it can't;
- ✔ We don't have time to mess around with things that don't matter—let's get this moving!

Some of these meetings were the dreaded "scrubs" … cancelling parts of AGC software that were desirable and well built, but just weren't critical enough to take up running time and memory space. Such was the fate of my own Routine 29 to make the LM's Rendezvous Radar search for the CSM. One scrubs meeting cast so broad a cloud that it got called "Black Friday." The crucial agenda item was how much of the AGC/LGC's running time should be held in reserve for unanticipated tasks. The representative from Kennedy Space Center remembered some numbers in George Silver's IDR, to the effect that a rare glitch in the Rendezvous Radar interface could waste up to 15% of the LGC's time by stealing memory cycles when the RR was not in use.

Bill asked, "Has this problem been seen in [Houston's] integrated test lab?" No, it hadn't. In the clarity of hindsight, we can see that he should have followed up by asking whether the problem was physically possible in that lab, which in fact it wasn't. Although the simulated gear there had a high degree of fidelity to the actual spacecraft equipment, they hadn't duplicated the fiendishly obscure corner of the RR interface where the two 800 Hz excitation supplies could be out of phase by a random amount. Houston's lab had only one 800 Hz supply, making a subtle difference that nobody in the meeting appreciated or even knew about.

Bill followed his usual practice of proposing a decision to see whether anyone might have a big problem with it. "If the real hardware at the Cape has been seen with a 15% problem and nobody has seen anything worse," he said, "let's make the cushion that size." MIT's representative at the Data Priority meetings, Malcolm Johnston, gulped at how much bigger that was than the time reserve we'd been seeing at the Lab. But he agreed to go home and find out whether we absolutely couldn't live with it. At the next meeting, Malcolm came back with an estimate that the mandatory processing during powered descent could be cut back to fit into the 85% allowance but optional display verbs might go over it by just a little. That meeting, like its predecessors, had higher-probability issues to deal with, so it accepted a compromise time cushion of "15% or maybe a tiny bit less."

Everybody had assumed that the RR circuit breakers, which fed power to the transmission and reception functions of the radar, would be open (off) in flight phases where the RR wouldn't be used—like the Descent phase. We also assumed that the RR mode, controlled by a rotary switch on the right side of the LM, would remain consistent with the spacecraft's mode. It would be in LGC while the primary system ruled, and either SLEW or TRACK while the Abort Guidance System ruled. The question, however, wasn't quite that simple. Buzz Aldrin, our own MIT-educated "Dr. Rendezvous," was training hard for his position as LM Pilot in Apollo 11, and he made sure to learn the lessons of Apollo 10. The biggest lesson was the temporary loss of control during the Abort Stage operation. Buzz realized that if Apollo 11 had to abort the mission in the Descent phase, he might not have as much time as planned to get the RR working. If anything like that control problem happened, he didn't want to have to go through the big extra step of closing the circuit breakers and waiting for the RR to warm up, or even the little extra step of changing the RR mode from LGC to either of the backup modes. So he asked for the procedures to specify that the RR should be powered up and in the AUTO mode during normal descent operations. It was a prudent and thoroughly rational decision by a man who had no way of knowing it opened a window of vulnerability to an improbable glitch.

TOUCHDOWN AND EXTRA POINT: 1969

Flight controllers at Houston were training intensely for Apollo 11, seeking out any possibilities they may have overlooked. Dick Koos, known as "Sim" for his role in setting up simulations for this training, discovered that the AGC software had a group of alarm codes they'd never seen at MSC. That was logical, because those alarms had been created at the Lab to aid in debugging the software. But, "Sim" asked us, could any of them happen in flight anyway? We told him that while we couldn't imagine any way they would arise, there was nothing in the software to block them. So he started putting the alarms into likely places in the training sequences. One that intrigued him announced "executive overflow," meaning that the AGC was trying to do more jobs in parallel than it had the capacity for. Wearing his evilest grin, "Sim" put it into the LGC's busiest phase, powered descent. For White Team Guidance Officer ("GUIDO") Steve Bales, it was his busiest phase also, and the appearance of "Program Alarm 1201" was a bolt from the blue. "What's a 1201," he wondered, "and what the hell am I supposed to do about it?" There wasn't much time for wondering during powered descent, so he called an abort.

Flight Director Gene Kranz ran the post-mortem session and asked Steve, "Was there any anomaly in the flight path, any problem besides the alarm code?"

"No, there wasn't," Steve replied, realizing he'd allowed himself to be pressured into an unnecessary abort. Kranz called on Jack Garman, who'd worked closely with the Lab on all aspects of the software, to make a list of all the Program Alarm codes, what they meant, and what would be a good response. Jack quickly put together a "cheat sheet" and made copies for all the controller stations. "Sim" never again succeeded in hornswoggling a controller with an alarm code.

I personally had no role in these last-minute preparations for Apollo 11. At work, I was busy designing the computer for the advanced Strapdown Inertial Reference Unit. At home, my first child Robby was born on June 19, a launch that put Vicki and me into a happy orbit of our own. My only preparation for the Apollo 11 mission was buying our first color television, a modest unit with a 12-inch screen.

The Apollo 11 crew consisted of Commander Neil Armstrong, CM Pilot Mike Collins, and LM Pilot Buzz Aldrin. Despite the intensity of their training, they had time to pick call signals—names—for their spacecraft, and settled on *Snowcone* for the CM and *Haystack* for the LM. These, coming on top of *Charlie Brown* and *Snoopy* in Apollo 10, were too much for NASA's public relations people, who insisted on something more dignified. Fortunately, Jules Verne came to the rescue. In *From the Earth to the Moon*, he gave the name *Columbiad* to his spacecraft fired from a huge cannon in Florida. So the more familiar form *Columbia* became the call sign for the CM. On a similarly patriotic theme, the crew named the LM *Eagle* for the national bird, thankful that Benjamin Franklin had not succeeded in promoting the turkey for that role.*

On July 3, 1969, the largest artificial non-nuclear explosion in history rocked central Russia as an N-1 booster with its 30 engines devastated its launch site, crippling the Soviet Union's ability to send cosmonauts to the Moon. Ten days later, the Soviets launched Luna 15 toward the Moon and briefed NASA on its flight path. They didn't initially tell us the full mission, a last-ditch attempt at a historic first. They'd programmed their robot to land, scoop up some samples, and return them to Earth before Apollo 11 would get back.

Apollo 11 lifted off on July 16, 1969, at the businesslike hour of 9:32 EDT, achieving orbit by 9:44. The third stage S4B performed its Trans-Lunar Injection burn flawlessly. In the Transposition and Docking maneuver, the crew pulled the LM out as planned. Houston controllers made the S4B vent its remaining fuel and dodge away, entering a "slingshot" path on the way to the Moon, not too near the spacecraft. Of the two mid-course corrections scheduled for the outbound leg, one was unnecessary and the other needed only a three-second burn. That was on July 17, the day Luna 15 entered a rather high-altitude Lunar orbit. The Russians made major changes in its orbit on July 18, to reduce its altitude and better align it for a landing in the Sea of Crises—a name that would later seem to have been a bad omen.

Apollo's Lunar Orbit Insertion on July 19 went as planned, with no sighting of Luna 15. The S4B stage sailed silently on to

---

*Think about it. Can you keep a straight face while saying "Tranquility Base here. The Turkey has landed"? I sure can't.

swing partway around the Moon, using its gravity as a slingshot to change course and become an eternal empty voyager around the Sun. After circularizing the orbit at 60 miles above the Lunar surface, the crew performed another round of system checks and tucked in for the night. The Russians made more changes in Luna 15's orbit, apparently having some difficulty with preparing it for descent, or they would have landed it before the end of July 19.

Passing again behind the Moon on July 20, Neil and Buzz moved into *Eagle* for the duration of its part of the mission, and powered up everything including the LGC. There was no sign of a time-wasting glitch, but it wouldn't have been detectable anyway because of the 15% time pad built into the software as a result of Black Friday (Chapter 23). They ran system tests for more than two orbits and gave the LGC a time-of-ignition for the next burn, also behind the Moon. The LGC calculated a new V_G, the velocity the burn should take out of the LM's trajectory to achieve DOI (Descent Orbit Insertion). The new orbit would keep its 60-mile high point (apolune), and its low point (perilune) would be just 50,000 feet—about 9 miles— above the Moon. That perilune point was calculated to be exactly the right place and time for a nominal Powered Descent phase to bring the LM down to the selected landing spot in the Sea of Tranquility. Buzz read the numbers to Houston, received go-for-separation, and told Mike they were ready.

Mike ordered his AGC to maneuver the combined spacecraft to align the LM's Descent engine with the required retrograde burn, and roll it so the LM's triangular windows looked down at the Moon. Then he released the tunnel latches from the CM end, and both crews got busy on nearly half an hour of running down the pre-DOI checklist. The LGC quietly recorded an extra push speeding up the LM. What nobody had thought about was how the oxygen in the tunnel, at about five pounds of pressure, would push the two spacecraft apart as soon as the latches were released. It had happened in Apollo 9 and in Apollo 10 also, but Apollo 11 was the first time it mattered.

Mike commanded a backing-off move that ran two of the SM's RCS jets for a long nine seconds. He had to get the CSM far enough away to prevent any chance of a collision when the LM began slowing down. Nearly an hour later, the LGC's displayed countdown was approaching zero. Neil took a last look around, got a thumbs-up from Buzz, and punched the PRO key to give the LGC permission to go ahead with the DOI burn. It ran two of the LM's RCS jets for a seven-second ullage thrust to settle the fuel and oxidizer in the bottoms of the tanks. Then it fired the Descent engine and sampled the Inertial Measurement Unit every two seconds to update the velocity-to-be-gained. After 30 seconds, it found V_G to be rapidly approaching zero, and shut off the engine. Like any good computer, it had done exactly what it was told to do—and nobody had told it to increase the amount of slowdown to compensate for the released tunnel's oxygen venting.

There was no fault in the inertial navigation. The LGC's readings of the IMU faithfully captured the velocity changes from both the venting and the burn. It combined them with its math model of Lunar gravity to yield the LM's actual velocity and position. But the velocity was higher than intended by about one part in a thousand, because the venting hadn't been figured into the V_G. That was enough to make a noticeable difference after traveling halfway around the Moon.

Although Neil had no way to know what effect the tunnel venting would have, his thorough preparation enabled him, once they'd come around to the well-mapped front side of the Moon, to time their passage over known craters with his wristwatch. He announced that they were a little west, a few miles, of where they should have been. That really impressed Buzz, who remembers, "How in the world can he really, at this point, tell that we're gonna be a little long? But sure enough, we were."

Arriving at the 50,000-foot perilune altitude, Neil selected the Powered Descent program and the LGC again ran an ullage thrust and lit the Descent engine to begin the twelve-minute descent-and-landing sequence. A little more than five minutes later, the master alarm horn sounded and "1202" appeared on the DSKY. Neither of the astronauts knew what the hell a 1202 was. Listening at home, I also had no idea—but it didn't sound good. The time-wasting problem had returned … at the worst possible moment. And nobody in Houston except Jack Garman even knew for sure that's what it was.

Neil, concentrating on flying, asked Houston for advice. The Houston controllers had seen the alarm too, and Steve Bales hailed Jack, who instantly replied, "That's a Go, Steve." He knew it was an executive overflow and had no idea what had caused it either, but it was nearly the same alarm that "Sim" had thrown at them a few weeks before, just a less severe level that affected a smaller subset of the LGC's work. Steve watched the LM's flight path and saw no problem with it. Flight Controller Gene Kranz was polling the room: "GUIDO?" Steve yelled "Go!" and astronaut Charlie Duke as Capsule Communicator (CapCom) relayed, "We're Go on that alarm, Eagle."

After 20 seconds, there was another 1202 alarm, and again Neil was able to keep flying. Buzz had been running display verbs to track distance and time to go to the final approach point, and was shocked to see them vanish from the DSKY. Houston agreed to supply that data and explained that the LGC was overloaded and was dropping low-priority tasks like the display verbs. "OK, what else around here is gonna get dropped as 'low priority'?" the LM crew wondered, but two whole minutes passed without further alarms. Then Neil selected the LGC's Automatic Guidance mode, and in less than a minute there was a 1201 alarm, exactly the one "Sim" had put into the test run. "We're Go. Same type. We're Go" was the calming word from CapCom. That was an unintentionally overbold conclusion, since 1201 was the more severe overflow condition. The LGC rebooted itself, picked up its stored indicators of what it was supposed to be doing, and carried on operating the Descent engine and the RCS jets in response to Neil's hand controller "pickle-stick" actions. There were two more 1202 alarms at 15-second intervals, and Buzz, motivated to do everything he could to make this nightmare stop recurring, cut back to the essential display verb for altitude and altitude rate, the only way to monitor that data from the landing radar. That reduced the LGC's workload to where the time-wasting was again absorbed into Black Friday's 15% time cushion, and there were no more alarms. Watching at home, I figured it was OK to stop sweating and breathe.

The LGC kept displaying numbers that Buzz read out loud so Neil could look through the correspondingly-numbered LPD graticule lines on his window to see where the predicted landing point would be. Since they were four miles west of the originally designated (and remarkably smooth) site, he kept finding boulders in the way and had to use his pickle-stick to redesignate the landing point and move horizontally like a helicopter to get there. That's the mode we had called "manual" despite the continued essential role of the LGC in carrying out the commands.

While the level in the Descent engine's fuel tank was dipping troublingly low, Neil chose a fairly reasonable place and let the LGC reduce the altitude gradually. His view of the surface was totally obscured by dust fanned out by the engine's exhaust, so he had to trust the LGC's ability to continue straight down to the chosen spot. One of the feelers extending down from the LM's saucer-shaped footpads hit the surface and lit the Contact light. After a second's hesitation that wasn't in the plan, he shut off the Descent engine, and the LM settled down so gently that the crushable shock-absorbing material in its legs was scarcely dented. After verifying that they'd landed just about level, Neil was able to say, "Houston, Tranquility Base here. The Eagle has landed."

CapCom Charlie Duke was so flabbergasted by Neil's creation of the new call sign he couldn't pronounce it straight at first: "Roger, Twan ... Tranquility, we copy you on the ground. You got a bunch of guys about to turn blue. We're breathing again. Thanks a lot."

In *Columbia*, 60 miles above the surface, Mike was not idle. Hoping to spot Tranquility Base from orbit, he ran AGC's landmark tracking program to point the sextant's telescope at the estimated location. He repeated the attempt many times in response to updated estimates from Houston but never could find it.

Neil and Buzz spent the next two hours going through a long checklist to make the LM ready for liftoff, even if it had to be premature. The LGC went into its idling loop (Program 00, or "Pooh") to be ready for action at any time. For the humans, there was a scheduled rest period, but they weren't interested. The twelve minutes of powered descent had been even more exciting than planned but not physically exhausting, and Neil and Buzz wanted to go outside and play. The rest period, never intended to be mandatory, had been put into the plan primarily so that if they did want to rest, the drama-hungry media couldn't headline it as a setback.

They took their time putting on the life-supporting backpacks, double-checking everything, and carefully backed out of the hatch, Neil first. At home, Vicki and I got our son Robby out of bed and propped him up in front of the TV. Being just one month old, he didn't react much to what was happening, but he was there, witnessing.

Neil made his way down the ladder and carefully planted the weight of his left foot on the lunar dust. "That's one small step for a man, one giant leap for mankind." That's what he said, calmly and precisely, yet back on Earth we all heard it without that little word "a" occupying its quarter of a second. In following the path of the electronic signal representing that sound, from the microphone in Neil's helmet to the loudspeakers in our TV sets, I found a place where about a quarter of a second's worth of signal could simply vanish. It depends on a certain action—not an uncommon one—by a NASA technician taking place at a key moment. Here's how it works. The low-power radio transmission from his backpack to a receiver in the LM was relayed by a higher-power transmitter through the LM's high-gain antenna to a huge dish antenna on the Earth, whichever one could face the Moon at the time. Next, the signal traveled by one or both of the global space-dedicated networks to Mission Control in Houston. Since there were multiple paths in the global network, a switch at MSC selected which path would feed the worldwide loop on its way into the commercial TV network. Actually, there were three switches, one each for data, voice, and TV.

Based on Neil's somewhat optimistic forecast of how long the Extra-Vehicular Activity (EVA) preparations would take, NASA planned to set all the switches to select the dish at Goldstone, California. That seemed highly advantageous because the operationally vital data and voice signals would use only domestic land lines, of known reliability, to reach Houston. The TV signal was more a matter of public relations and could be selected on picture quality alone, with lower reliability concerns.

As the EVA preparations went on longer than predicted, the Moon sank lower in the California sky and rose higher at Honeysuckle Creek in Australia. Neil's televised progress down the ladder looked better and better through the Honeysuckle feed, compared to Goldstone's. By the time Neil was ready to take his step and make his speech, the difference drove Houston to throw the selection switches hastily to Honeysuckle. All three signals came in satisfactorily, but somebody in Houston suddenly remembered the policy of feeding voice and data through Goldstone whenever possible. Since the Moon wasn't going to set at Goldstone until an hour after the EVA would be over, it was indeed possible, so they switched those two signals back while Neil was speaking. The timing of that reselection is the key to my solution of the mystery.

Traveling at nearly the speed of light, electromagnetic signals cover a thousand miles of wire in just over 5 milliseconds, making the trip from Goldstone to Houston in about 8 milliseconds. Even when receiving signals from the third big-dish antenna in Spain, the Atlantic undersea cable made the length of the trip about 20 milliseconds. But Australia had no undersea cable connections to the global communications net at that time. Signals from Honeysuckle had to take a 50,000-mile detour through a geosynchronous satellite (Intelsat III), at its inevitable altitude of 22,236 miles, nearly one-tenth of the distance to the Moon. That added 300 milliseconds to the trip.

Houston's reselection from Honeysuckle back to Goldstone must have come just after Neil's words "That's one small step for a" arrived at Honeysuckle, so that the first word through the Goldstone channel was "man." Instantaneously shortening the path by 50,000 miles simply chopped 300 milliseconds out of the speech's perceived time span. Neil's word "a" went from Tranquility Base to Honeysuckle and up to Intelsat, but by the time it got back down to Earth nobody was listening to that path. These reselections of receiving stations—and their exact timing—are my conjecture and are not stated in the official transcripts, but all the other factors are based on a careful reading of those transcripts. In space flight, the speed of light does matter, a lot.

Buzz joined Neil on the surface and they set to work, easily adjusting to the Moon's one-sixth gravity. They quickly collected contingency samples, unveiled and read the plaque, *We came in peace for all mankind*, set up the American flag, and talked with President Richard Nixon. They laid out the scientific instruments, collected more samples, and had no sighting— indeed no thought—of Luna 15. Watching at home, I was spellbound and very proud and happy about how things were going. However, I also knew that it wouldn't be over until the three astronauts were back on the Navy carrier. It wasn't quite time to go dancing in the streets, yet.

After two hours of EVA, they climbed up the ladder, stowed the precious samples, and repressurized the cabin to wriggle out of their backpacks and Moon boots. That made it possible to take their helmets off and have supper. Once dressed for traveling again in pressurized suits, they depressurized the cabin, dumped all the equipment they wouldn't need out the hatch, closed it tight, and repressurized the cabin. *Then* they were ready for a rest period, in fact a good night's sleep, on and around the Ascent engine cover. Neil's ability to sleep was compromised by the superb quality of his landing. He'd put the LM down so level that blue light from the half-lit Earth beamed down through the LM's Alignment Optical Telescope. Seen from any fixed position on the near side of the Moon, the Earth stays put forever in one place in the sky. Its light came down on the only place Neil could comfortably lay his head ... and stayed there.

But there was no rest for the Russians, as their difficulties in regaining control of Luna 15 were running up against two limits. There wasn't much maneuvering fuel left. If they didn't try to land soon, their chance to beat Apollo in returning Lunar samples to Earth would be gone. They managed to put it on a risky descent course for their original target in the Sea of Crises. British astronomers at the huge Jodrell Bank observatory, who had been tracking Luna, concluded that it wasn't likely to make it over the surrounding mountains. And indeed, at the time they predicted, signals from Luna 15 ceased. The crash, hundreds of miles away, didn't even register on the seismic recorder at Tranquility Base.

In the afternoon of July 21, CapCom Ron Evans woke Mike in *Columbia*, where he'd had five hours of good sleep, and Neil and Buzz in *Eagle*, where they hadn't done quite so well but were ready to get going. He asked them to use the Rendezvous Radar to track the CSM for a while before launch, to allow Houston to get a better fix on their location by working backward from the CSM's precisely known orbit. Then Houston wanted them to open the RR's circuit breakers during Ascent—meaning just the burn required to get back into Lunar orbit—and then close them again for the RR's role in the Rendezvous phase. The controllers' purpose was to avoid any more program alarms, a measure we understood later to be totally ineffective against the time-wasting problem. Buzz—intending only to be humorously cranky—commented that during Descent he'd had the RR in Slew mode rather than the LGC mode that would be used in Ascent. Saying that, he was accidentally hitting the truth about what had triggered the alarms. Houston consented to leaving the RR powered up during Ascent to avoid the warm-up time issue, but asked Buzz to set the RR mode to LGC during Ascent anyway, thereby (inadvertently) preventing any more program alarms.

Eagle lifted off and rose gently and quietly for over seven minutes, feeling somewhat like a long elevator ride. They shut off the Ascent engine after achieving an orbit just a little lower than their Descent orbit, 10 miles high and headed for an apolune of 48 miles. After rendezvous and docking, Neil and Buzz used a vacuum cleaner to reduce the amount of Moon grit clinging onto the sample containers. With everything stowed in the CM, they cast off the LM, leaving it powered up to see how long the Primary GN&C system would work without cooling— four hours for the IMU and seven for the LGC, as it turned out. Early on July 22, Apollo 11 passed behind the Moon for the last time, and performed a precise Trans-Earth Injection burn.

Entry and splashdown in the Pacific were on July 24, 1969, as scheduled, and the Apollo 11 astronauts were safe on the USS Hornet within an hour. *Then* it was time to say "Touchdown! We did it. Jack Kennedy, we did it. For you, for our country, for everyone on this good Earth. We did it."

Nearly all the world's nations had joined in the media

coverage and in the rejoicing. The spirit, echoed again and again when the Apollo 11 astronauts went on their world tour, was "We—not just the USA but all mankind—have completed the greatest achievement of all time." Only the most rigidly closed societies tried to keep their people from even knowing the mission had taken place: Albania, China, North Korea, and North Vietnam. Perhaps to humor them, the creaky Soviet propaganda machine rumbled into life and started suggesting that Neil and Buzz and Mike had survived only by blind luck in a foolishly risky venture using that stupid failed computer. After all, hadn't NASA been openly uncertain about the exact location of Tranquility Base, and wasn't it several miles off target?

At the Lab, we had to figure what really caused those program alarms, and what to do about them, while listening to widespread ignorant folklore that was saying, "The stupid computer failed, so the brilliant human had to take over and do everything manually." Even President Nixon, who for all his constitutional challenges was bright enough to know better, seemed to swallow that one. Well, at least he didn't join the conspiracy wingnuts who said the whole thing had been faked in a movie studio. To put accurate facts before NASA and even some of our in-house people, the Lab's George Cherry wrote an excellent memo, which I have reproduced in the Appendix. He called it an "exegesis," sending his readers scrambling for their dictionaries.[47] Don Eyles made a detailed study, with timeline graphs, showing exactly which jobs and tasks encountered problems with starting a new cycle when the previous cycle had not yet ended.[48]

George Silver's Interim Discrepancy Report finally got the multi-disciplinary attention it deserved. We just had to stop seeing it as a hardware design issue for Grumman to deal with (or not), and reinterpret it as asking for a procedural or software workaround for the hardware issue it described.

We considered two procedural approaches. One recognized that the critical phase difference resulted from the exact time interval between powering up the LM systems in general and powering up the LGC-centered Primary GN&C system. If George could see the effect of the time-wasting by examining the stream of down-telemetry data, why couldn't we do the same during the mission and ask the crew to recycle the LGC power switch if we saw it? As a random event with only a 1% probability, one recycling would be very likely to fix it, and we could still do it again if necessary. The fatal flaw in that idea was that powering up the LM was done behind the Moon, where nobody on Earth could see the telemetry.

The other procedural approach was to insist that Buzz Aldrin was wrong in powering on the Rendezvous Radar and setting its mode to the abort-oriented SLEW rather than LGC during a normal Descent, and this view is visible in many archives today. But as I said above, his setting was a wise and practical way to apply the lessons of Apollo 10's abort rehearsal. There was a further misapprehension about whether opening the RR's circuit breakers would prevent the problem. But no, they only affected the RR's pulse transmission and reception circuits.

One software approach would be making the LM, on initial power-up, run some routine that would show whether the time-wasting was going on, and display an alarm then, to cue a power recycle with no need for examining telemetry. But another approach was much simpler. Whenever the RR mode was powered off, or in either of the abort-system modes instead of LGC mode, we knew its shaft and trunnion angles were of no interest to the LGC. That meant it would be correct to check for the RR power and mode settings at regular intervals and send a command to "zero" (reset) our Coupling Data Units for the RR whenever it wasn't powered up and in LGC mode. The abnormal state of the resolvers would still be there, but it wouldn't be stealing any memory cycles from the LGC.

The simpler way was clearly the better way, but there wasn't time to apply it in time for Apollo 12, which was set to launch in mid-November, following Apollo 11 by a scant four months. Testing of Apollo 12's software was too far advanced to allow any change that wasn't essential for safety. Those program alarms were pesky but highly improbable and evidently not life-threatening—so perhaps the decision to ignore the problem wasn't totally wrong after all. But NASA and Grumman really should have followed up to understand it better before the flight.

———— ∞∞∞ ————

The importance of accurate landing was a lesson that could be applied to Apollo 12 procedurally. First, NASA figured out how to operate the venting of the CM-LM tunnel so that the oxygen pressure wouldn't give the LM that forward push. Second, an intensified use of Earth-based radar, when it first saw the LM in its Descent orbit, allowed improved timing for Powered Descent Initiation. With these tools in hand, it made sense to announce an ambitious target, just a few hundred feet away from the unmanned Surveyor 3 that had landed successfully in April 1967.

Finding the Moon a little out of reach, the Soviet manned space program had to do something as spectacular as they could in Earth orbit. On October 11, 12, and 13, they launched three Soyuz spacecraft, numbered 6, 7, and 8, with a record total of seven cosmonauts. Soyuz 7, with three cosmonauts, was supposed to take the active part in a three-vehicle rendezvous. But consistency in rendezvous guidance was also a little out of their reach. All three returned to Earth after five-day flights with no rendezvous achieved.

The Apollo 12 mission had acquired a considerable urgency which made it easy to downplay a dubious weather picture as the scheduled launch time approached. Because it would have been the first Lunar landing if Apollo 11 failed, everyone connected with it had gotten used to the importance of completing its mission before the end of 1969. That momentum was not diminished by the success of Apollo 11, partly because the Soviets were still actively competing, and partly because of its more ambitious scientific goals.

On November 14, Pete Conrad, Dick Gordon, and Al Bean settled into their CM, *Yankee Clipper*, and launched into a rainy sky with a mid-level cloud deck around 10,000 feet. Just thirty-six seconds after liftoff, there was a lightning bolt. Some sources say it hit the spacecraft's Launch Escape Tower and passed through all the spacecraft and booster stages before going to ground through nearly a mile of the Saturn booster's exhaust. That seems unlikely to me, because it didn't burn a hole anywhere and ignite any of the tons of kerosene and hydrogen being carried.

My interpretation is that the bolt's electrical current passed through the rocket exhaust plume and never touched the vehicle. It was close enough to deliver a substantial EMP—an Electro-Magnetic Pulse. The EMP was big enough to induce abnormal electrical currents in parts of the vehicle, but not big enough to actually fry the circuits. A second discharge fifteen seconds later induced more abnormal currents and no apparent damage.

In the transcripts, all the recorded dialogue for the boost period is about electrical power supply events, with no mention of a burst of sound or any indication of scorching. The first pulse tripped all the surge detectors in the Service Module, shutting down the fuel cells without damaging them. Amazingly, the automatic switchover of all spacecraft systems to battery power was so quick and smooth that none of the comments suggest a blink of the cabin lighting.

CM Pilot Dick Gordon's reaction to the alarm lights was, "What the hell was that?" Commander Pete Conrad responded with a puzzled "Huh?" showing that he hadn't noticed anything abnormal. The only anomaly during those fifteen seconds was instrument readings showing that the fuel cells had gone offline. Then the second discharge made the IMU stable platform tumble, which in turn made the Flight Director Attitude Indicator (or "eight-ball," an artificial horizon for three dimensions) spin randomly. The AGC, with its RAM protected against the surge, restarted instantly and lit an alarm light on the DSKY indicating Inertial Subsystem failure.

Despite all the alarm lights, this wasn't a catastrophe requiring a panicky abort. All the voltmeters for the power supply busses showed low but usable voltages. It was a classic case of a backup system working so well that it was hard to figure what had gone wrong. Loss of attitude reference in the CM was a nuisance but not a disaster because its Primary GN&C System was only backing up the Saturn's Instrument Unit in the S4B. The launch vehicle computer didn't have to restart because it was on battery power the whole time, and its two-out-of-three voting architecture was sufficient to cancel out any single-point data errors induced. There was plenty of time left in the boost phase to sort things out.

In Houston, electrical specialist John Aaron remembered how an obscure switch had been seen to reset all that sort of chaos in a test months before. Less than a minute after the second strike, he passed the suggestion through CapCom Jerry Carr: "Try SCE [Signal Conditioning Equipment] to auxiliary." In the spacecraft, Pete had no idea what Jerry was talking about, but Al remembered a test in which a similar failure had been simulated, and knew where to find the switch. It restored the fuel cells to operating condition, but they postponed hooking them up to the power busses until orbit. During their first Earth orbit, the crew went through the regular stable platform alignment using star sights. As the second orbit began, they ran the AGC self-check program written by the Lab's Ed Smally and sent down a copy of all the data in the Erasable Memory (RAM). Eldon Hall's surge protection for the Erasable had kept the transient currents from corrupting any data.

After pulling the LM *Intrepid* out of its shelter, Pete and Al made an extra visit there to check on the condition of its systems. Everything in the LM had been unpowered throughout the excitement, and they found no evidence of any electromagnetic intrusion. All the circuit breakers had their proper settings, the LGC ran its self-check, and a dump of its Erasable found no corruption.

How could the lightning's current miss the metal-skinned vehicle, which would seem to be a good lightning rod? I think it was because the one-mile column of ionized air, created by the rocket exhaust, was a much better lightning rod. Lightning science has advanced since 1969 and often describes a cloud-to-ground strike as including an "upward leader" from the ground, a column of ionized air reaching partway to whichever cloud is serving as the static charge reservoir. A "return stroke" coming down from the cloud meets it and completes the path. Historians agree that the launch of Apollo 12 in the rain actually caused a lightning strike that wouldn't have occurred otherwise. The Saturn booster's ionized exhaust seems to have played the role of upward leader.

If any substantial fraction of the cloud-to-ground current had hit the vehicle, it would have passed first through the Launch Escape System, which includes the tower with its canted rockets and the Boost Protective Cover, a conical shape fitting snugly over the CM. Then it would have gone down the length of the SM, possibly damaging one of the exposed RCS jet quads on the way, and along the adapter shroud covering the LM. Then down the three booster stages with their interstage adapters, before jumping to the ionized exhaust column. Only the CM came back from any Apollo mission, and it was the one piece completely shielded from such a current, so there was no opportunity to look for scorch marks after the mission. There was an opportunity in flight to examine the SM, when the LM undocked in Lunar orbit in preparation for Descent, but none of the recordings mention such an attempt.

Apollo 12 continued on its designed timeline, the only major difference being the crew's conversation returning again and again to their remarkable experience with the lightning strikes. They even asked Houston to replay the recorded dialogue from that period as entertainment one evening in place of music. With the improved techniques for undocking and last-minute radar tracking, Pete and Al landed *Intrepid* within an easy walk of Surveyor 3. Their light-hearted banter was such a change from the businesslike exchanges between Buzz and the taciturn Neil that it produced a headline, "Al Bean brings laughter to the Moon." During the second of their two EVAs, they clipped off some pieces of it to bring back for research into the effects of long exposure to space. Rejoining Dick in *Yankee Clipper*, they made the trip home with no further anomalies.

Their pinpoint Lunar landing, combined with the triumph of good engineering over a potentially disastrous event, took the remaining wind out of the Soviet propaganda machine. There could be no more snide talk about lucky flukes. The Cold War was a long way from being over, and much of the Space Race was still to be run. But beyond any doubt, the United States of America had scored a touchdown with Apollo 11, made the extra point with Apollo 12, and won the Race to the Moon.

Space Race Highlights of 1969

(All manned flights are indicated in bold.)

14 Jan **Soyuz 4. 3 days. Crew: Vladimir Shatalov. Achieved dock with Soyuz 5.**

15 Jan **Soyuz 5. 3 days. Crew: Boris Volynov, Aleksei Yeliseyev, Yevgeniy Khrunov. First docking of manned spacecraft. First crew transfer, of Yeliseyev and Khrunov to Soyuz 4 for entry.**

21 Feb First test of Soviet N-1 booster, counterpart of Saturn 5, failed. Destroyed one minute after liftoff.

03 Mar **Apollo 9 (AS-504). 10 days. Crew: Jim McDivitt, Dave Scott, Rusty Schweickart, first manned LM with internal crew transfers, of McDivitt and Schweickart to LM and back.**

16 May Venera 5 returned data from Venerian atmosphere for 53 minutes.

17 May Venera 6 returned data from Venerian atmosphere for 51 minutes.

18 May **Apollo 10 (AS-505). 8 days. Crew: Tom Stafford, John Young, Gene Cernan. "Dress rehearsal" including everything but Lunar landing.**

03 Jul Second test of N-1 booster failed seconds after liftoff. Fell back on launch pad and exploded.

13 Jul Luna 15. Unmanned. Launched as a Lunar sample return mission. In Lunar orbit 17–20 July. Crashed on Moon 21 July.

16 Jul **Apollo 11 (AS-506). 8 days. Crew: Neil Armstrong, Mike Collins, Buzz Aldrin. First manned Lunar landing 20 July, first spacecraft launched from Moon 21 July.**

05 Aug Mariner 6 and Mariner 7. Unmanned. Took photos on flyby of Mars.

11 Aug Zond 7. Unmanned Soyuz. Lunar flyby and free return; would have been first Soyuz to safely return a cosmonaut if it had been manned.

11 Oct **Soyuz 6. 5 days. Crew: Georgi Shonin, Valeri Kubasov. Failed passive rendezvous with Soyuz 7 and Soyuz 8.**

12 Oct Soyuz 7. 5 days. Crew: Anatoly Filipchenko, Vladislav Volkov, Viktor Gorbatko. Failed active rendezvous with Soyuz 6 and Soyuz 8.

13 Oct Soyuz 8. 5 days. Crew: Vladimir Shatalov, Aleksei Yeliseyev. Failed passive rendezvous with Soyuz 6 and Soyuz 7. First three-spacecraft simultaneous mission.

14 Nov Apollo 12 (AS-507). 10 days. Crew: Pete Conrad, Dick Gordon, Al Bean. Second manned Lunar landing, 19 November. Second spacecraft launched from Moon 20 November.

Complete detailed data on other flights is not available for 1969.

FAILURE IS NOT AN OPTION: 1970

As 1970 opened, the Moon Race had been settled but the Space Race was far from over. Automated Soviet exploration of planets was ahead of ours, and they expressed a firm dedication to developing long-term space stations. Superpower politics required us to assure parity and seek superiority in both areas, if we were not to lose the advantage we had gained.

If anything, the Space race now expanded. Even the January 4 cancellation of plans for Apollo 20 could be considered a positive since the idea was to reassign its Saturn 5 to launching the "dry" version of the space station Skylab instead. "Dry" meant fully assembled and furnished on the ground before flight, and thus heavy enough to need the big rocket. The older "wet" version would have been assembled in orbit from the empty shell of an S4B second stage booster. Studies had indicated that the "wet" version would be more expensive and complicated.

In February, the Japanese space agency succeeded in launching a long-term scientific satellite, Ohsumi (named for a southern province), into orbit where it remained for 33 years. Toward the end of April, the People's Republic of China launched Dong Fang Hong 1 into permanent orbit, carrying a heavy radio transmitter that played its eponymous song, *The East Is Red*, for nearly a month. But between those two came a much bigger story.

North American Aviation's design for the Service Module provided spherical tanks for the cryogens, liquid hydrogen and liquid oxygen. In combination, they fed the fuel cells to produce electrical power and water. The oxygen had the additional job of providing breathable atmosphere to the spacecraft. These tanks, when no longer full, tended to separate into liquefied gas and a sort of froth, which meant a spotty unreliable flow when their valves were opened. Electric fans inside the tanks solved the problem by stirring the contents into a uniform texture. Since it would use too much power to run the stirring fans full-time, Houston would ask the crew for a "cryo stir" at opportune times.

Obtaining gas from a tank required more than just opening a valve. To maintain adequate gas pressure, each tank had a heating system with a thermostat. There were sensors to report quantity and temperature to CM instruments. NAA and their contractor Beech Aircraft designed these heat management units to use the standard spacecraft electrical power supply, 28 volts DC, but somehow failed to account for the later use of KSC's launch-complex power supply, 65 volts AC.

One of the LOX tanks had a checkered history including being dropped two inches at the factory in 1968. It required more use of the 65-volt supply than the others to get it to fill and empty properly in the Apollo 13 prelaunch drills. The thermostat-controlled switch to cut off the heater power did not work with 65 VAC, allowing that tank to reach about 1000°F. Unfortunately, the highest reading the temperature sensor could display on the instrument panel was the designed maximum of 80°F. The strongly built tank showed no problem with that extreme (and completely undetected) temperature. Inside it, the Teflon insulation on the stirring fan's wiring quietly melted.

Test engineers wrote a discrepancy report about the tank's known symptoms, but the officials reviewing it felt that was no reason to delay the launch. They wrote a waiver, which was signed off by several people including Commander Jim Lovell. In defiance of triskaidekaphobes—those with a morbid fear of the number 13—everywhere, Apollo 13 was launched at 13:13 CST, Friday, April 11. The first cryo stir would be ordered a few hours before the spacecraft crossed into the Moon's sphere of influence, 200,000 miles out, on April 13.

I was at home that evening, with no radio or TV going. My mother called from the Cape (Cod in her case, not Canaveral). "Isn't it awful what happened to Apollo?"

"How awful was *what*?" I wanted to know, and she gave me what she could glean from the TV coverage. An explosion had jarred the spacecraft on its way to the Moon and caused a total loss of fuel cell electrical power. "Houston, we've had a problem"—and this time there was no one-minute fix using an obscure switch. I considered going in to the Lab immediately to see if I could help but realized it wasn't any kind of a computer problem. Anyway, I didn't have any special knowledge of the Trans-Lunar coast phase or of the free-return trajectory. There were plenty of Lab people in the loop, manning our local SCAMA room as well as in Houston. It would be better on the whole to stay out of their way. If anybody wanted me they knew where to get me, only four miles away.

Flight Director Gene Kranz quickly determined that continuing around the Moon, with a course correction to achieve free return, was the only workable abort option. As a 1966 study on possibly using the LM as a "lifeboat" had noted, there was plenty of oxygen for breathing in the combined spacecraft. There wasn't a lot of water, but enough. Most of the lithium hydroxide canisters, to scrub carbon dioxide out of the air, fit the CM's Environmental Control System, but not that of the LM. As anyone who has seen the *Apollo 13* movie knows, jury-rigged adapters made up out of miscellaneous materials on board solved that problem, and assured an almost religious respect for duct tape.

What there wasn't enough of was electric power, at least for normal operation of the spacecraft. It would just do for an abnormal operation, shutting down everything in the CM for several days to conserve its battery power. All the crew and their activity had to be in the LM, with only its most essential systems turned on. The CM was going to get quite cold over the next few days but still had to wake up in time for entry, and we'd never started up either the AGC or the IMU in such cold. Unlike Houston, MIT had a convenient "thermal test chamber," that is, the chill of New England nights in early April. Eldon Hall put an AGC in his car trunk, and Jerry Gilmore did the same with an IMU. Both units woke up successfully after their overnight cold soak. This result was quite encouraging even though the actual spaceborne cold soak had three more days to run.

It was a strange-looking spacecraft that whipped around the Moon and headed back to Earth. All three modules remained together, as they had been for the outward trip, but the loss of all the liquid oxygen killed all the critical functions of the normally powerful SM. It couldn't supply breathable oxygen to the CM, it couldn't oxidize hydrogen in the fuel cells to generate electricity, and it couldn't oxidize hydrogen in the SPS engine to provide thrust. It was up to the LM's Descent engine to supply thrust for the mid-course corrections, pushing a much larger and heavier object than it had been designed to do. There was some concern about whether that mass, resisting the thrust, could compress the LM's featherweight structure enough to rupture the skin and depressurize the cabin. No such concern was communicated to the crew for the very good reason that they had no choice but to try it.

Steering the long awkward combination using only the LM's RCS jets was well outside the designed performance envelope, mainly because the center of mass (and therefore the effective pivot point) was several yards outside the LM. A Mississippi pushboat captain would recognize the situation. It would be like the difference between steering his boat by itself and steering it while pushing a nest of twelve heavy barges. This was a good demonstration of the virtuosity of inertial navigation. The LGC read the IMU gyros continually to assess the turning actually achieved by RCS burns, and deduced the location of the center of mass without any prejudice about where it ought to have been.

I liked the book and the movie on Apollo 13, and happened to be at the Smithsonian Air and Space Museum in Washington in 2006 when Fred Haise gave a presentation and answered questions, especially from kids. Fred's love for kids is evident; he gives them his full attention and is duly worshipped as a favorite uncle. One of the questions was, "How did you like the movie?" Fred said the only false note was the amount of profanity and tension in the conversations among the crew. A true representation would have looked and sounded like a technical meeting of businesslike engineers. Fred figured the movie people had to inject the usual tokens of drama to help audiences understand what was going on emotionally behind those calm exteriors.

My tiny part in the recovery, like thousands of other people's, had no frames in the movie or even made it to the cutting-room floor. Among the new situations, in the period just before re-entry, was separating the LM from the CM. Normally the LM would have separated from the CSM in Lunar orbit. This time, all three modules were in the entry corridor to the edge of Earth's atmosphere four days after the accident. The SM was separated from the CM first, to allow the crew to take photos of the damage. In a normal final LM-CSM separation, certain RCS jets on the SM made the CSM back off away from the LM. The CM's own RCS jets were oriented to perform roll and pitch maneuvers during entry, and none of them fired in a direction that would help this backing off. The only jets that *could* help were on the corners of the LM, which would be unmanned when it was time to fire them.

I was called in to the Lab's SCAMA room while this problem was being discussed. Our flight monitors asked me to write a tiny LGC program to fire the appropriate LM RCS jets after separation. Houston would send it via uplink to the LGC's erasable memory just before separation, and run it afterwards. This task was fairly straightforward, though I spent about half the time in reading the output channel tables three times over to be *quite* sure I was firing the right jets!

I was just getting ready to take it for a Digital Simulator run when somebody remembered an important fact: "You know what we found in Eleven when they were on our case about running long at the beginning of descent? It wasn't a fault in our guidance equations. When they separated, there was oxygen in the tunnel connecting the vehicles. When the latches were popped, the gas pressure blew the spacecraft away from each other. That added enough speed to the LM to account for the discrepancy. *The tunnel is going to be full of oxygen for this sep too. Why not let it do the work?*"

I wish I remembered who came up with that ultra-simple solution. What a great demonstration of the benefits of unity and continuity in an engineering organization! Sure, I would have been glad if my little scrap of code had been used to solve this problem, but the simplest way is the best way.

So in a strict sense, I didn't do anything to save Apollo 13. But in a broader sense, we all did—the hundreds of thousands of us all around the globe who set about doing any impossible thing to bring that crew home. Failure was never an option because in all that multitude, the ruling spirit was, *We can do this.*

Neither Gene Kranz nor anybody else at NASA said "Failure is not an option" during the Apollo era. The quote was coined for the film by screenwriter Bill Broyles, paraphrasing a background explanation by Kranz's FIDO (Flight Dynamics Officer), Jerry Bostick. Broyles instantly recognized it as an ideal tag line for the movie, to be spoken by the Kranz character. Kranz himself happily borrowed it for his book title, and I have just as happily borrowed it for the title of this chapter.

Like the Apollo 1 fire but at a much lower cost, this accident pulled the covers off weaknesses in the management of our manned space program. The response to dropping the tank at North American Aviation was halfhearted at best. Leaving 28-volt circuits in place to be operated at 65 volts was slipshod. Writing waivers against valid discrepancy reports, in a rush to launch on schedule, was foolish. Nearly everybody involved was guilty in some way. And I won't listen to anything about the number 13 working mysterious magical mischief on their minds.

The accident and its happy conclusion form the most tightly woven combination of disastrous failure and heroic success in history. The weaknesses revealed by the accident jarred NASA out of the habit of mounting an Apollo mission every few months. They had to back off, investigate, and fix the problems. There were also budget cuts due to the decreased urgency after the Moon race was won. Those cuts resulted in a September 2 cancellation of Apollo 18 and 19, and postponement of the Skylab launch into 1973.

At this point, the Soviets finally hit their stride, sending successful robots to the Moon and establishing themselves as a continuing manned presence in Earth orbit. Soyuz 9 maintained two cosmonauts in orbit for a record 18 days in June. In September, Luna 16 succeeded where Luna 15 had failed, landing on the Moon's Sea of Fertility and returning a hundred grams of basaltic material to a soft landing in Kazakhstan. In October, Zond 8 carried a man-rated (but unmanned) Soyuz craft around the Moon and returned safely. In November, Luna 17 delivered the first Lunar roving robot, Lunokhod 1, to the Sea of Rains, where its eight wheels kept it busy exploring for nearly a year. And in December, Venera 7 arrived at Venus after a voyage of only four months. It entered that planet's hellish atmosphere, landed hard, and sent temperature data back home for 23 minutes. At 887°F, Venus was shown to be not quite as hot as an overcooked SM LOX tank.

A friendly exchange took place, a sign of things to come. The Soviet scientists swapped some of their Luna 16 samples for some of our Apollo 12 samples. Perhaps it was both sides' way of showing that neither mission was faked, or perhaps it was just a case of scientists being a world community. Either way, it was a glimpse beyond the space-race mindset.

Another successful launch occurred just before the New Year. Our daughter Caroline was born, and it seemed to us that she had hurried the process along, perhaps to assure us of another tax exemption for all of 1970. Even more than big brother Robby, Caroline showed us that children are substantially who they are from birth, long before stumbling parents can mess them up. Vicki and I soon learned to wonder, "Who are these small people who have come to live with us?" Apparently, we managed to help them to discover and express their best selves, because our answer to that wonderment became "These are people we are privileged—and glad—to know."

Space Race Highlights of 1970

(All manned flights are indicated in bold.)

11 Feb   Ohsumi. Orbited for 33 years. Unmanned. First launch to orbit by Japan.

11 Apr   Apollo 13 (AS-508). 5 days. Crew: Jim Lovell, Jack Swigert, Fred Haise. SM crippled by explosion. Used LM as "lifeboat" for safe return.

24 Apr   Dong Fang Hong 1. Orbited. Unmanned. First launch to orbit by China.

01 Jun   Soyuz 9. 18 days in orbit. Crew: Andriyan Nikolayev, Vitali Sevastyanov. Longest one-spacecraft flight to date.

12 Sep   Luna 16. Landed on Moon. First robotic return of a sample to Earth.

20 Oct   Zond 8. Unmanned Soyuz. Rounded Moon, returned safely.

10 Nov   Luna 17. Landed on Moon. First robot Lunar rover, Lunokhod 1.

12 Dec   Uhuru (U.S. launched). Orbited unmanned. First satellite built by Kenya.

15 Dec   Venera 7. Landed on Venus. First to land on another planet. Sent data.

Complete detailed data on other flights is not available for 1970.

THE GHOST IN THE BUTTON AND THE ROVER ON THE MOON: 1971

Murphy's law was certainly a regular participant in the Apollo program. He'd set up the checklist error in Apollo 10. He'd produced the critical phase difference between the 800 Hz excitation voltages in Apollo 11. He'd invented a new way for lightning to strike in Apollo 12. He'd outdone himself in blowing up a LOX tank in Apollo 13. What could he do for Apollo 14, the first space event of 1971?

Kennedy Space Center conducted Apollo 14's launch a little more circumspectly, holding the January 31 liftoff forty minutes to make sure the heavy cloud cover didn't present any lightning threat. The boost and Trans-Lunar Injection were normal.

Transposition and Docking presented a challenge when the hard docking, required for the CSM *Kitty Hawk* to pull the LM *Antares* out of its adapter, wouldn't happen. After nearly two hours, CM Pilot Stu Roosa was able to promote soft dock to hard dock by thrusting the CM's nose against the

LM's docking collar while Commander Alan Shepard and LM Pilot Ed Mitchell removed the docking probe from the tunnel. With whatever was wrong with the probe out of the way, the docking latches activated correctly. Perhaps that was all that Murphy wanted.

Well, no, it seemed Murphy had been at work in the switch-and-button factory making controls for the LM. Inside every push-button assembly there's a certain amount of space between the connections, and one of the most common quality problems is a loose bit of something in that space. A plastic fragment there could block the effect of pushing the button, or a tiny ball of loose solder could make a short circuit, inadvertently producing the effect of pushing the button. Murphy's choice for Apollo 14 was a red circular button in an angry-looking diagonal striped border, labeled "ABORT." Fortunately, like other GN&C-oriented buttons in the LM, all it actually did was place a one or zero in just one bit position in one of the input channels of the LGC. Two parts of the LGC software looked at this bit. A routine scan periodically copied it, along with everything else in the input/output channels, to Mission Control via down telemetry. The software for operating the *normal* Powered Descent phase was the only thing that checked the bit to see if an abort was being commanded. Note that word "normal," which was the weapon we used to defeat Murphy.

When *Antares* was powered up preparatory to Descent Orbit Insertion, the telemetry suggested that a clumsy astronaut had accidently pushed the ABORT button ... but he hadn't. Houston asked LM Pilot Ed Mitchell to tap the panel, which made the false signal go away for a little while, but then it came back. A random event—undoubtedly a solder ball wandering around in zero-G—was the culprit and would keep happening. If it was still there when the Powered Descent burn started, it would abort the mission by thrusting the LM into its rendezvous orbit.

Don Eyles, the Lab's wizard in how the LM abort logic worked, set about devising a software workaround. There was no way to modify the program wired into the LGC's rope ROM, but there was a way to make the LGC execute a small amount of code in the erasable memory. In the LGC's multitasking Executive software, not every task had to know what flight phases other tasks thought they were in. Don figured out how to add a little program, in erasable memory, that would fool the task whose duty included watching the input bit from the Abort button. All he had to do was change its memory location that held a program number identifying the flight phase. Specifically, his code would put in the program number for the case that an abort sequence had already started. That would keep it from looking at the input bit.

Don's intimate knowledge of how the descent guidance tasks talked to each other showed him that the false program number would not have any side effects as long as there were no further anomalies. But what if other things went wrong during Powered Descent and the crew really needed to abort? Happily, all they had to do was the verb-noun pair that restored the correct program number. That would require seven additional DSKY keystrokes before pushing the Abort button, but saving the mission from that ridiculous ball of solder was worth the risk.

Don created a "short" sequence of 84 keystrokes to enter his mini-program into erasable and change a task address to make the Executive take the detour. He tested it for as long as he dared, then CapCom fed the steps by voice to Ed to perform. While that was completing, the countdown for Powered Descent approached single digits on the DSKY. Alan Shepard took a deeper Commander breath than usual before pressing the PRO key. It must have been the increased adrenalin flow that enabled him to make the most accurate Lunar landing of the whole project, at Fra Mauro.

Alan and Ed performed both the scheduled EVAs over two days, taking the longest walks on the Moon of any mission. They lugged equipment around in a two-wheeled pull cart they called the "Lunar rickshaw." They called it other things when it proved to be as unstable as most small trailers on rough ground, tipping over and making nearly more trouble than it was worth. Alan took his famous pair of golf shots with his smuggled six-iron club head. He demonstrated that although test pilots and astronauts may be absolutely reliable when reporting technical facts, they can exaggerate the length of their shots like any other golfer. It wasn't "miles and miles" as he first said, but about 400 yards.

Apollo 14 returned home safely and triumphantly, with all scientific objectives achieved. The crew saluted Don Eyles as "the guy who saved the mission single-handed." Murphy seemed to have gone on a well-deserved vacation, but Earthlings were to learn, later in the year, how frustration and even tragedy still stalked space explorers.

In April, the Soviets confirmed our understanding of how they wanted to continue the Space Race. The Americans can have the Moon, they seemed to say, but we'll lead the way to the planets, and we'll take the lead in occupying the LEO (Low Earth Orbit) region. Salyut 1 became the first space station, launched unmanned on April 19. Three days later, Soyuz

10 with three cosmonauts followed and rendezvoused with it successfully. Like Apollo 14 at first, they had trouble promoting a soft dock to a hard dock. Nothing they tried worked. After two frustrating days, Soyuz 10 had to come home without even a glimpse of the inside of Salyut.

In May, the USSR launched two Mars probes. Mars 2 launched on the 19th and eventually achieved Martian orbit, where it detached a lander, but the lander crashed. Mars 3 launched on the 28th, also eventually orbited Mars, and its lander module did survive the descent but stopped transmitting after 20 seconds. Our Mariner 9 launched on the 30th and made the trip somewhat faster, becoming the first to orbit Mars. It carried no lander module.

On June 6, Soyuz 11 took three cosmonauts up to Salyut and docked successfully. That crew became the first humans to staff a space station, where they stayed for the rest of the month, setting a new space endurance record and feeling like the wave of the future. But on their way home, communications with their Earthbound controllers unexpectedly ceased while they were in the entry corridor, several minutes before the heat of re-entry would block radio transmissions. The spacecraft landed automatically, using its parachutes and retro rockets as intended, within sight of one of the recovery helicopters. That helicopter landed and its crew jumped out, not really concerned by the signal break, just muttering about cruddy Soviet radio gear. They got ready to greet the cosmonauts, watching for them to open the hatch from inside. Nothing happened. Puzzled and by then a little alarmed, the helicopter recovery crew ran up, knocked sharply on the Soyuz's side, and called the cosmonauts' names. No answer. They got out their tools and opened the hatch. There lay the bodies of Georgy

Dobrovolsky, Vladislav Volkov, and Viktor Patsayev, intact except for signs of death by suffocation. A vent that should have been closed during entry was flapping open. It had somehow become unlatched by the separation of their descent module from the orbital module, and let all the air out—another ill wind that blew death to brave men.

———— ∞∞∞ ————

My new home in the Lab, the Digital Development Group (DDG), had been looking for a new direction since the completion of AGC design engineering in 1965. Other groups had bigger roles in Apollo-related projects. One was called DFBW, or Digital Fly By Wire, a Navy carrier-based F-8C fighter plane in which we replaced all the mechanical cabling for moving the rudder, elevators, and ailerons. We installed small motors, controlled by electrical wiring from a standard AGC, to move those "muscles." Neil Armstrong was a leader in that project because he felt the reliability and performance advantages of computer mediation he'd seen in the Apollo spacecraft would benefit both military and commercial aviation.

There were a number of space station concepts, of which the only American one then viable was Skylab, a joint project with the new European Space Agency. Development had started in 1967, and it would use an Apollo CSM as a taxi. We took pride in how little the Apollo software had to change to prepare for those flights.

The possibility of cooperation as well as competition in space between the United States and the Soviet Union was getting some preliminary exploration in the second half of 1971. That would come to something four years later.

There was no sign that any of these efforts would need

innovative computer hardware design by the Lab, partly because many aerospace companies had developed the ability to do that for government projects. Ray Alonso and Al Hopkins noticed that the new generation of space computers could not incorporate the extreme approaches to reliability we'd adopted for the AGC. They saw an opportunity for us in the DDG to get involved by re-inventing ourselves as experts in fault tolerance, the art of designing systems that continue to perform even after individual hardware units suffer glitches or fail altogether.

Where there's enough built-in redundancy, full performance can continue, like the way the U.S. electric power distribution system is supposed to work and usually does. One step below that is "graceful degradation" of performance, like a brownout, buying time for humans to change the way they use the system to something the lower levels will support. We studied how adding small amounts of extra hardware, like the memory parity checking we included in the AGC, would "cover" some faults but not others. Full-scale duplication and even triplication of hardware would cover very close to every type of fault if the "voting" logic was carefully designed, as it was in IBM's Launch Vehicle Digital Computer for the Saturn.

As in any technical discipline, we coined some curious jargon. Any piece of checking hardware that failed to notice problems with its computer host, we said had a "Pollyanna failure," referring to the fictional naïve little girl who started saying "It's all good" long before Martha Stewart was even born. Any checking hardware that was caught reporting false alarms, we said had a "Cassandra failure," after the gloom-and-doomer of ancient mythology. Strictly speaking, that was unfair to Cassandra, but then, so was everybody else.

We read widely in the literature and presented our own

papers to Fault Tolerance conferences, getting to know many of the top players. UCLA Professor Algirdas Avizienis was a large man with a magisterial manner and a considerable Lithuanian accent. Herb Hecht was a continuing author and consultant in the field. Nick Murray of NASA/Langley had monitored many contracts in the discipline. Lynn Killingbeck and others at IBM's Federal Systems Division in Owego, New York, published papers on fault tolerance.

One of our trips took us to RCA's research-and-development establishment in New Jersey early in 1971. While there, we met a lead engineer in a mini-project which was being kept quiet, but obviously excited the RCA man considerably. All he would tell us was that we would enjoy the upcoming Apollo missions in a new way, especially the end of the Lunar stay.

⸺ ◌⟩⟨◌ ⸺

Apollo 15 launched on July 26, with Commander Dave Scott, CM Pilot Al Worden, and LM Pilot Jim Irwin. It was a flight full of new things, both good and bad. The S1C first booster stage continued some thrusting after staging, threatening to damage the S2's engines. However, the S2 stayed out of reach and "defended itself" by frying an S1C telemetry unit with its exhaust.

So far from having docking problems, this LM, *Falcon*, seemed reluctant to leave its mother ship *Endeavour* to begin Descent Orbit Insertion. Al had to fix the seal in the tunnel hatch.

All three astronauts had received more extensive geology training, including Al, who had to operate several new science instruments mounted in a Service Module bay that hadn't previously had any function. He made observations during his solo cruise in Lunar orbit. Dave and Jim landed on target, not on a flat "sea" like the previous flights, but by a long valley shape called Hadley Rille. With three days of Extra-Vehicular Activity (EVA) ahead of them, they tucked into bed on arrival, though not before they briefly depressurized so that Dave could stand on the Ascent engine cover, stick his head and upper body out the docking hatch, and take a panorama of photos.

Over the next three days, they performed long-distance, long-duration EVAs, made possible by an elegant electric "car," the Lunar Roving Vehicle (LRV), which they unpacked from one side of the Descent Stage on the first morning. The LRV carried all their geological tools and had an RCA TV camera and a dish antenna to provide real-time video of their expeditions. Their enhanced training enabled them to identify and collect a so-called "Genesis Rock" much older than the rest, about the age of the Solar System itself. There was a little spare time on the third day for a set-piece TV presentation, in which Dave dropped a feather and a hammer at the same time. The feather plunged to the ground in a dead heat with the hammer, demonstrating Galileo's claim that the acceleration of gravity is the same for light and heavy objects. He then drove the LRV a little distance from the LM and placed a plaque and statuette honoring the eight astronauts and six cosmonauts then known to have died while training for or performing space exploration. The list of names was incomplete because the Soviets had kept two deaths secret.[49]

As soon as *Falcon* lifted off, we fully understood what our contact at RCA had been talking about. The camera on the LRV had some automation to make it track the rising LM for a way, the first live coverage of a launch from somewhere other than Earth. With a frame rate slower than a regular TV camera, the moment of liftoff seemed to show differently colored pieces of debris flying sideways from where the Ascent Stage had sat on the Descent Stage, some red, some green, and some blue. The color of each piece depended on which color scan was happening when it flew out.

After rendezvous, docking, and stowing of treasure, there was more to do than just come home. Al's science bay in the SM also held a "subsatellite" named PFS-1, which they released before doing their Trans-Earth Injection (TEI) burn. PFS-1 had sensors to observe charged subatomic particles and the Lunar magnetic field. As proof that Murphy's law was asleep for most of the Apollo 15 mission, they happened by sheer luck to leave PFS-1 in one of the four Lunar orbits that were later called "frozen" because all other low orbits were so disturbed by Lunar mascons as to become unstable, making satellites crash. PFS-1 became one of many spacecraft that revealed how powerfully the mascons affected the Moon's gravitational field.

The day after TEI, Al added to his record as the busiest CM Pilot by taking a deep-space walk (another first) to retrieve exposed film from his instrument bay in the SM. Most of entry went normally, but Murphy woke up in time to collapse one of the three parachutes for the splashdown part. There was no damage, though, because the system had been designed for two parachutes to be enough.

After landing and recovery, NASA called Apollo 15 the most successful space flight in history, a well-deserved accolade. We liked how they didn't have much to say about the AGCs and the Lab's GN&C systems, which just hummed along doing their jobs.

Then Murphy got in one farewell shot. The crew had taken 398 unauthorized commemorative "postage stamp covers," in addition to 243 authorized ones, and thus got into a mini-scandal because they meant to sell them. It blew over before too long, but left a dent in the perceived moral purity of astronauts.

In September, the Soviets sent two more unmanned spacecraft to the Moon. Luna 18 was intended to collect another sample and return it to Earth, but it crashed on the Moon. Luna 19 stayed in Lunar orbit for a year, studying the effects of the mascons.

And in October, the UK launched a satellite named *Prospero* into Earth orbit, the only time a UK rocket performed that feat. They'd named the satellite for the protagonist of Shakespeare's play *The Tempest*, set in a remote island which many think was in the Bahamas, close to Cape Canaveral.

CHANGES IN THE COLD WAR; CHANGES IN THE SPACE RACE: 1971

We at the Lab had been so fully occupied as to be somewhat insulated from the turmoil at home and abroad that characterized the '60s for so many people. Student protests against the Vietnam War, and against the establishment's general mean-spiritedness, did not leave the Lab untouched. It was the era in which Al Capp's final years of drawing *Li'l Abner* occasionally featured a protest group with the acronym SWINE, for Students Wildly Indignant about Nearly Everything.

MIT's Division of Sponsored Research—the sole sponsor being Uncle Sam—had two well-known components, Lincoln Lab out in the western suburbs and Instrumentation Lab on the Cambridge Campus. On rational grounds, MIT student unrest in 1969–71 should have been directed against Lincoln and its focus on missile systems, and not against us. Our Lab's NASA work was the greatest demonstration anywhere of peace-promoting high technology, and even our Navy work was then on a submarine rescue vehicle. The protesters' simplistic ideology was: "Labs do (or did) missiles, therefore labs are bad."

Our IL-7 building, a block or so east of East Campus, was the obvious site to deploy a thousand students to shout slogans. Even there, the only place for a crowd was around the loading dock and emergency exit in back, so we reinforced those. As it turned out, there never was an attempt to invade the building. The main upshot of the unrest was to supply a handy weapon to a faction of the Aero-Astro Department faculty that wanted to break with both labs because they felt like a small dog being wagged by its two huge tails. That's how the MIT Instrumentation Laboratory became the Charles Stark Draper Laboratory Inc., an independent non-profit company—allowing the students to take credit for "disarming" the Institute. CSDL remained, however, a part of the "MIT Community." Even though we had to get new stationery, our membership cards were still valid at the MIT Faculty Club, the most comfortably furnished bar in that part of town.

Our lives inside the Lab (by whichever name) were filled with purpose and meaning. Long hours were the self-directed norm, somewhat like the atmosphere in Data General Corporation depicted years later in Tracy Kidder's book, *The Soul of a New Machine*. Like those computer designers, we weren't motivated by the money, nor particularly by being in a competition. We were artists, excited by the activity of design and the triumph of seeing our creations work correctly. We were a community like the builders of cathedrals, bonded by the joy of seeing our works coordinated into a supreme achievement. And like Kidder's DG people, the greatest reward we could imagine would be an opportunity to do it all over again from our higher base of knowledge and skill.

If we were allowed to play again, what would the new game be? Visionaries were conceiving a permanent Lunar base, as a place to learn how to settle an alien world, or as a jumping-off place for travelers to Mars and beyond. But visionaries don't turn up in any quantity as political leaders, or budget-minded congressmen, or even voters.

For many Americans, the Space Race was the race to the Moon, and beating the Russians brought it to a satisfactory conclusion. Enthusiasm for scientific research on the Moon was waning even before the last two flights. The reliability of the systems making it possible became so great as to diminish the perceived drama of the missions. President Nixon, though content to share photo ops with astronauts, focused his attention on re-election and other political matters. He didn't provide any leadership in expanding the human adventure further into space until he had to, just a little.

For the Soviet leaders, meanwhile, the Space Race didn't begin with the Moon Race and couldn't end there. It began as an adaptation of the arms race, and another adaptation would be needed for the '70s.

Soviet foreign policy grew up in the Bolshevik era as a tree with two trunks. The older one, Leninism, was centered on the Marxist idea of a world in which indigenous Communist revolutions would rise up and destroy capitalism everywhere. A perceived decadence was supposed to collapse the capitalist West when faced with the righteous wrath of oppressed workers. The Soviet Union's role would be the fountainhead of Communist ideology, leading the parties of all other nations through the Communist International, or Comintern.

The other trunk was Stalinism, an obsession with making Russia so strong that no nation would ever again invade. An armor plating of Communist states all around Russia—all friendly and even subservient to the USSR—looked like a good solution. As it became clear that indigenous revolutions weren't going to blossom like dandelions, even there in the neighborhood, the Soviets made heavy investments in subversion.

Western powers turned out to be not so decadent. As economic entities, their capitalists abhorred any "ism" threatening them with expropriation. As political entities, their statesmen objected strenuously to subversion. Frustrated by determined opposition to both policy trunks, the USSR had to re-invent itself as a militaristic superpower. The arms race, specifically the ballistic missile race, was the expression that best used the captured German talent after World War II, as mentioned in Chapter 9.

Korolev's inspired suggestion of Sputnik made an ostensibly peaceful Space Race an effective proxy for the unattractive arms race. It served the Leninist policy trunk by promoting an image of Soviet rocket scientists as leaders in world technology, and thus exemplars of the New Soviet Man. It served the Stalinist trunk by providing many opportunities to use big rockets for something more interesting than parades through Red Square, and more compelling as demonstrations of capacity to propel heavy warheads.

President Kennedy's conversion of the Space Race into a Moon Race, as something the USA could win, had another side that I like to think was clearly in his mind. That side was the consequences to the USSR of losing the Moon Race. Once Khrushchev picked up that challenge, one he couldn't readily avoid in any case, he was betting the whole Leninist trunk on winning.

Soviet propaganda throughout the Moon Race focused

on how Communist ideology made Soviet rocket scientists necessarily superior to those of the decadent West. It was supposed to help Third World people decide to reject Western ideas and seek their ideal future in the Communist way. The decisive ending of the Moon Race by Apollo 11 and Apollo 12 splintered the Leninist policy trunk into matchsticks.

With only the Stalinist policy trunk left standing, Soviet space policy was reduced to showing that the USSR was not markedly *inferior* to the USA in manned spacecraft technology. Lacking Saturn-class boosters, their arena was necessarily low Earth orbit, and the most hopeful direction was development of space stations. And in fact, Salyut 1 was the first station to go into operation, putting the ball back into the American court.

That made it our turn to meet a challenge we couldn't easily avoid. Having won a great victory in space, and having no political will to expand the arena to Mars, we couldn't very well let the losers dominate the space near home. Among other things, many people worried about strategic weapons in space. Most engineers agreed that a spacecraft is the most ineffective possible place for such weapons, but it takes more than that to assuage a really world-class worry. We needed to figure out how to maintain a presence in Earth orbit in a way that showed some superiority over the USSR, while keeping it financially sustainable.

Apollo CSM spacecraft were expensive and complex and had no way to be reused. Even before the Apollo 11 landing, conceptual design of a reusable spacecraft—a Space Shuttle—had begun. The Lab was involved in those studies, in a consultant role. After a great deal of thinking and rethinking by NASA, a viable design began to emerge. "Viability" meant, primarily, the ability to get funding from a Congress that felt nothing like the urgency of 1961. The Air Force, long shut out of spaceborne activities unless you count missiles, agreed to provide some of the funding if the vehicle was large enough to carry USAF equipment on highly classified "blue flights." That helped President Nixon support it. However, he needed assurances that for civilian operations it would carry valuable cargo much more cheaply than existing space technology. Also, the turnaround time after each flight had to be kept short, to experience those savings frequently. The result was an effective agreement to proceed, provided that the annual development cost did not exceed three billion dollars.

A president who asks for assurances usually gets them, and so it was. Nobody asked pointedly how expensive it would be to get a Shuttle ready for a new flight in only a couple of weeks. Nobody asked pointedly where the demand was going to come from, to take so many tons of material up into orbit and back down again, in quantities that could produce the "assured" savings. On the other side of the world, the Soviets asked those questions about the U.S. Space Shuttle and were very concerned with the answers they could deduce out of publicly available data.

───── ∞ ─────

While many engineers at the Lab worked to support the continuing Apollo flights, others including the Digital Development Group participated in the Shuttle studies. We in DDG wrote up designs for an architecture called "distributed computing" in which a highly fault-tolerant vehicle data bus would serve many small computers in strategic locations around the vehicle. The question remained: When the study phases gave way to actual development, what role would the Lab play?

The aerospace industry in general and the avionics industry in particular had by that time made it clear to Congress that the indignity of handing a major sole-source contract to a unit of a university—not to mention the foregone profits—would no longer be acceptable. In fairness, a variety of flightworthy computers were at least ostensibly available. One thing that really bothered us was a statement from somewhere in NASA to the effect that it had been such a difficult job managing the Lab's participation in Apollo that something different had to be done this time.

Elsewhere in NASA people knew better. Bill Tindall was as disappointed as we were that they couldn't have us pick up the same role as in Apollo. "You guys are the best" is the way he put it. But, he added, Congress wasn't going to fund anything that cut out their corporate constituents. And if anybody knew how much (or how little) trouble we had been to manage, it was Bill. But many others in NASA, more fully equipped with project management theories than with Bill Tindall's wisdom, felt that the software development work on Shuttle avionics should be done right there in Houston where they could keep a close eye on it. By that time, the selection of a vendor of on-board General Purpose Computers (GPCs) had probably been wired for IBM's Federal System Division (FSD), despite a pro-forma competitive bid process. The presence of FSD's software arm, just across NASA Road 1 from MSC, seemed ideal.

A good deal of thought went into how to exploit the Lab's combination of expertise and real-project experience. The fault tolerance expertise we'd been building up in Eldon Hall's DDG was an obvious match for NASA's need to cope with flight computers that were more complex, and less inherently reliable, than the AGC. Aging of circuits would be more of an issue in avionics that would have to go on operating as a reliable system for many years. Fortunately, the Shuttle's mission objective of operating in low Earth orbit allowed NASA to relax their draconian restrictions on the weight of components. They could devote more space and mass to increasing reliability by duplicating, not only electronics, but also the instruments and even parts of the hydraulics that moved the aerodynamic control surfaces.

Many other forms of valuable Lab expertise included the digital autopilot, rendezvous and other on-orbit maneuvering, and re-entry. The bottom line was that we would function as consultants to NASA in all those areas. It would be just about as much work as if we had been the prime contractor in our area again, but the effort would be directed toward a more educational purpose. Our role would be to convince first NASA and then the contractors of the right ways to do things.

Space Race Highlights of 1971

(All manned flights are indicated in bold.)

31 Jan **Apollo 14 (AS-509). 9 days. Crew: Alan Shepard, Stu Roosa, Ed Mitchell. Software patch to work around faulty Abort button. Third manned Lunar landing, 5 February. Lunar golf.**

19 Apr Salyut 1. First space station. Unmanned. Orbited until 11 October.

22 Apr **Soyuz 10. 32 orbits. Crew: Vladimir Shatalov, Aleksei Yeliseyev, Nikolai Rukavishnikov. Failed to achieve hard dock with Salyut 1.**

19 May Mars 2. Unmanned. Started for Mars; later achieved Martian orbit. Lander part crashed.

28 May Mars 3. Unmanned. Started for Mars; later achieved Martian orbit. Lander part landed, but failed after 20 seconds.

30 May Mariner 9. Unmanned. Started for Mars; later achieved Martian orbit.

06 Jun **Soyuz 11. 24 days. Crew: Georgy Dobrovolsky, Vladislav Volkov, Viktor Patsayev. Docked with Salyut 1. First to occupy a space station; cabin depressurization just before entry killed all three.**

26 Jun Third test of N-1 rocket failed. Destroyed one minute after liftoff.

26 Jul **Apollo 15 (AS-510). 12 days. Crew: Dave Scott, Al Worden, Jim Irwin. Fourth manned Lunar landing, 30 July. Lunar Rover.**

02 Sep Luna 18. Failed robotic return of a sample to Earth. Crashed on Moon.

28 Sep Luna 19. Unmanned. Orbited Moon for a year measuring mascons.

28 Oct Prospero. Unmanned. Permanent orbit—the only UK launch to orbit.

Other flights where a vehicle entered space, mostly orbital:

USA	46
USSR	84
Canada	15
France	2
UN	2
Japan	2
China	2
UK	1
Italy	1
NATO	1
Total	**156**

Of these, 133 went into Earth orbit or beyond. Country names identify where payloads were made. Most boosters were made by USA or USSR. These numbers count spacecraft, regardless of how many were launched on a single booster (up to 8 or 9). Three of the Soviet Kosmos series were anti-satellite tests, impacting and destroying earlier Kosmos craft.

GOODNIGHT MOON: 1972

On January 5, 1972, President Nixon announced the kickoff of the U.S. Space Transportation System program, otherwise known as the Space Shuttle. He itemized a number of ways in which it would be more efficient than any prior space program. First, each spacecraft would be reusable for as many as one hundred missions. Second, the refurbishment cycle, from landing to launch readiness, would be less than a month. Third, its capacious payload bay, sixty feet long and fifteen feet across, could carry over 50,000 pounds into orbit—and could bring back over 30,000 pounds. Fourth, scientists, engineers, and their equipment could ride along without doing the rigorous training for "old-style space flight." Fifth, a small fraction of the flights would accomplish U.S. Air Force space missions cost effectively. With such frequent and high-capacity missions, the cost of sending people and cargo into space could be reduced by 90%. He expected manned test flights by 1978 and full operation "a short time later."

The aerospace industry, NASA, and MIT were glad to

wrap up the "Phase A" design studies that we'd been working on for three years and finally get going on development. The two biggest problems to achieving reusability, we knew, were the thermal tiles covering the vehicle's entire body (to absorb the heat of re-entry and then re-radiate it without being damaged), and the main rocket engines that would have to be restartable hundreds of times. At MIT, the most interesting parts were the guidance for this heavy-set glider that could veer over a thousand miles to either side of the straight-line re-entry path on its way to a mostly-automatic runway landing, and the fault tolerance for all its critical mechanical as well as electronic systems.

The Soviet Union picked this moment to score *their* Lunar extra point. Luna 20, launched on February 14, repeated the robotic success of Luna 16 in bringing back a sample of the Moon. Then it was our turn to score in the interplanetary arena. On March 3, we launched Pioneer 10, which would be the first spacecraft through the asteroid belts, the first Jupiter flyby, and, in 1983, the first to travel beyond all the planets in the Solar System.

Between those launches, President Nixon launched something significant too. His visit to the People's Republic of China and the reopening of relations changed the balance of the Cold War. The Soviet Union, then having an additional Cold War with Mao's China, saw this détente between their chief rivals as another blow to their Leninist dreams of world leadership.

While these world-changing events were developing, the momentum of Apollo carried on, with less urgency and more caution. Apollo 16 launched on April 16 after a month's delay in coping with glitches. Prelaunch testing detected damage to a Command Module fuel tank, and no hasty waivers this time. The whole stack was trundled back on the Crawler Transporter to the Vehicle Assembly Building so the tank could be changed out properly. Commander John Young's space suit had places that moved too stiffly. Lunar Module batteries gave inconsistent readings on charge level. It wasn't clear that the CM would cast off its docking ring correctly after the final separation from the LM. This was no time to ignore even "minor" problems; we'd learned that in manned space flight, very few problems are truly minor.

On the outbound trip of Apollo 16, the guidance was so accurate that the mid-course correction required only a two-second burn. Young, CM Pilot Ken Mattingly, and LM Pilot Charlie Duke took some time to study the phenomenon of occasional light flashes that earlier crews had reported. They confirmed that the most likely cause was the response of human eyes to the passage of cosmic rays through the eyeballs, apparently not doing any damage.

On April 20, John and Charlie landed their LM, *Orion*, within a thousand feet of the target point in the Descartes Highlands. The first Extra-Vehicular Activity (EVA) had good news and bad news. The bad news was a Lunar surface experiment cable that got caught around John Young's boot and broke. The good news was the biggest single hunk of Moon ever brought back—four-billion-year-old "Big Muley," a twelve-kilogram rock weighing 26 pounds on Earth but happily only four pounds on the Moon.

In the second day's EVA, John and Charlie drove the Lunar Roving Vehicle up to an elevation 500 feet above the landing site. Those were full working days of over seven hours, with no lunch break, though they did have access to less than a pint of water and a fruit bar in their suits. The third day was shorter, and featured a rare opportunity to reach under the overhang of "Shadow Rock" (very carefully) and collect some surface material that hadn't been touched by sunlight in a billion years.

After rejoining Ken in Lunar orbit, they got busy with the vacuum cleaner, sucking as much Moon dust as possible off the sample containers before transferring them to Ken for stowage. John particularly was impressed by the abrasive clingy qualities of that dust. Where there is no erosion, every speck has all the sharp corners dictated by its atomic structure. Where there is no moisture, every speck picks up static electricity when disturbed, and clings tight to anything metal, especially the sliding-ring joints that gave flexibility (such as it was) to his space suit. It gave a whole new meaning to "true grit."

Like Apollo 15, this crew released a Lunar sub-satellite, PFS-2, to continue studying what little Lunar atmosphere there is. In all innocence, they put it into nearly the worst possible orbit, where gravitational variations due to mascons quickly degraded its stability. In two and a half weeks, its perilune distance had shrunk to six miles, so low that ground controllers thought it might hit the next mountain range. They backed it off to a 30-mile orbit, hoping for stability while still close enough to take its measurements. But after another two and a half weeks, mascon gravity destabilized it even faster, and it crashed. NASA scientists made it a priority to study the mascon anomalies and determine where Lunar orbits are stable. The correct safe level was ultimately determined to be 60 miles, happily where the CSM orbits had been routinely placed without any knowledge of the problem.

The Soviet leadership was having some hard years. They were still smarting from the loss of the Moon Race. Their new emphasis on space stations had been ravaged by the loss of three cosmonauts in Soyuz 11. And now Nixon's opening to China sliced away most of the credibility of the "Soviet Bloc" concept.

At least one of these problems had a straightforward engineering solution, a redesigned Soyuz to eliminate the depressurization failure mode. They put it through an unmanned orbital test just a little over a year after the tragedy. But the geopolitical issue was tougher to handle—they didn't want China's overt defection from the Soviet Bloc to have the effect of isolating Russia. Premier Alexei Kosygin's government found an approach by looking back a decade and a half, to the late 1950s when Khrushchev had started talking about détente and peaceful coexistence between the United States and the Soviet Union. Idealistic people on both sides had spent years trying to figure out how to attach something concrete to those hopeful words, but now there was a pragmatic motivation as well. A technological rapprochement with the United States, in an arena which the Chinese were completely unprepared to operate in, would restore some balance. That's my interpretation of how Nixon and Kosygin came to sign the agreement to create the Apollo-Soyuz Test Project (ASTP), to be at least one space flight with US astronauts and Soviet cosmonauts working together.

The opening to China and the agreement on the ASTP were Nixon's best efforts to burnish his legacy, the high points of his presidency. Within a month, the burglary in Watergate began the long slow debacle ending in his resignation in 1974.

———— ∞∞∞ ————

The NASA-oriented part of the Lab didn't need to do much more for the Apollo program. Routine support was enough while our hardware and software went about its work with no "interesting" problems. With the presidential and funding commitments in hand, we focused increasingly on our new consulting role in Space Shuttle development.

The architecture of the Shuttle as a reusable spacecraft had settled down after dropping two concepts. One was a fully reusable booster that could come back to base and land, ready for refueling. In the compromise design, two Solid Rocket Boosters (SRBs) would be reusable but only because the Navy would go and pick them up out of the ocean. The External Tank (ET) supplying liquid fuel and oxidizer to the spacecraft's own main engines would be jettisoned to re-enter at speeds sufficient to burn it up. The other dropped concept was jet engines to give the Orbiter normal aircraft-style powered flight after entry.

The reusable Orbiter part took the form of a fat delta-winged glider. Its body and wings would share a broad, nearly flat bottom to accommodate a reusable heat shield. Instead of ablating away like previous heat shields, it would consist of ceramic "thermal tiles" that would absorb the heat of re-entry without damage and re-radiate it after landing. Developing these tiles was one of the two most challenging engineering problems, one in which the Lab had no role.

Like other delta-wing designs, the Orbiter would have no separate horizontal tail surfaces with control surfaces called "elevators." The trailing edges of the wings would extend all the way to the back of the vehicle, and their control surfaces would be called not "ailerons" but the compound word "elevons." There would be a normal vertical stabilizer surface with an unusual split-rudder design. As long as the rudder's two faces were pressed together, it would look and act like any airplane rudder. In final approach and landing, the two faces would be pushed apart to serve as an aerodynamic brake.

Unlike any airplane, the back end of the vehicle was an open cavity containing three large rockets ("main engines") arranged in a triangle to take part in the boost phase, and two smaller rockets for use in orbit. To protect all those engines from the heat of re-entry, a unique surface called a "body flap," covered with thermal tiles, extended the bottom from the forward bulkhead of the engine cavity to the end of the vehicle. It was moveable by hydraulic actuators, like the rudder and elevons, to function as a central elevator control surface.

The key to a spacecraft reusable for a hundred missions was making all those rocket engines reusable, much more so than the few stops and restarts of Apollo's Service Module and LM Descent engines. That was the other highly challenging engineering problem, again with no role for the Lab.

"Fatness" of the Orbiter's body was dictated by the payload requirement, to accommodate a cylindrical shape 60 feet long by 15 feet in diameter. Access was provided by two curved doors opening upwards and outwards like an upside-down bomber. Forward of the payload bay was a three-level space accommodating up to five crew in addition to the Commander and Pilot on the flight deck. The ungainly shape of the vehicle inspired people to call it a "rock" rather than a "glider."

The good news about the broad flat bottom was that it formed a powerful air cushion after final flare. It would take a relatively long time to settle down onto the runway, landing more gently than a typical rock. The bad news was a reduction in aerodynamic stability, especially in the yaw axis, making it riskier to fly than a typical glider. The key specification— the elephant in the fault tolerance room—was this: A lack of computer control lasting only 0.4 seconds during aerodynamic flight could put the vehicle into an unrecoverable flat spin. To the consternation of the astronauts, that's nowhere near enough time for a manual switchover from a primary to a backup system, so the computerized fault tolerance had to do the job.

I found it a wrenching change to stop thinking creative thoughts about making an unprepossessing computer do six impossible things before breakfast. Instead, we had to think creatively about errors, faults, and failures. A governmental jargon phrase "FO-FO-FS" (pronounced foe-foe-fuss) became our theme song. The acronym expanded to Fail-Operational, Fail-Operational, Fail-Safe. A FO-FO-FS system could suffer any failure and carry on the complete mission with no noticeable hesitation. It could then suffer a second failure (even of the same type of unit) and carry on the mission similarly. Finally, it could suffer a third failure (again, even of the same type) and still support a safe mission abort. Daunting as this may sound, there were some escape clauses, primarily that we could assume that multiple *simultaneous* failures would not affect any one type of unit (such as a computer). Specifically, we could count on enough time to clean up the configuration after one failure before the next one hit.

The hardware configuration to support this rule involved quadruple redundancy of the most critical units. General Purpose Computers, data buses, and local microprocessors to interface subsystems to the data buses were the electronic elements quadruplicated. For each of the aerodynamic control surfaces (elevons, rudder, body flap) there was just one "big muscle," a primary hydraulic actuator. But each of those received its hydraulic fluid from a set of four smaller secondary hydraulic actuators, electrically valved. Whatever a majority of the active secondaries commanded was what the primary actuator would do.

For important units whose function could be approximately covered by other means (e.g., IMUs), triple redundancy was considered enough, and there were a few dual-redundant units such as pitot tubes to measure air speed.

We also had to analyze transient fault modes and recover from any number of them that didn't coincide. These might include cosmic rays corrupting a single bit or even lightning strikes like the one on Apollo 12.

But the first job was to make sure of what the avionics part of the architecture actually was. The selected designer and builder of the Orbiter vehicle, the former North American Aviation, wasn't even "North American Rockwell" any more. The corporate digestive juices had redefined it as Rockwell International Space Division (RISD).

The RISD leaders had made some decisions about how to implement the FO-FO-FS rule, and we worked with them to settle on how many redundant copies there would be of each type of unit. We couldn't persuade them to unify the many quad-redundant buses into our concept of a universal quad-redundant bus. I suspect that each of their bus systems was controlled by a different department, so we were shoveling sand against political surf. Their approach to engineering management took a little getting used to, though it had been so well received by the management theorists at NASA as to be a significant factor in their getting the contract. All the mid-level managers had offices on a sort of mezzanine floor around the edges of a vast square building. Within that border, a large "bullpen" area at ground level had rows and columns of desks in a completely open-office arrangement. That was the management method: the officers sitting at their physically elevated stations could watch all the grunt-level engineers. It sure didn't feel like our autonomy-centered culture at the Lab.

There were six individuals we saw the most of in the early days: Bob D'Evelyn, John Peller, Gene O'Hern, Ron Loeliger, Sy Rubenstein (boss of the above), and Ken McQuade (Rubenstein's boss) ... all mezzanine-level workers.

Ken McQuade was a physically powerful-looking man with an Australian accent and an assertive manner suitable for the Outback. Sy Rubenstein was a big guy, though not what you'd call athletic, with a wicked sense of humor and an impressively broad grasp of the Orbiter design issues. Ron Loeliger's average size and lean frame suggested a marathon runner, though I don't know whether he actually did that. He was one of those we worked with most directly on fault tolerance. Gene O'Hern was a stocky, fiercely red-haired Irishman whose specialty was airframes. John Peller was a tall dark-haired drink of water, concentrating on instrumentation.

Our favorite, a free spirit we'd have hired into the Lab in a heartbeat, was Bob D'Evelyn. A bit smaller than average and compactly built, he had the open manner and sunny disposition ideally suited for the great spaces of the West. On the less traditional side, he had a special midday habit of his own: While the rest of us piled into cars to go and eat unhealthy things for lunch, Bob went into a sort of anteroom part of the men's room and stood on his head for half an hour, then nibbled on an apple or two. He said it was very beneficial for him, draining all the morning's annoyances and irrelevancies out of his head, leaving him refreshed to start a highly productive afternoon. It also cured him of carrying change in his pockets.

These six Rockwells traveled to Houston and Washington and other relevant places to present their design concepts, but they didn't always coordinate their stories and often seemed to be conducting interdepartmental debates while on the road. That was a surprise to us because my boss Alan Green made sure we were all on the same page before each trip. The shortage of harmony in Rockwell's Space Division group put me in mind of the lyric to *MacNamara's Band*. My version went like this:

> There was O'Evelyn, Loeliger, Peller, O'Hern,
> Rudenstein and McQuade;
> And niver an agrrreement was,
> The six of them had made.
> Whiniver they got togetherrr,
> The shoutin', it was grand,
> Whin shuttlin' round the counterrrs as
> The Space Division Band!

I kept looking for an opportunity to perform this masterwork for them, but never found one, which was doubtless just as well.

One of the bright young people who joined NASA around this time was Clay McCullough, a trim, handsome dark-haired chap who could pass for Gregory Peck in a dimly lit bar. Clay was tasked with traveling around the country, visiting companies that were developing flight computers, and producing assessments of the candidates for the GPC job. As he was a little new to the spacecraft computer game, I was assigned to travel with him, which was a great pleasure. Most of our stops were in southern California, where new efforts in this area tended to concentrate. We went into plants to see what the companies were developing. Sometimes we'd see production models, sometimes working prototypes, sometimes little more than paper.

There was one leafy campus, up the coast a way from Los Angeles, where we went to see a machine that looked, from the pictures we'd seen, a lot like the experimental "cubic inch" microcomputer we'd developed at the Lab. I expected great things from that company and was terribly disappointed. After passing through security and being directed to a place where we would find a host to take us around, we wandered through vast rooms divided into mostly empty cubicles. One occupied cube contained a man reading a newspaper with his feet up on the desk. We never did find our assigned host, just wandered out again to find a tavern with enough good beer to restore our heavy hearts.

We had a somewhat different experience at Hughes Tool Company, the only place I've ever visited where the guards searched a visitor's briefcase on the way in as well as on the way out. Howard Hughes was running his empire personally in those days, and the stamp of his famously secretive character was everywhere. There were some prototypes, but they told and showed us no more than we'd already seen in the brochures.

More normal was the busy site of Autonetics, where we saw what looked like production models of their D232 and were given a fairly detailed pitch on the technology involved. I asked the presenter how they screened their chips for Purple Plague and got a wide silent grin. It reminded me of Dr. An Wang many years before, when I'd asked him how his Logarithmic Computing Instrument desktop calculator (LOCI) was able to compute anti-logarithms so fast. In this case, the silent grin meant either "You don't need to know that and I'm not about to tell you" (like Dr. Wang) or "I haven't the foggiest notion what you're talking about and I'm not going to admit it."

Our travels did not include Owego, New York, where

IBM's Federal Systems Division developed the "4π" series of aerospace computers. I suspect that someone senior to Clay had already done that and picked IBM's AP-101 of that series to be the Shuttle's GPC. Our tour was a token search for competition, open to any "Wow, look at this" finding that we might have brought back … but we didn't.

NASA spent a lot of effort generating requirements specification documents, and asked us to review them. As each document turned up at the Lab, we parceled it out and went through it with red-ink pen in hand, noting internal contradictions, inconsistencies with other specs that we understood to be still valid, and occasionally some weird things. For the quadruple-redundant data bus, they specified a reliability level that caught my attention. They wanted the probability of an undetected error in data transmission to be capped at 10^{-25}. I knew that our approach to checking for bus errors by a compare/vote scheme should find every error short of a systematic failure of the whole bus system, and I couldn't resist doing the math to see what they were really saying. Since the data rate on that bus was to be one million (10^6) bits per second, I figured out how long 10^{19} seconds was and reported, "I see that the average interval between undetected errors is to be about 75 times the age of the Solar System. How shall we test the bus system for compliance?"

Looking at the long parts at the back that had been copied from older specs for military electronics, I discovered that nobody had checked to see whether the conditions mentioned were part of a spacecraft computer's environment. Finding a requirement for how heavy a load of snow the computer's case had to withstand, I suggested there should be separate snow load requirements for the different mission phases, especially the maximum-dynamic-pressure (max-Q) part of boost. For the part about the computer having to survive impact by two-inch hailstones, I commented that surely it was time to start stating hailstone diameters in metric units, and five centimeters would be close enough here. There was a lot of silence from Houston in response to these sallies, but later Clay told me there had been some good laughs.

When not poking fun at mindless number games and cut-and-paste absurdities, we did consider some serious requirements-spec issues, many concerned with timing. Two phrases we became very familiar with were "transport lag" and "jitter." Transport lag is the time from the observation of a change in a parameter to the application of force required by that change. In automotive terms, that's the time from when you see the brake lights come on ahead to when your brake calipers hit the rotor disks. Engineering to bring transport lag down to a value consistent with safety of flight involves a chain of parameters: the interval between samplings of a sensor; the delay in getting the computer's attention redirected; running time of the code to calculate a suitable response and send a command to an effector; and finally how long it takes the effector to make a suitable difference in the vehicle's motion. That last item is a given from the computer system's point of view, but all the rest is grist for the software designer's mill. Jitter is a measure of how far a periodic activity's starting times deviate from perfectly uniform intervals, like an orchestra player wandering from the correct tempo.

Unlike computer results, data from redundant sets of sensors such as Inertial Measurement Units should track closely but can't be expected to be exactly the same. We had to decide what level of checking to apply: reasonableness checks on data from individual units, auto-correlation tests to catch impossibly abrupt changes over time, or comparisons between like sensors to take a serious outlier out of further consideration.

———— ∞ ————

To close out the year and the Lunar landing program, Apollo 17 lifted off after midnight on December 7, the only Apollo launch at night. On board were Commander Gene Cernan, CM Pilot Ron Evans, and LM Pilot Harrison "Jack" Schmitt, the only professional geologist to visit the Moon. Their flight from Earth parking orbit to Moon parking orbit was routine except for one dazzling feat of photography. Two hours after the TLI burn, Jack was ready with his Hasselblad camera when their side of the Earth was fully sunlit. His photo showing the whole Earth has become the most widely distributed image in history, known everywhere as *The Blue Marble.*

Gene and Jack in their LM *Challenger* left Ron in his CM *America.* They landed on target, by the Taurus-Littrow valley, on December 11. Like the Apollo 11 explorers, they skipped a rest period and set out on their first EVA four hours after landing. They unpacked the LRV efficiently but committed the same faux pas as the Apollo 15 crew, breaking off part of a rear fender. A duct tape repair reduced the showers of clingy dust for part of the day.

Besides setting out the science experiment packages and collecting samples, Gene and Jack took seven measurements with the new "Gravy Meter," our nickname for the only Lunar-surface scientific instrument designed and built by the Lab. Properly called the Traverse Gravimeter, its high-precision gravity measurements contributed much to understanding the effects of mascons.

In preparation for the second day out, they built a respectable LRV fender out of four stiff-paper maps held together with duct tape, eliminating the flying-dust problem. The day's samples included some unusual orange-colored soil from down in the valley. They set out more explosive charges for later detonation, made more Gravimeter measurements, and drove to a point nearly five miles from the LM.

At the end of the third excursion of over seven hours, Gene was conscious that his situation was exactly the other bookend to Neil Armstrong's first small step. He took a moment to reflect:

As I take man's last step from the surface, back home for some time to come—but we believe not too long into the future—I'd like to just [say] what I believe history will record. That America's challenge of today has forged man's destiny of tomorrow. And, as we leave the Moon at Taurus-Littrow, we leave as we came and, God willing, as we shall return, with peace and hope for all mankind.

Space Race Highlights of 1972

(All manned flights are indicated in bold.)

14 Feb   Luna 20. 11 days. Second robotic return of a Lunar sample to Earth.

03 Mar   Pioneer 10. Unmanned, to outer planets and beyond.

16 Apr   Apollo 16 (AS-511). 11 days. Crew: John Young, Ken Mattingly, Charlie Duke. Fifth manned Lunar landing, 20 April, in highlands.

26 Jun   Kosmos 496. Unmanned orbital test of redesigned, safer Soyuz spacecraft.

22 Jul   Venera 8. Landed on Venus; sent data for 50 minutes.

23 Nov   Fourth and final test of N-1 booster exploded two minutes after liftoff.

07 Dec   Apollo 17 (AS-512). 12 days. Crew: Gene Cernan, Ron Evans, Jack Schmitt. Sixth manned Lunar landing, 11 December. Traverse Gravimeter.

The USA launched 17 other satellites into Earth orbit. Complete detailed data on other flights is not available for 1972.

SPACE STATIONS AND SHUTTLE
COMPUTERS: 1973

From the American operational side, 1973 was the Year of
Skylab. From the Soviet operational side, it was a year of great
frustration in space stations and Mars probes. They had one
disaster, a modest comeback in manned flight, and a huge
expansion, over a hundred, in unmanned orbital flights. For the
Lab's Space Shuttle work, it was a manifold exercise in "dog-
and-pony shows" to put across our ideas about fault tolerance in
the Shuttle's General Purpose Computer system.

The Soviets led off in January with Luna 21 taking their
second rover Lunokhod 2 to the Moon. It was a good piece of
engineering and good Moon science, but didn't draw a lot of
attention. Some people felt the USSR was just working through
their remaining inventory of Moon Race gear. They had less
luck in April with Salyut 2, actually a military Almaz space
station in disguise, which attained orbit but was wrecked by a
small explosion and depressurized before it could be staffed.

Three days later, NASA launched Pioneer 11 toward the outer planets. It would become the first Earthly visitor to Saturn. On May 11, the Soviets launched what should have been Salyut 3—a real Salyut space station this time, not a disguise—but it suffered crippling failures in orbit and was hastily renamed Kosmos 557 to hide the embarrassment.

Three days was the charm again, up to a point. The U.S. Skylab space station was launched unmanned on May 14, and suffered major damage during staging. One "wing" full of solar cells was torn off, the other was jammed with debris and couldn't unfold, and an insulating outer body panel broke off. Aside from that, the "windmill" array of solar panels deployed correctly and everything worked fine.

Instead of launching the first Skylab crew the next day, NASA took ten days to design repair procedures and train the crew in them, while inventing bizarre ways to keep the station alive. The controllers experimented with pointing the station one way for a while to keep the unprotected side out of direct sunlight and prevent solar heating from spoiling the stored food supplies or even damaging plastic parts. Then they pointed it another way for a while to put the windmill solar panels back into direct sunlight and get enough power to run the temperature control. Jack Kinzler invented a large parasol made of aluminized Mylar for the crew to take up.

NASA determined that the "can-do" spirit could prevail and on May 25 launched an Apollo Command/Service Module set named *Skylab 2*. It took Commander Pete Conrad, Pilot Paul Weitz, and Science Pilot Joe Kerwin up to rendezvous with Skylab, where they went on a spacewalk and tried without success to pull out the jammed solar panel wing. After another spacewalk to take the CM's docking probe apart and reassemble it, they achieved hard dock and moved in. The first task was to poke the furled parasol through an instrument hatch and open it to shade the exposed area. That brought the heat problem under control and allowed an orientation that made the windmill solar panels produce enough power to be sustainable though not fully operational.

After two weeks of performing low-power experiments, Pete and Joe went out to apply their training in Houston's neutral-buoyancy pool to the stuck wing. As soon as they pulled out the obstructions, the wing sprang open and tossed them away. Happily, their tethering cables halted their flight with a mighty jerk. They pulled themselves back to finish one of the greatest demonstrations of what "Right Stuff" means. With all station resources restored, the crew were able to use the Apollo Telescope Mount as a solar observatory.

After 28 days in space, Pete, Paul, and Joe climbed back into their CM, closed the Skylab's docking hatch, and re-entered. Their splashdown marked the first safe return of humans from a space station visit.

During that summer, Soviet spacecraft showed us more failure modes that we fault-tolerance experts might have to cope with. A spy satellite, *Tselina-O*, was on its launch pad in June when the booster's fuel tank was accidentally overfilled. The tank developed a leak that stopped the countdown at T-15 seconds. Valiant attempts at deactivating the vehicle failed, and an explosion killed nine Red Army technicians. Two Mars orbiters were sent off in July. One failed to establish a Martian orbit. The other did achieve Martian orbit but was disabled by a computer failure within a few days.

Our consultant role in Space Shuttle avionics included a design review of the flight computer selected as the Shuttle's General Purpose Computer. It was IBM Federal Systems Division's System 4π Model AP-101, and a team from FSD's headquarters in Owego, New York, came to the Lab to present the design. We knew it wasn't totally a "paper tiger" because models bearing that number had been used in military aircraft. But we had some clues that the AP-101, as configured for the Shuttle, was well short of a production model. NASA's political need to say they were purchasing "off-the-shelf" equipment may have led to the curious packaging, two breadbox-sized units called Central Processing Unit and Input-Output Processor. The CPU and IOP were connected by a cable with many conductors, an arrangement that would lead to a bad-news/good-news event in the first approach-and-landing test flight in 1977. The CPU part could be characterized as a generic machine and therefore "off-the-shelf," while the IOP was necessarily customized to the Shuttle's architecture of several special-purpose data buses.

The word lengths of 16 bits, 32 bits, and 64 bits were very far from what we would have chosen, but there was no help for it because of a techno-political requirement. GPCs had to do their calculations to exactly the same precision as the IBM 360s in the Mission Control Center, and the AP-101 design was a perfect clone of the 360 architecture in matters of word length and almost all of the instruction set. Floating-point arithmetic would be used for all calculations that weren't obviously simple integer operations, so the important word formats were a "short" floating-point word of 32 bits and a "long" floating-point word of 64 bits.

Each of these word formats included a sign bit and a 7-bit exponent field representing a power of 16 ranging from +64 down to −63. That left 24 bits in the short format, and 56 bits in the long format, for the mantissa part that provides the precision. Having used 28 bits of precision for navigational variables in Apollo, we judged 24 bits to be inadequate. That meant keeping such variables in the long format with twice the required precision.

As long as the selection of computer type had seemed to be up in the air, I'd been campaigning for floating-point formats of 24 and 48 bits, providing long and short mantissa precisions of 16 bits and 40 bits respectively. But all such analysis was steamrollered by the mandate to have exactly the same word lengths as the 360. To this day, I haven't heard any detailed justification of how this sameness was beneficial in any practical way. It seemed to be a political posture that "sounds nice" to anybody with scant understanding of the subject.

The execution speed of AP-101 instructions was generally state-of-the-art, with most of them taking one to three microseconds—in modern terms, roughly half a Million Instructions Per Second (MIPS). There was, however, one glaring exception, the long floating-point division, which ran for over a hundred microseconds. We knew that the short floating-point division, at ten microseconds, would be inadequate for many of the critical guidance and navigation calculations. Having lived through developments where people twisted the logic into gnarly shapes to avoid performing divisions, I decided to be The Mouse That Roared and persuade IBM to take a second look at this design.

I had a good handle on the problem because I'd built for the AGC a very good double-precision division subroutine that included just two single precision divisions and a multiplication, achieving very close to full double precision. During IBM's presentation, I thought about how I could do likewise in floating point with the AP-101 instruction set. When they paused for comments, I said, "I can beat the running time of that long division with a short subroutine."

"Well," one IBMer replied, "I guess you better show us." I devoted a week to the effort and mailed them the result, a subroutine that did the job in about 90 microseconds.

The next thing I knew, they announced that their newer model, the AP-101B, had a long division instruction that took 18 microseconds. The original design had been overly sensitive to a principle that program interrupts, which have to be held up while an instruction is in progress, should not have to wait too long. The FSD architect had given the AP-101 long division an architecture that *could* be interrupted after the development of each bit of the quotient, and would pick up where it left off afterwards. That feature had stretched out its running time by a factor of about six. Once they realized that the slowness could cause all that beautiful design work to go unused, they came around and did it right.

Skylab 3, again an Apollo CSM, was launched on July 28, taking Commander Alan Bean, Pilot Jack Lousma, and Science Pilot Owen Garriott up to rendezvous with the repaired Skylab. This time, Murphy's Law fingered the Reaction Control System of the Service Module, which developed a leak of dangerous hypergolic fuel. After shutting off the affected RCS jet quad, they docked successfully with Skylab and set up an improved sun shade over the parasol from the Skylab 2 mission. With a two-month stay planned, a lot of the science work was medical studies. Much of the human body's design is dedicated to control of internal fluids in a gravity field, so the fluids wander about in microgravity causing symptoms like "puffy face syndrome" that needed better understanding.

Six days into the mission, another SM RCS quad developed a leak and had to be shut off, which alarmed the analysts in Houston. There just aren't supposed to be two failures of the same kind occurring close together. If there are, the suspicion arises, "Is this a systematic failure that's going to affect *all* the subsystems of this type?" KSC responded by rolling the next booster-CSM set out early to its launch pad, the first time readiness for a possible rescue was implemented. It wouldn't have been a difficult rescue, since NASA had provided two docking ports in Skylab to cover such cases. But Murphy was done with the SM, apparently. It was only slightly awkward to fly the CSM with two RCS quads shut down, because the AGC software had been engineered to work around a variety of subsystem failures. There were no more leaks, and no rescue was required.

The Skylab 3 mission included a number of scientific experiments designed by high school students, as well as trials of a new type of "personal spacecraft" called a Manned Maneuvering Unit. The astronauts performed evaluations of subsystems for long-term space living such as keeping haircuts under control with a vacuum cleaner, and a shower stall. After a record 59 days in orbit, the crew returned safely.

During the mission, the Soviets launched two Mars lander spacecraft which later proved to be more disappointments. One stopped transmitting shortly before landing and presumably crashed on Mars. The other suffered a malfunction in separation from its booster and missed Mars altogether. Then their luck changed. The new model Soyuz spacecraft, redesigned to fix the deadly air leak that had doomed Soyuz 11, had been through an unmanned test flight in 1972. Now, on September 27, Vasili Lazarev and Oleg Makarov put Soyuz 12 through a successful two-day orbital test flight, cautiously keeping their space suits on the whole time. Their only missed objective was docking with a Salyut station because, despite the springtime efforts, there wasn't one in orbit.

With the exception of a few people monitoring the AGC's "commuting" operations, the Lab focused on Space Shuttle design, no more connected to all these operational events than anyone else. As we in the Digital Development Group worked out our fault tolerance strategies for the Shuttle (in partnership with astronaut Bob Crippen, who later flew in the first orbital flight test), NASA kept up a running critique. "Don't make it too complicated," they said. "You'll outsmart yourselves and bring the whole system down with a software bug." Knowing that IBM's FSD programmers were new to the art of multi-tasked spacecraft control, they applied the same thought to the mission software. Their solution was to split the avionics up into a Primary Avionics Software System running IBM software and a Backup Flight System running software written by a different contractor using a different compiler. The BFS code would run on the same type of GPC as the PASS, but any of the five GPCs on board could be assigned the BFS role.

This approach wouldn't cover the worst of worst cases, a systematic PASS failure during those parts of aerodynamic flight when the manual switchover couldn't be done fast enough, but at all other times it would provide a way to recover from problems. This kind of backup supported a rule we called FO-FO-FSM, where the 'M' stands for "Mostly." Having gained some confidence from that thought, NASA decided they would actually operate the missions using a FO-FS rule. The mission would continue as long as no more than one unit of any type had failed, but abort and run for home as soon as a second failure of any one type occurred.

Yet another form of backup was the provision of magnetic tape drives, a byproduct of NASA's new approach to needing more memory for PASS programs than could feasibly be installed. There were just two of them, twinned to make a primary-backup pair, and they were loaded with program files, one per major mission phase. Their typical normal use would be to reload PASS computers with on-orbit software after Earth orbit insertion and again to reload them with entry software before the de-orbit burn. Both occasions were relatively relaxed periods with enough time to repeat the loadings if anything seemed squirrelly.

For fault tolerance purposes, the presence of the tapes meant that any glitch affecting a computer's ability to retain its program in memory could be dealt with fairly promptly, at the next relatively relaxed moment. They were also the key to changing which GPC would be assigned to the BFS role, by replacing its PASS code with BFS code.

In November, NASA launched Mariner 10 to make a double flyby, first passing close to Venus and making observations. Then it would use Venerian gravity as a slingshot to steer it toward Mercury, where it would become the first Earthly visitor, making several flyby passes. On November 16, Skylab 4 lifted off for the final visit to the Skylab station. The all-rookie crew, Commander Gerald Carr, Pilot Bill Pogue, and Science Pilot Ed Gibson, had trouble keeping to the timeline for refurbishing the station on arrival, mostly because Bill suffered space sickness and they tried to prevent Houston from knowing it. After some testy exchanges, mission controllers had a heart-to-heart talk with the crew and they worked out a more forgiving timeline.

The Skylab station had a novel type of attitude control in place of RCS jets. Control Moment Gyros were much larger and heavier than the miniature gyros used in the navigation systems, and were effectors rather than sensors. To change the station's orientation, its computer commanded a light braking of a CMG's spinning wheel, causing a reactive opposite torque to rotate the station's structure. The rotation was halted by applying power to bring the wheel's rate of spin back to normal speed. There were three CMGs, any two of which were enough to perform the function. So when one of them started overheating, a week into the mission, the crew had to shut it down and investigate. The problem, insufficient lubrication, seemed non-threatening until a second CMG started showing signs of distress a few weeks later. Houston controllers worked out a way to reduce its workload to what its lubrication would support. With two working CMGs, the mission continued for its planned period of nearly three months.

The crew trained high-resolution optics on the Earth for detailed images to take back to scientists. Among the photos was an image of the infamous Area 51, which they'd actually been ordered to skip. They claimed it had been included by accident, and pointed out that no harm was done since it didn't show any flying saucers or alien spaceships. So in the end, that image was published along with the rest, hiding Area 51 in plain sight. In December, they took advantage of Comet Kohoutek's passage, making images in the far ultraviolet as well as the visible spectrum. They even caught it coming back into view after its rapid dash around the Sun.

While taking tens of thousands of solar images with the

Apollo Telescope Mount in January 1974, Ed Gibson spotted a bright spot on the Sun's left edge. As he kept the camera rolling, it grew into a gigantic flare, the first observation from space of a flare birth.

Returning home, the Skylab 4 crew bade farewell to their station, as well as the entire Skylab program. From its unpromising beginnings, it had developed into a major success. At the Lab, we noted that the Apollo CSM, its Primary Guidance, Navigation and Control System, the AGC and its software, had quietly performed its space-taxi role for Skylab with a minimum of issues.

While the Skylab 4 crew were working, the Soviets launched Soyuz 13 with Pyotr Klimuk and Valentin Lebedev aboard, evidently unconcerned about the number 13. In this second manned test of the upgraded Soyuz craft, a space observatory named Orion 2 replaced the docking apparatus made unnecessary by the absence of a Salyut station. The crew were able to spend a week making astronomical observations.

In another area of U.S.-Soviet relations, 1973 was the year all American troops left Vietnam, allowing the Soviets to be more demonstrably cooperative in the joint design of special docking gear for the Apollo-Soyuz Test Program. The adapters on each spacecraft presented to the other a sort of thumb-and-two-fingers ring around the tunnel, so that active docking could be done from either craft. For that reason, they were termed "androgynous."

Space Race Highlights of 1973

(All manned flights are indicated in bold.)

08 Jan   Luna 21. Landed on Moon. Second robot Lunar rover, Lunokhod 2.

03 Apr   Salyut 2. Unmanned military space station. Orbited; failed by depressurization.

06 Apr   Pioneer 11. Unmanned; to outer planets and beyond.

11 May   Kosmos 557. Unmanned space station. Intended to be Salyut 3; failed.

14 May   Skylab. Unmanned space station. Damaged in launch but repairable.

25 May   Skylab 2 (an Apollo CSM, booster SA-206). Docked with Skylab for 26 days. Crew: Pete Conrad, Paul Weitz, Joe Kerwin. First repair of an orbiting spacecraft. First safe return of a crew from a space station.

26 Jun   Tselina-O. Unmanned spy satellite. Exploded on launch pad, killing 9.

21 Jul   Mars 4. Reached Mars but failed to orbit there.

25 Jul   Mars 5. Reached Mars. Orbited. Computer failed within days.

28 Jul   Skylab 3 (an Apollo CSM, booster SA-207). Docked with Skylab for 58 days. Crew: Alan Bean, Jack Lousma, Owen Garriott. Use of Apollo Telescope Mount. First real-time preparation of a possible rescue mission.

05 Aug   Mars 6. Mars lander. Went silent before landing, probably crashed.

08 Aug   Mars 7. Mars lander. Missed Mars due to boost malfunction.

27 Sep   Soyuz 12. 31 orbits. Crew: Vasili Lazarev, Oleg Makarov. Test of new safer Soyuz design. Wore space suits throughout.

03 Nov   Mariner 10. Unmanned. Dual flyby of Venus and (a first) Mercury.

16 Nov   Skylab 4 (an Apollo CSM, booster SA-208). Docked with Skylab for 83 days. Crew: Gerald Carr, Bill Pogue, Ed Gibson. Overwork issues after docking. Comet astronomy. Final Skylab mission.

18 Dec   Soyuz 13. 7 days. Crew: Pyotr Klimuk, Valentin Lebedev. Second test of new safer Soyuz design. Astronomy with Orion 2 Space Observatory.

The USA launched 20 other satellites into Earth orbit. The USSR launched 102 other satellites into Earth orbit. France and China each had one failed launch.

END OF THE SPACE RACE: 1974–1975

Manned space flight in 1974 was entirely a Soviet affair. American activity was design and engineering, both the long-term Space Shuttle work and the near-term Apollo-Soyuz Test Project (ASTP) work. ASTP became more of a joint project in the greater openness that followed our departure from Vietnam, with American astronauts going to Star City for familiarization with the Soyuz systems.

The Soviets, having not entirely forgotten the Moon, sent Luna 22 on May 29 to orbit and perform both photographic and magnetic-field studies. On October 28, they launched Luna 23 to collect and return another sample, this one from the Sea of Crises where Luna 15 had crashed during the Lunar-surface time of Apollo 11. Unluckily, the name still held its curse, as the Soviet craft landed softly enough to keep communicating, but with very low energy. Decades later, the Lunar Reconnaissance Orbiter took a picture showing Luna 23 tipped over on its side.

The space station Salyut 3 launched on June 25 … only it didn't. What actually launched was Almaz 2, the first spaceborne

Red Army post to reach orbit. The Soviets, unwilling to admit to having a military space station, gave it the civilian Salyut name and disclosed practically nothing about the station or its mission. Later, we learned that it packed heat, a Rikhter R-23 gun for "self-defense."

On July 3, Soyuz 14 carried Commander Pavel Popovich and Flight Engineer Yuri Artyukhin to dock with it, though without testing a new automatic docking system. They spent two weeks doing a little medical research and a lot of high-resolution photography of the Earth's surface, possibly including Area 51, but did not fire the gun for fear of damaging the station with the vibration. The Soyuz 14 crew returned safely from what turned out to be the only visit to Salyut 3.

Soyuz 15, launched on August 26, was intended to continue the secret military studies, but also depended on the automatic docking system as part of the development cycle for their unmanned space truck, Progress. Commander Gennadi Sarafanov and Flight Engineer Lev Dyomin tried for two days to make it work, but ran low on maneuvering fuel and had to return home with no accomplishment but a detailed critique.

An upgraded automatic docking system was quickly installed in Salyut 4 in preparation for its late December launch. The Soviets retired Salyut 3 with a special salute, firing its self-defense gun until the ammunition ran out.

In a rehearsal for ASTP, Soyuz 16 was scheduled to launch on December 2 with Commander Anatoly Filipchenko, Flight Engineer Nikolai Rukavishnikov, and one of the special androgynous docking ring adapters. Soviet authorities, edging warily toward increased openness, offered to give NASA the launch data and time in advance, with the (unacceptable) condition of withholding that information from the media.

Rebuffed, they published the flight an hour after launch, when it was already in orbit. The crew tested the adapter successfully and performed a full-length dry run of their side of the ASTP mission.

We didn't know then that some Soviet Salyut stations were genuine space science facilities and some were secret "Almaz" military bases in space. Happily, Salyut 4 was the genuine article, launched into orbit on December 26.

———— ✇ ————

NASA's people in the Johnson Space Center (the Manned Spacecraft Center, renamed in 1973 to honor President Johnson) initially liked where IBM's Federal Systems Division (FSD) had set up their software office on NASA Road 1, just across from JSC. It put their software contractors right where they could keep an eye on them, rather than having to communicate with MIT "scientists" 1,500 miles away.

Wary NASA officials sometimes called us "scientists" with a tone that indicated no compliment was intended. In fact, however, we started hearing from our NASA friends that setting up meetings in the FSD building, and getting FSD folks to cross the road to come to meetings at JSC, was no easier than dealing with us at MIT had been and, in some ways, was harder. FSD would plead that too much interfacing (read: interference) was out of the scope of the contract.

The FSD people we found there seemed less like engineers as we understood the term and more like programmers, some distinctly run-of-the-mill. Coming from a place where the air we breathed was "Never mind what's impossible, we can do this," we felt the FSD air was "Give us a spec and we'll implement it." To a degree, it was inevitable in a site devoted entirely to constructing software on exactly that basis. We'd been spoiled by working in a place where the programmers and hardware engineers lived in each others' pockets and the dirt under our fingernails was of many different compositions. Our opinion, fair or unfair, was that many FSD/Houston programmers were just available, and not a group carefully picked for that assignment.

Where we'd settled into reviewing avionics system *requirements* specifications with Rockwell, we found ourselves reviewing, and frequently editing, software *design* specs with IBM. They were quite systematic about making comprehensive flowcharts from which to write the code, much more so than we'd been in Apollo. That was a good thing, especially considering they couldn't just trot across the hall to consult with an expert in vehicle systems. Other groups around the Lab worked with the FSD people on matters of Guidance, Navigation, and Control. In the Digital Development Group, we gravitated to the Flight Computer Operating System (FCOS), since that's where the logic for full GPC synchronization had to reside. Most General Purpose Computer (GPC) programming was done in the high-level compiler language *HAL/S*,[50] but FCOS (which resembled more a "kernel" than a modern broad-scale operating system) had many places where intricate time-critical logic had to get done in assembler language.

Since the AP-101 had not been designed from the beginning to operate in tightly synchronized redundant sets, achieving that goal in software was a major issue. Most of our attention was on synchronizing a Redundant Set (RS) of four GPCs because that's what was required for the dynamic phases, the transitions between Earth and space. Synchronization wasn't only about when the calculations got done. Making the GPCs use exactly the same inputs to produce exactly the same outputs required us to look beyond the computer boxes, at where the data came from and where it had to go.

In the Space Shuttle, as in a scientific view of the human body, everything other than the brain was classified as either a sensor or an effector. Sensors included IMUs, "air data" measuring altitude by pressure and airspeed by pitot tubes, status information for engines and aerodynamic control surfaces, plus digital inputs like crew commands and uplink from the ground. Effectors included engines and the hydraulics that moved the aerodynamic control surfaces, plus digital outputs like crew displays and downlink data to the ground.

The Shuttle's avionics system had three layers: the computer-controlled sensor and effector subsystems with redundancy levels of two, three, or four identical units; simple local processors called MDMs to interface each group of related subsystem units with one of the quadruple-redundant data buses; and at the other end of the buses, five GPCs. MDM stood for Modulator-DeModulator (like the modem on your computer), which was an understatement, since MDMs contained logic to command or sample multiple different types of subsystem units.

One way to configure the sensing and effecting would have been the "separate-string" model in which each GPC in the RS would listen to only one of each kind of sensor and command one of each kind of effector. There were several problems with that concept, particularly on the sensor side where not all sensors had quadruple redundancy. Also, we couldn't bear to make the usability of each GPC stand or fall with the correct functioning of *every* unit on its string. The solution was a "cross-coupled" configuration in which every reading from every sensor was received simultaneously by all the GPCs in the redundant set. On the effector side, every GPC was capable of commanding any string of units, but was in fact assigned to only one string until response to a failure required a different assignment. The effect of cross-coupling was that you could continue the mission fully operational after many failures, provided only that no two of the failures affected the same type of unit. If that sort of double failure did occur, the crew could still abort the mission and get home safely based on the system voting two-out-of-three.

We had to make sure all the measurements from each redundant set of any type of sensor were delivered to all GPCs in the redundant set, picked up there at the same point in the program flow in each GPC, and that the resolution of those redundant measurements into a single best estimate was done the same way in all GPCs. Additionally, the GPCs' real-time "alarm clocks" to schedule events based on the passage of time had to be treated as sensors in the same way.

The only element of the AP-101 design that directly supported synchronization was a set of "discretes," wires that could be electronically latched to 28V for ones or 0V for zeros, interconnected so that three discretes set by each GPC could be read by all the other GPCs. This cross-strapped exchange of 3-bit codes became part of the system design long before we began our extensive discussions of exactly how GPC synchronization should work. Either it was a judicious design because it was just enough to support the sync scheme we worked out, or we elaborated the sync scheme until it used up all the possibilities of those codes—your choice. I'd say both are fully true and that credit for the "judicious" part goes to an IBM gentleman named Lynn Killingbeck, who had designed both hardware and software for the military and aerospace computers developed at FSD in Owego, New York.[51]

The scheme had two parts, or levels. The base level kept the GPCs in a Redundant Set doing everything in the same order when no faults are occurring. That sounds like a trivial task until you realize that input/output operations were not going to reach completion at a predictable point in the program flow, and the same was true of each GPC's "alarm clock" timer. What these events did was to "wake up" whatever piece of the program was waiting for them. For example, a navigation job had to wait while data was gathered from the redundant inertial measurement units, and an engine-firing job had to wait until the time-to-go for its ignition ran out. But the GPC had other jobs to do while that waiting was going on, and some of those things could affect data used by the waiting jobs. That's why the "predictable point" was so important. We used signals exchanged on the discretes to make faster GPCs wait for slower ones, with limits on the waiting time to detect the case of a GPC that wasn't merely slow but actually stopped by a failure.[52]

The higher level of sync logic had to determine whether faulty input data looked the same to all GPCs. If that were the case, the sensor needed to be corrected or discarded. If it looked different in different GPCs, it must have been a GPC fault.[53]

That's a brief summary of the fault tolerance scheme we persuaded NASA to accept and IBM to implement, to keep missions operating through even a wide sprinkling of scattered failures. Our memos and slide shows were only a conceptual design; the other half of our work in this area was going through IBM's design flowcharts with a very fine-tooth comb to make sure their implementation was correct.

The year 1975 opened with Soyuz 17 taking Commander Aleksei Gubarov and Flight Engineer Georgi Grechko up to dock with Salyut 4 on January 11. This crew achieved a remarkable feat, repairing a Solar Telescope mirror after automatic pointing failed in a way that let sunlight burn off the original coating. Then they devised a workaround method of pointing it, using a stopwatch, a stethoscope to listen to motor noises inside the case, and (apparently) no duct tape. Gubarov and Grechko were able to perform their research program in astrophysics for the rest of the month, and then land safely in a snowstorm.

Generally, failures in Russian space systems were kept rigidly secret by the Soviet authorities, but a special circumstance allowed us to hear about "The April 5th Anomaly." The imminence of the Apollo-Soyuz Test Project, then in its fourth year of development, required a mutual openness unprecedented in the Cold War. The anomalous event was supposed to be Soyuz 18 docking with Salyut 4 and testing systems to be used in ASTP. But the launch ran into trouble when the second booster stage was cast off to let the third stage ignite. The casting-off was only partial, so the third-stage engine had to blast it away; but by the time that worked, the spacecraft was thrown so far off course that it couldn't recover. Commander Vasili Lazarev and Flight Engineer Oleg Makarov had to separate their Soyuz abnormally from the third stage and use the spacecraft's engines to dive steeply into the entry corridor. Their couches were designed to keep them fairly comfortable at an acceleration 15 times that of Earth gravity. However, in that situation, the multiple went up to 21g. Their effective weight went over a ton and a half each, breaking many of their ribs. The parachutes worked, and after landing on a steep mountain slope, they rolled and slid some distance in deep snow, narrowly missing a fatal tumble off a sheer cliff. They couldn't tell right away whether they had landed in China, a bad place for Russians to be in those days. Luckily, they were 500 miles north of the border. They were rescued eventually and airlifted home to Star City, where Makarov recovered and returned to space several more times. It was the first *manned* flight in history to suffer a booster failure, and remained the only one where the failure occurred at high altitude.

Historians have identified that mission with numbers like Soyuz 18-1 or Soyuz 18B, but the Soviets gave numbers only to successful flights and insisted on a somewhat arch phrase, "The April 5th Anomaly." Its connection to ASTP produced one of the strangest moments in the Cold War, when the Congress of the United States held an investigation into the anomaly and demanded a more detailed account from the space agency of the Soviet Union.

Better news for the Russians that spring was launching Aryabhata, a research satellite built by India. Getting into the business of launching satellites for other countries had some Cold-War value in a neo-Stalinist way. This one forged a link with the biggest Third World country, correspondingly weakening India's link to America.

At the Lab, we had to sell our fault tolerance concepts to Rockwell as well as to IBM and NASA, which involved a good deal of travel, mostly to Downey, California. One contractor engineer, whom I'll call Moody because he *was* as moody as he was bright, explained that he was on vellum, a statement that puzzled us. Studying the matter later by ourselves, we realized he meant Valium.

On one of our trips to Houston, we sat in the bar one evening while a local band was battering eardrums. A contractor team led by Moody had joined us there. Moody happened to set his beer bottle down where the drummer's flying elbow knocked it over, and the storm clouds gathered ominously across his face, portending retaliation. He got another beer and we carried on more or less as usual, but his throat was full of muttering and grumbling, a noise somewhat like rolling thunder. We finished our beers, went up in the elevator, fanned out toward our rooms, and said goodnight ... but Moody's thunder was still rolling, as if his supply of Valium lay forgotten at home. I trotted down the stairs and crossed the pool area toward the bar, just in time to intercept my friend Moody, who still had a vengeful glint in his eye. "Hey, man, I got a question. What's it really like to work for Fussy?" naming a man who had been Moody's uneasy boss for a year or so. To my great relief, Moody allowed himself to be distracted, and we sat at a little metal poolside table where he recounted the tribulations of reporting to Fussy. After a while his tempo slowed considerably, his head sagged down toward his folded arms, and a small dribble of vomit appeared on his sleeve, so I knew that his cargo of alcohol had completed its merciful work. I walked him to the elevator and up we went again, this time for the night. Ah, the oddly assorted duties of consultants.

On May 24, 1975, the "real" Soyuz 18 carried Commander Pyotr Klimuk and Flight Engineer Vitali Sevastyanov to a successful docking with Salyut 4. They had to repair a number of scientific instruments and other gear, then settled down to their program of astrophysical and Earth science observations and a variety of experiments, primarily medical and biological.

In anticipation of their ability to continue the mission right through the time span of ASTP, Soyuz 18 reported, not to Baikonur, but to the Crimean mission control center that had been last used for Soyuz 12. The men proved more durable than the Salyut when its environmental control system lost the ability to reduce humidity in July. Their physical preparations for homecoming—more sweaty time on the exercise machines— didn't help matters. The green mold grew thicker on the walls, and windows became nearly opaque. The crew's 63 days in orbit was a record for cosmonauts, in second place behind the 83 days of Skylab 4.

July 15, 1975, was Day 1 of the Apollo-Soyuz Test Project mission. Soyuz 19, reporting to the newer Baikonur mission control center, lifted off seven and a half hours before Apollo did. But that wasn't about competition, it was about the fact that Baikonur's time zone is ten hours ahead of Kennedy Space Center's. Both launches were televised live, a first for the Soviet space program, at convenient hours for their home time zones. Soyuz, with Commander Alexey Leonov and Flight Engineer Valeri Kubasov, orbited independently for the first two days. They reduced their sea-level air pressure to ten pounds to meet Apollo's five-pound oxygen atmosphere halfway. The Apollo CSM, carrying Commander Tom Stafford, CM Pilot Vance Brand, and Docking Module Pilot Deke Slayton, had to perform a Transposition and Docking to collect the ASTP docking adapter/airlock from its place where the LM would have been for a Moon mission.

On July 17, Apollo took the active role in the first international docking. It took three hours to move things out of the way of the transfer tunnels at both ends of the airlock. Then Tom floated from Apollo to the midpoint, Alexey floated from Soyuz to the midpoint, and they shook hands. In that moment, the Space Race was over.

The two crews exchanged gifts, socialized, shared meals, and conversed in both languages. Tom's Russian was strongly flavored with the drawled accents of the Great Plains, leading Alexey to count "Oklahomski" as a third language in use. They received a statement from Premier Leonid Brezhnev and a phone call from President Gerald Ford. The moment had a special sweetness for Deke Slayton. He'd been selected as one of the original "Mercury Seven" astronauts at the very dawn of the Space Race, and for medical reasons had not been allowed to fly until this mission, the end of the Space Race.

The two spacecraft also cooperated on science while undocked. Apollo backed away, up-sun, until it exactly blocked the disk for Soyuz, making photography of just the corona possible. Soyuz returned home after five days, and Apollo orbited four more days, making Earth science observations.

Murphy's law produced one last swipe at Apollo. Everybody knows that the layer of superheated ionized air around an entering spacecraft blacks out radio communication for about four minutes.[54] Less well known is the amount of audio noise that entry generates in the cabin, creating a sort of audio blackout. In this flight, Vance couldn't hear Tom reading the end-of-entry checklist item for shutting down the CM's RCS and popping the drogue chutes. By the time he realized it was time to switch it off, some of the RCS's hypergolic oxidizer, nitrogen tetroxide, leaked out of one of the jets and made its way into an air intake. Vance passed out before Tom could whip out the oxygen masks. He revived when Tom put the mask on him. All three received treatment at a Honolulu hospital.

Space thus became as international as Antarctica, where

cooperation replaced hostility because it had to. It was the moment when the twentieth century finally decided it had better start behaving itself. Americans and Russians took off their demonization blinders and began to understand what it takes to live together on a small Blue Marble glowing against the infinite blackness of space.

Space Race Highlights of 1974

(All manned flights are indicated in bold.)

29 May   Luna 22. Orbited Moon. Photographic and magnetic studies.

25 Jun   Salyut 3. Unmanned (secretly military, armed) space station. Orbited.

03 Jul   **Soyuz 14. 16 days. Crew: Pavel Popovich, Yuri Artyukhin. Docked with Salyut 3, secretly investigating military presence in space.**

26 Aug   **Soyuz 15. 31 orbits. Crew: Gennadi Sarafanov, Lev Dyomin. Failed to dock with Salyut 3 using only automatic docking system.**

28 Oct   Luna 23. Intended sample return. Landed hard on Moon and tipped over.

02 Dec   **Soyuz 16. 6 days. Crew: Anatoly Filipchenko, Nikolai Rukavishnikov. Tested docking ring for Apollo-Soyuz Test Project.**

26 Dec   Salyut 4. Unmanned space station. Orbited.

Space Race Highlights of 1975

(All manned flights are indicated in bold.)

11 Jan   **Soyuz 17. 30 days. Crew: Aleksei Gubarev, Georgi Grechko. Docked with Salyut 4, astrophysics research.**

05 Apr   **"April 5th Anomaly," 21 minutes. Crew: Vasili Lazarev, Oleg Makarov. Booster failure caused Soyuz to abort. Crew suffered 21g deceleration.**

24 May   **Soyuz 18. 63 days. Crew: Pyotr Klimuk, Vitali Sevastyanov. Docked with Salyut 4. Controlled independently of Soyuz 19 in ASTP.**

15 Jul   **Soyuz 19, 5 days. Crew: Alexey Leonov, Valeri Kubasov. Docked with Apollo CSM-111 to form Apollo-Soyuz Test Project.**

15 Jul   **Apollo CSM-111. 9 days. Crew: Tom Stafford, Vance Brand, Deke Slayton. Docked with Soyuz 19 to form Apollo-Soyuz Test Project.**

Other Space Highlights of 1975

19 Apr   Aryabhata. First Indian satellite. Launched by USSR.

20 Aug   Viking 1. Mars orbiter and Mars lander. 10-month trip, 4 years operation.

09 Sep   Viking 2. Mars orbiter and Mars lander. 11-month trip, 2 years operation.

LESS SEPARATE AND MORE TOGETHER: 1976–2001

The Space Race was over, and the Cold War had lost its way, stumbling along with no clear idea of what its aims were. It had become a habit more than a campaign.

With no follow-ons planned for the one ASTP mission, our AGC retired from active duty and became a museum piece. I suppose we should have given it a retirement party, but we'd gotten too busy with the Shuttle systems and didn't look back. Rather than disappearing into the dustbin of history, however, the AGC has found a second home in the hearts and minds of Space-Age hobbyists around the world. These people spend vast amounts of time and ingenuity creating accurate simulations of the AGC on their laptops, complete with perfectly photographic working reproductions of the DSKY on their screens. Most of these clones run an LGC program (*Luminary*), used in the Apollo 13 "lifeboat" flight, that is posted on the Web in its entirety.[55] Early in this century, I participated in a conference where astronaut John Young was the featured speaker. At a lunch meeting, Julian Webb of the University of Western England brought his AGC clone over to show him. John, usually notorious for never giving autographs, was so impressed that he took out a permanent marker and autographed the outer surface of Julian's laptop. I guess Julian had to apply a coat of varnish to preserve it.

Most of what took place in space after ASTP was internationally neutral, often cautiously moving toward greater cooperation. NASA launched Viking 1 and 2 on a year-long trip to Mars, where they landed and did Martian science for years. Voyager 1 lifted off the next year and eventually sent back data from far beyond its 2012 crossing of the *heliosphere*, where the Sun's influence over charged particles in space is exceeded by interstellar influences. The Soviets sent an unmanned Soyuz 20 to dock automatically with Salyut 4, where it stayed for three months exercising spacecraft systems and doing biological science, then came home. It validated the concept of the unmanned Progress missions that would supply later space stations. And just to Moon the western world once more, they sent Luna 24 on a successful mission to return a six-ounce sample from the Sea of Crises—finally overcoming the apparent negativity of that name.

Salyut 5, another Almaz military outpost in disguise but without a "self-defence" gun, was staffed twice for a total of nine weeks. Its "published" activities included sun observations, other science, and a televised conference with school children. A third visit was aborted due to an avionics failure. The station ran low on maneuvering fuel after fourteen months and was de-orbited destructively. There were no more Almaz stations, since little or no useful military activity for them was identified.

Salyut 6 represented a major advance in Soviet space stations and operated for five years, welcoming foreign crew from eight Soviet-bloc countries. Its second docking port received logistic support visits, including refueling, from robot Progress vehicles.

Salyut 7, the last in the series, was similar to Salyut 6 but with a more modular architecture to test systems for the much-delayed new type of space station. With occasional crew from outside the Soviet bloc (France and India), it operated during the first five years of the Space Shuttle era.

The Soviets named the new type of space station *Mir* (Russian for Peace), in a significant change from the military tone of *Salyut* (Russian for Salute). It was put together from seven modules over a decade, most of which was under the aegis of Russia after the dissolution of the Soviet Union. Crew members came from many countries for twelve of its fifteen years of operation, 1985 to 2001. Most significantly, Mir provided a docking port used by the U.S. Space Shuttle.

Unlike most manned spacecraft, whose orbits are more nearly equatorial than polar, Soyuz 22 was a self-contained research mission that was guided into a nearly polar orbit so as to pass over high latitudes, including all of Siberia. With that exception, each Soyuz, from 21 to 40, served as a taxi to and from a Salyut station. In the middle of Salyut 6's career, an upgraded "T" version of Soyuz entered service, beginning a new series of mission numbers starting with Soyuz T-2. The T version could take a *Troika*, a crew of three, like early Soyuz models before the depressurization disaster limited them to crews of two.

Soyuz T-10 suffered a major but not fatal fire and explosion on the launch pad. The crew survived when launch controllers were able to fire their launch escape system by radio command, two seconds before the booster exploded. That was the only time a launch escape system had to do its job for real.

The final T-series flight was Soyuz T-15, the first spacecraft to dock with two space stations, Salyut 7 and the new one, Mir. A new "TM" series then entered service, of which TM-13 was the only spacecraft to change flags (USSR to Russia) during its mission.

TM-21 was part of the first flight in the Shuttle-Mir program, a new high in space cooperation. TM-30 made the final visit to Mir, and TM-31 made the first Soyuz visit to the International Space Station.

⸻ ⊗⊗⊗ ⸻

Our fault tolerance work at the Lab focused in on microscopic possibilities of sync failure in the Space Shuttle's General Purpose Computers (GPCs). Since we had to emulate in software what should ideally have been implemented in super-fast hardware logic, there were loops of about ten instructions (about ten microseconds) for sampling the sync discrete signals exchanged between GPCs. If the rise from zero volts to 28 volts on those wires was slow or wobbly, the signals could in principle be sampled at a "wrong" time and misinterpreted. NASA was concerned about such cases—what we called "sync holes."

I did a little unauthorized research into a suitable logic circuit to serve as a hardware solution, but was rebuffed. The Lab's Digital Development Group wasn't going to be allowed to develop anything digital for the Shuttle project. So we went on thinking up more and more obscure possibilities, and tweaking our sampling logic to cope with them. Fortunately for us, the company developing thermal tiles that could absorb the heat of entry, re-radiate it, and be ready to do that 99 more times was struggling with a hard problem. And the company developing medium-large rocket engines with that same level of reusability was also struggling. That gave us plenty of time to refine our software solution.

The intractable tile and engine problems had other interesting consequences with respect to the schedule President Nixon had announced in 1972. One was a clever NASA approach to beating the goal of manned Shuttle test flights by 1978. Verifying that this spacecraft/aircraft, shaped like a streamlined rock, could land safely and controllably was important, and could properly be done without going into space at all. It wouldn't need working thermal tiles or working rocket engines, just things of the same weight in the right places on the vehicle. There was already a plan for a Shuttle Carrier Aircraft, a Boeing 747 with special fittings to carry a Shuttle on its back from wherever it landed to Kennedy Space Center for its next launch. All it took to perform Shuttle Approach and Landing Test flights was devising a pyrotechnic way for the SCA to pop the shuttle off its back for the two-man crew to fly it down from 20,000 feet or so to the ground. Five such flights occurred in 1977. In the first one, our sync software lit up a flight deck display to show that one of the four synchronized GPCs had failed sync. Commander Fred Haise shut off that GPC and the landing continued flawlessly. Post-flight analysis found a broken connection in that computer, thereby validating our fault tolerance logic. Actual space flights of the Shuttle started four years later, in 1981, not quite fulfilling Nixon's phrase "shortly thereafter."

The other consequence of our tile and engine problems was in the Soviet Union, where Nixon's expression of unrealistic economic hopes for the Shuttle had triggered an intense paranoid worry about what he really meant. In a dictatorship where a policy decision would be carried out with little or no concern for its cost, it was hard to appreciate how much bending of truth it takes to get anything funded in a checks-and-balances democracy. Soviet analysts felt certain (correctly) that launching dozens or hundreds of satellites per year, for years on end, was unlikely to be justified or accomplished. Noticing the Air Force involvement, they could imagine only one rational purpose for such a launching capability: deploying a weapon system threatening the USSR. Scratch their heads as they might, they couldn't figure out what such a weapon would be or how it would work. But if the public case for the American Shuttle didn't make any sense, there had to be a covert case that did. In anticipation of discovering what this secret weapon might be, and thereby having the capability to match it, they set about to build a Soviet Space Shuttle.

There wasn't an independent existing vision among Russians as to what a Space Shuttle should look like, and they couldn't take a lot of time catching up, so *Buran* ("Snowstorm") looked almost identical to the U.S. Space Shuttle. The size was much the same, as were the delta-wing configuration, the color scheme of black heavy-duty thermal tiles and white lighter-duty ones, the shape of the nose and flight deck, the payload bay, orbital maneuvering engines, the rudder and body flap … just about everything, with one large and interesting exception. There were no main engines in their orbiter, so an easy way to tell a Buran from a Shuttle was a rear view. Or you could read the name painted on the side.

Soviet designers finessed the difficulty of developing large reusable steerable rocket engines by not trying. The Energia booster, the world's heaviest liquid-fueled boost vehicle, had the usual steerable engines, which did not have to be reusable. It would take Buran all the way to orbit and be discarded, just as it did with Soyuz spacecraft. The other major problem of reusable thermal tiles was greatly simplified by not worrying much about the "reusable" part. Unlike the U.S. Shuttle, it was never intended for the same extensive reuse for civilian purposes. Being built for no purpose other than to take its part (whatever that might turn out to be) in Armageddon, the Soviets felt no need for hundredfold reusability. One more difference was adopted. It could be flown unmanned, a mode always appreciated by the Soviets with their passion for *Telemekhanika*, remote control. We always thought that trend was a good match for their political system.

Development started in 1974, as soon as the design of the U.S. Shuttle became fairly stable. Buran was mounted on the Energia much as the Shuttle was mounted on its External Tank. For intra-atmospheric trips it was carried on the back of a 747-like plane, the Antonov An-225 with its six jet engines and wide double tail.

Buran did fly in space just once, unmanned, on November 15, 1988. It maneuvered into a higher orbit after booster separation, completed two orbits, swung around to perform its de-orbit burn, and finally landed in a stiff crosswind with commendable accuracy. Its next public appearance was at the 1989 Paris Air Show, sitting atop the An-225. The dissolution of the Soviet Union killed any chance of further flights. In 1993, Buran was mothballed and stored at Baikonur, in a hangar that collapsed in 2002, crushing the spacecraft and eight technicians.

One Buran prototype, which never flew, now sits by a lake in Gorky Park, Moscow, a forlorn souvenir of the Arms Race in space.

To the Soviets' surprise, our Space Shuttles spent almost their whole lives doing the sort of civilian activities we'd announced, though without bringing the cost of space transportation down nearly as much as Nixon had promised. When *Challenger* suffered a Solid-Rocket Booster failure in 1982, in which flame shot through a cold-stiffened O-ring and blew up the External Tank, nobody could miss the thoroughly civilian significance of schoolteacher Christa McAuliffe being one of the seven victims.

Only eleven missions were to any degree "Blue" flights for Air Force purposes. Twice as many carried the European Space Agency's Spacelab, a habitable scientific module that made the Shuttle into a series of short-term space stations simply by staying in its payload bay. Its grandest scientific achievement was orbiting the Hubble Space Telescope, designed as the largest possible object that would fit in the payload bay. Five later Shuttle missions visited the Hubble to make repairs and upgrades.

The Space Shuttle's ultimate contribution to world history was taking the lead role in constructing the International Space Station. That project began as an American national effort with the decidedly Western-World vehicle name of *Freedom*.[56] When the Soviet Union collapsed, they were getting ready to replace the Mir space station with Mir-2. In the improved world climate, the United States and Russia merged their projects. Other countries have contributed modules and equipment, notably Japan and Canada; perhaps China will join in. Although it uses *Alpha* as a radio call sign, the result is known to everybody as the International Space Station or simply ISS, the global facility whose crews have come from fifteen countries.

Rocket science, navigation science, computer science, and good system engineering have given us the opportunity to live and work in space indefinitely. History has given us the realization that the space near our lonely Blue Marble can and should belong to everybody.

NOTES

PROLOGUE

1. NASA's Research Steering Committee on Manned Space Flight first met on May 25, 1959, exactly two years before Kennedy's challenge to Congress. Harry J. Goett, director of NASA's Ames Flight Research Center, chaired the discussions of how the still infant NASA should plan its manned space operations beyond the already established Mercury program. They discussed expansion of Mercury to a larger two-man craft—the concept that later became Gemini. Controversy centered on the relative priorities of a space station, circumlunar missions, and a lunar landing. George M. Low, who had been one of NASA's organizers and was then Chief of Manned Space Flight, argued strongly for the lunar landing. Just a month later, the committee made their decision. Goett's minutes contained an ironic prescience of how the Space Age would play out:

> *A primary reason for this choice was the fact that it represented a truly end objective which was self-justifying and did not have to be supported on the basis that it led to a subsequent more useful end.*

In July 1960, NASA Administrator T. Keith Glennan and the Goett committee agreed on the name Apollo for the lunar landing program. At that time, there was no geopolitical aspect of the program. It was just a worthy goal for manned space flight, and had no likelihood of urgent funding in President Eisenhower's budget-balancing administration.

CHAPTER 3

2. When Global Positioning System (GPS) technology was new, the U.S. Coast Guard's Aids-To-Navigation command got carried away with the ability to average hundreds of measurements of the location of each buoy, and published latitudes and longitudes stating those locations to an absurd precision of about the nearest inch. In the first place, buoys swing around on chains many yards long. In the second place, continental drift can change the physical facts by inches per year. Achievable accuracy of measurements and adequate precision to represent relevant data—while leaving enough extra room to mitigate round-off errors without wasting resources by providing too much precision—govern a computer designer's choice of how data is stored in the machine's memory. If a machine is to "eat its own tail," one of the key decisions is determining how much of that tail is consumed in a single bite. Our modern term "byte" is arguably derived from that thought, but byte-centered architecture isn't the only way. Babbage's data quantum of 40 decimal digits remains the all-time giant, and the sizes have been going mostly down ever since, with a variety of methods to access several quanta at once:

> ➤ 1944—Harvard's Mark I kept data "words" of 23 decimal digits and sign.

> ➤ 1950—Harvard's Mark IV kept data words of 16 decimal digits and sign.

> ➤ 1951—Univac I kept data words of 11 decimal digits and sign.

> ➤ 1950s—IBM and Univac "scientific" computer data words were 36 bits ~ 12 digits.

> ➤ 1950s—IBM "business" computers used arbitrary-length strings of 6-bit characters.

> ➤ 1960s—MIT spacecraft computer words were 15 bits ~ 5 digits, with a little logic to support double precision (30 bits) and even triple precision (45 bits).

> ➤ 1960s—IBM System 360 introduced strings of 8-bit bytes, with logic to process 2, 4, 8, or even 16 of them at a time for scientific calculations.

Chapter 5

3. Figure 5-1 is one of many items obtainable from the Internet, where articles of a technical nature generally demonstrate the potential for reliability in crowd-sourcing. This one, courtesy of Jorge Stolfi who released it into the public domain, is from en.wikipedia.org/wiki/Cartesian_coordinate_system.

4. In aviation, a term "vectoring" is used in a less mathematical way for the changes of position and velocity required to meet some requirement like alignment with a runway for landing.

CHAPTER 6

5. There are two main kinds of IRU, called gimbaled and strapdown. In the gimbaled kind, the stable platform to which the gyros and accelerometers are secured is supported by three or even four gimbals, pivoting rings like those that allow the magnetic compass card to remain level in a boat. The computer literally stabilizes it by changing the gimbal angles to precisely compensate for any change in orientation detected by the gyros. This has the advantage that the directions of the forces measured by the accelerometers are always aligned with the three axes of inertial space described in Chapter 5. Gyros in IRUs are nowhere near massive enough to stabilize the platform all by themselves like a toy gyroscope; that's why the computer has to tweak the gimbal angles.

In the strapdown kind, which requires a considerably faster computer, the platform is fastened rigidly to the spacecraft. The computer performs a virtual stabilization by passively keeping track of changes in orientation detected by the gyros, then using that information to project accelerometer readings trigonometrically onto the standard inertial axes. Both types were used in Apollo's Lunar Module, in the primary and abort guidance systems respectively.

CHAPTER 7

6. Each of the 80 columns represented a character in 12-hole positions to give each possible digit value its own time slot: first 9-time, then 8-time, and so on through 0-time, followed by X-time for minus signs and Y-time for other control purposes. Letters and punctuation marks were coded as combinations of two or even three holes to control printing on ledger paper. Programming of a very limited sort was possible: Wires plugged into a plugboard steered particular card columns to particular print positions or adders, and could use control codes to dump a multi-wheel adder's content into selected print positions.

7. In 1989, Zuse and some colleagues completed a replica of the Z1 for the German Museum of Technology.

8. This patent infringement trial, Honeywell, Inc. v. Sperry Rand Corp., 54 F.R.D. 593 (D.Minn.1973), occurred in Minneapolis instead of Washington because of a finding that Honeywell's suit had been filed just minutes earlier than the one filed by Sperry Rand. Judge John

Sirica, whose decision on this "race" gave Honeywell the home-field advantage for the actual trial, later gained fame when he brought the gavel of justice down on the heads of President Nixon's Watergate conspirators.

9. Mark I was the first computer for which I learned, in 1956, to write programs (Chapter 4). Nobody told me it was known to its close friends as "Bessie" because so much of the mathematics in the programs was solving Bessel equations. Most of the machine is on permanent display in Harvard's Science Center, where its presentation as a museum piece was significantly upgraded in 2014.

10. The word "bug" had been in use for centuries to mean a Bad Thing to be feared, but this was the first time it was applied to the functioning of a computer. Figure 7-1, courtesy of Naval History & Heritage Command, is from www.history.navy.mil/research/histories/bios/hopper-grace.html#david.

11. An *instruction* is an "atom" of a stored program, just enough information to specify one arithmetic operation on one piece of data—nothing close to such modern commands as "Siri, direct me to a nearby Chinese restaurant."

12. Boris Artzybasheff's idiosyncratic illustrations for the covers of *Time*, some two hundred between 1941 and 1965, placed him among the world's best-known artists. Sometimes he morphed people into machines, but more usually he morphed machines into people. The Mark III portrait is archived at content.time.com/time/covers/0,16641,1101500123,00.html.

13. There are several on-line archives that include such "giant brain" images. One of the best cartoons, drawn by Michael Ffolkes for *Punch*, can be found by searching for "punch cartoons out of copyright" and then searching for "ffolkes computer."

14. Ken Thompson of Bell Laboratories may have been thinking of Hopper's "A" when he created a simplified high-level language called "B" in the late '60s. Then, with other Bell Labs stars including Brian Kernighan and Dennis Ritchie, he set aside "B" and created the "C" language we know today in its many variations.

CHAPTER 8

15. Close observation reveals that the number of ferrite cores in this unit

was twice the number required to store the information. To solve the problem of having to erase ferrite core memory while reading it, this unit simply copied the data from half the cores into the other half and then remembered which half contained the data. Figure 8-1 is a Harvard Mark IV memory register, courtesy of the Collection of Historical Scientific Instruments, Harvard University.

16. The letter K (for Kilo, Greek for one thousand) is used by many scientists, including electrical engineers, to stand for exactly one thousand. Computer scientists, living in a world of binary numbers, often need to use numbers that are a power of two: 2, 4, 8, 16, 32, 64, ... They also need to use abbreviations to express large numbers in approximate form. By a happy coincidence, the tenth power of two (1,024) is acceptably close to the third power of ten (1,000), so they have adopted the letter K to mean "literally 1,024 but, you know, like 1,000." I use "K" in this book consistently in that sense, except as noted.

Similarly, M (for Mega, Greek for big) is used by many scientists to stand for exactly one million, but computer scientists use it as the square of K, for "literally 1,048,576 but, you know, like 1,000,000." The next step, G, is for Giga (from the Greek for giant) stands for a billion, the 9th power of ten or the cube of K (30th power of two). Like "K," I use "M" and "G" in the computer-science fashion, but knowing that won't materially affect the reader's understanding.

17. The *FORTRAN* compiler gave me my first taste of a software diagnostic message that was correct, specific, expressed in irrelevant terms and nearly useless: "Error in Fortran input record 1146." Well, at least it pointed me to the defective equation, in which I had written an expression like "$(a + (b - c)))$". See the problem? One extra closing parenthesis—*FORTRAN'S* creator John Backus had been prepared to make it say something sensible about one too few, but not about one too many.

18. The title was *Design of Water Resources Systems; New Techniques for Relating Economic Objectives, Engineering Analysis, and Governmental Planning* (1962). The authors were project leader Professor Arthur Maass, my genial manager Maynard Hufschmidt, Professor Robert Dorfman of Economics, my faculty advisor Professor Harold Thomas of Engineering, graduate student Stephen Marglin, and Professor

Gordon Fair of Sanitary Engineering (nicknamed "Flush Gordon"). My name appeared only in footnotes, but it was my first credit in hard covers.

19. IBM 650s found homes in many universities, functioning as precursors of the mini-computers of the 1970s. Figure 8-2 is courtesy of IBM Archives.

20. IBM 407s could be called the MS Office suites of their time, combining a small subset of the functions of word processors and spreadsheets. Figures 8-3a and 8-3b are courtesy of IBM Archives.

21. Charlie Werner briefed me on the procedures for programming the Lab's 650, which were nearly identical to those I'd used with a standard 650 at Harvard. It certainly was a lot more physical work than our modern way of clicking to select a word processor, writing and editing some code with a whole page in view, summoning assembly or compilation with another click, getting any diagnostic feedback instantly, making the test run with another click. Here's what I had to do to start a new program:

➤ Create flowcharts and other parts of a very informal design document.

➤ Decide whether to use the high-level compiler language *MAC* or the low-level assembly language *FLAD*. Pull a pad of the corresponding coding sheets (printed by the Lab's Technical Publications Department) from a supply shelf.

➤ Working from the design document, compose and write the source code on ledger-size coding sheets. The printed form established rectangles so that every character I wrote was assigned to its particular punched-card column. Shading printed on the form distinguished fixed-width fields such as location, operation code, address, and remarks.

➤ Cross the hall to the machine room and get a cardboard box of two thousand blank punched cards from the supply shelves. Use an IBM "026" keypunch, equipped with a typewriter-like keyboard and tab stops for the fields marked off in the coding sheets, to enter the source code.

➤ After a keypunching session, take the deck of cards to the 407 printer to get a listing of my source code, one line per card. Proofread the listing against the coding sheets to catch typos.

➤ Get a time slot on the 650 and take the source code box to its card reader. At the beginning of the deck, place a special "bootstrap" card containing just enough object code to fetch the desired compiler or assembler from the hard disk. Press a Start button on the 650's console panel.

➤ Since the source code deck was usually much too big for the card reader's magazine, pull cards that had been read from the reader's stacker to place at one end of the box, while transferring the next batch of unread cards to the reader's magazine. Maintain total concentration to avoid getting parts of the source code deck out of order.

➤ When all the source code cards have been read in at 200 per minute, wait for the language processing program to begin punching the "load deck" containing numerical object code into blank cards fed from another magazine atop the card punch unit. This wait would be a few minutes for a *FLAD* program, or an hour or more for a *MAC* program. And what came out of the card punch, no faster than 100 per minute, wasn't always a load deck. Sometimes it was a small number of cards with diagnostic messages pointing to where the source code syntax was internally inconsistent, preventing the processing from being completed.

➤ When the output was diagnostic messages, yield the 650 to the next user and take the diagnostic cards to the 407 to make a listing of them to guide editing of the source code deck to correct the errors.

➤ When the output was a load deck, pull cards out of the punch's stacker and pack them into another card box. When necessary, add more blank cards to the punch's feeder magazine. Maintain total concentration to avoid getting parts of the load deck out of order, especially because nothing got printed on those cards.

➤ When the load deck is complete, put it into the 650's card reader magazine with a few cards containing test data behind it, and press the start button to dedicate the 650's central processor entirely to the test run. With luck and skill, it punched an output deck as directed by the program under test. With less luck, some error would make the machine stop and display only one clue, the address of the last instruction executed, in the neon indicator bulbs on the console panel.

➤ Yield the 650 to the next user and take the output deck to the 407 for visible results.

That was a lot of steps and a lot of time, yet it didn't seem particularly onerous.

22. I started by defining the *YUL* source language so it could use a dictionary that could be efficiently implemented by the IBM 650, with its 2,000 ten-digit words of memory. Since the 650's input logic provided a way to convert any character in a card column to a two-digit number, it made sense to define symbolic names as up to five characters—just what would fit in one word of memory. The *definition*, numerical information corresponding to each symbol, comprised the number to be substituted in the second pass and some coded information about the symbol's status (not yet defined, defined OK, or defined with error) or "health" as I called it. Thus a dictionary entry comprised two words, the symbol and its definition/health data. Since the biggest memory contemplated for a Mars computer in 1959 was only 512 words, and since not every location in an object machine's memory needs a symbolic name, a dictionary with 200 entries would be plenty big enough for those early machines. With such a short schedule to develop this assembler, I was very happy to let it live with these limitations in the initial phase, to get the simplicity—and especially the speed advantages—of an internal dictionary, one that didn't have to go through the complexity of residing partly in memory and partly on the hard disk.

23. Although the architects of the Mars computers had recently come from Harvard, they didn't choose to apply the Harvard architecture with its separate memories for data and program instructions. We preferred the von Neumann architecture with its greater flexibility based on sharing a single pool of memory for both purposes. The tradeoff was that the data and instruction memory cycles could not occur simultaneously but had to be consecutive, which meant accepting a longer running time to obtain the flexibility of allocation and to avoid the peak power consumption of running both memories at once. It's a little like our smart phones today, draining their batteries faster when we run complex displays and audio outputs simultaneously.

24. Such intricate optimizations have become a Web-based game for geeks today. It's called "Code Golf."

25. Regular infinitesimal calculus, as invented by Newton and Leibniz, doesn't meet this sort of problem because what that algebra models is an effectively *infinite* number of calculations of variables that change over time in a smoothly continuous manner (no instantaneous jumps). Each such change occurs in an *infinitesimal* period of time. "Infinitesimal" means, basically, "No matter how small you think it is, it's really very much smaller than that." That works if the equations involved—e.g., equations of motion of a spacecraft—can be expressed in "closed form," meaning the sort of formulas you see in any calculus textbook.

CHAPTER 10

26. These events, occurring at various times in the first year of the Apollo "Program" (NASA's word, taken from standard government jargon) or "Project" (everybody else's word, especially those concerned with computer programs), put all the players and their assignments on the field.

CHAPTER 11

27. These cartoons have acquired a sort of immortality, appearing in such books as Mindell's *Digital Apollo* with its focus on the history of man-machine interactions. Figures 11-1a and 11-1b are courtesy of the Charles Stark Draper Laboratory, Inc. Oddly, the version that Mindell obtained from the MIT Museum included a small but significant update: in the automated spacecraft, the astronaut on the right is smoking a cigar instead of snoring. Presumably, the astronaut corps objected to *any* suggestion that astronauts might sleep on the job, but smoking (in a cartoon) was acceptable.

28. Doing celestial navigation in space has other differences that are beyond the scope of this book. The sextant's line of sight in the Lower Equipment Bay was not fixed, but could be electrically turned in any direction under the control of joysticks. In addition, it could be controlled by its companion piece, a Scanning Telescope with a wide field of view to facilitate finding and identifying a star. When position finding in Earth orbit, it's possible to use major landmarks such as San Francisco Bay or the Kennecott copper mine pit in Utah instead of the horizon. That's why one of the sextant's optical paths was named LLOS for Landmark Line Of Sight, and the other was named SLOS for Star Line Of Sight. Doing fine alignment of the IMU gimbal angles with stars in both lines of sight was quite a novel use of a sextant, because the angle being "measured," between two stars, was effectively constant throughout the Solar System and well known. The angles of interest were the orientation angles of the sextant assembly in the spacecraft's wall, as determined by the joysticks. That worked because the geometrical plane defined by the two stars and the Solar System is fixed in inertial space. So the orientation angles, at the time the two stars appeared exactly in the sextant's lines of sight, determined one axis of the spacecraft's actual orientation. A second such observation, on a different pair of stars, determined another axis. Combining the data from these observations yielded the complete spacecraft orientation, usable to correct the gyros' idea of that orientation.

29. Internally, each key generated a 5-bit code that we expanded to 15 bits, two copies of the code at the left and right ends of a 15-bit word, plus an inverted copy (each one changed to zero and vice versa) in the middle 5 bits. That allowed for very high-confidence checking for valid codes, but not because there was any uneasiness about the wiring between the DSKY and the AGC. Sometimes such codes came from the ground via radio "uplink" because in certain situations (e.g., unmanned test flights), it was appropriate for ground controllers to operate the computer's interface exactly as onboard astronauts did. This demanding level of checking was important for "keystrokes" arriving from a journey of up to a quarter-million miles.

30. For some nice photos and engineering graphics of the DSKY, there's an informative article on the AGC published in the Computer History Museum's publication, *Core 3.2* (May 2002), archived at http://www. computerhistory.org/core/media/pdf/core-2002-05.pdf. Figure 11-2 is courtesy of the Charles Stark Draper Laboratory, Inc.

CHAPTER 12

31. A memory cycle with distinct read and write times was characteristic of ferrite-core RAM because it couldn't be read without destroying the information. The solution was to keep a copy of the information in an electronic register long enough to write it back a few microseconds later. If the purpose of the cycle was a simple read, that's all there was

to it. If the purpose was a simple write, the data from the read part was just ignored. But if there was a fancier purpose like exchanging a register's content with that of memory, the information obtained at read time went to one central register, and then data (from some other register) to be written was set up for write time. Exchange was a very cool instruction because it made one memory cycle do the work of three instructions. In the example given in the text, the value that was written was either one greater or one less than the value read. That made an input operation (when pushed in from outside) take the least possible time, one memory cycle, only half the running time of most instructions. Remember, a microsecond saved is a microsecond earned.

32. We're used to every computer having ultra-high-capacity disk drives now, both rotating and flash types, not to mention just keeping everything in "The Cloud." It feels strange to remember a time when magnetic tapes were the standard method of mass storage. The major limitation of tapes was called *serial access*, contrasted with the *random access* of an internal memory, the origin of our acronym RAM. Updating a file on a tape involved copying the entire tape onto a second tape, making the required changes on the fly as it were, because there was no way to write the new version back on the same tape without destroying access to all the files located "downstream" of that point. This fact had a significant advantage, however. The input tape automatically became a backup copy, current except for the latest updates.

Chapter 13

33. The design of the Block I Interpreter is preserved in Ron Burkey's comprehensive archive of Apollo details (http://www.ibiblio.org/ apollo/hrst/archive/1721.pdf). It's the document Tom and Charley put together for all of SUNRISE, the program they created to integrate the executive, waitlist, interpreter, and astronaut interface logic with some generic Block I GN&C code. It was as far as they could go before mission profiles were defined for any of the flights, and was enormously valuable in exercising all the software tools for creating and testing an AGC program. Don't worry about the upside-down image of the front cover; all the other pages are right-side up. Also be aware that the Optical Character Reader that scanned this as a searchable document guessed wrong in many places, and not all of those got fixed.

34. Figure 13-1 credit: Ted Polumbaum/Newseum Collection.

CHAPTER 14

35. This figure is from a NASA poster, courtesy of Kipp Teague's Apollo Archive. Specifically, it's at www.apolloarchive.com/apollo/sat5_ diagram.gif. For a slightly different approach, see also www.space. com/18422-apollo-saturn-v-moon-rocket-nasa-infographic.html.

CHAPTER 16

36. Al Hopkins obtained this and two other simple functions, one to temporarily inhibit program interrupts and one to release them again, by noticing that the one-cycle instruction Transfer Control (TC) could not sensibly be used with most of the central registers. The trick was simply to recognize three 15-bit words, which looked like TCs to three of the central registers, as special cases: EXTEND, INHINT, and RELINT. These two interrupt controls weren't new to Block II, just more efficiently realized. Whenever the multitasking control software (Executive) was notified that the priority of a waiting job had become higher than the priority of the running job—usually by a program interrupt triggered by a timer expiration—it would tuck the running job into bed and wake up the waiting job. That switch-over involved saving several data items belonging to the old job and gathering similar items for use by the new job. We couldn't let another interrupt cut off this Executive activity in mid-stream and overlap it with a different instance of itself. The solution was to provide a programmable way of blocking interrupts entirely for the sub-millisecond periods when this sort of pants-down transition was going on.

I raised an issue with the EXTEND logic. The Block I method, using the INDEX, allowed actual subscripting simultaneously with the Shift-key function, if you prepared the data word addressed by INDEX to have that effect. Now there wasn't a way to apply INDEX to any extracode, so I defined a second INDEX op code that was itself an extracode, with the special property that it repeated the Shift-key function to affect the instruction modified by the INDEX. Thus, the instruction sequences to perform a subscripted add and a subscripted multiply (an extracode) would look like this:

```
INDEX I
AD     ITEM    ADD CONTENTS OF (ITEM + CONTENTS OF I)
EXTEND
INDEX J
MP     FACTOR  MULTIPLY BY CONTENTS OF (FACTOR + CONTENTS
               OF J)
```

At the microprogramming level, these two INDEX codes had different behaviors, but programmers writing *YUL* source code didn't need to know that. This was a case where having the system software developer at the hardware design table kept things simpler.

37. Since we had the capability to shift any number 1 bit position left or right while copying it from one register to another, we could perform conditional shifting based on pairs of multiplier bits. The little logic machine for this function had two modes:

NORMAL MODE		
Bits	Do what to the partially developed product	Do what to the mode
00	nothing	nothing
01	add the multiplicand	nothing
10	add the left-shifted (doubled) multiplicand	nothing
11	subtract the multiplicand(!)	set to Borrow

BORROW MODE		
Bits	Do what to the partially developed product	Do what to the mode
00	add the multiplicand	set to Normal
01	add the left-shifted (doubled) multiplicand	set to Normal
10	subtract the multiplicand(!)	nothing
11	nothing(!)	nothing

Then if the Borrow mode is still set at the end, add the multiplicand in once more, making an eighth addition in some cases, but not taking any more time. For simplicity, I have omitted the shift of the developing product, two bit positions to the right, that winds up the processing of each pair of bits in the multiplier.

38. In 2013, I used some of the research for this book to sketch a paper design for a "Block III AGC," using the same technology but with a better architecture. I hoped to double the speed again. I chose a

Harvard architecture with fixed memory devoted strictly to program storage and erasable memory devoted strictly to data, so the two memories would cycle simultaneously in most situations. That made it possible to have instruction words of 19 bits and parity, providing logical space for plenty of instructions without obscure tricks, while the data words remained at 15 bits and parity. I plan to publish this fantasy on-line for the amusement of all the people around the world who enjoy building hardware or software replicas of the AGC.

Chapter 18

39. That little machine also starred in a unique competitive drama. Its architecture was quite a departure for Honeywell, and the H-200 was quite openly the "love child" of Honeywell and IBM, as the supermarket press might put it. Actually, there wasn't a lot of love lost, since it was created specifically to displace a similar IBM system called 1401, by being faster and cheaper. It came with a special program named Liberator that translated 1401 object code directly into H-200 object code. The hardware designs were sufficiently different that you couldn't call them clones (no patent violation on that ground), and the resulting programs weren't quite similar enough to charge copyright infringement.

It was a novel kind of intellectual-property alienation, and I never found any trail of legal bread crumbs on the subject. That's probably because IBM ignored the issue, knowing they were about to obtain a monopoly of the mainframe computer business with their 360 architecture that combined scientific and business computing features in one box. Adding insult to injury, Honeywell left their beige/brown/black color scheme to their 800 family and made the H-200's exterior panels a combination of innocent white and … IBM blue.

Chapter 19

40. Some details of these machines, but no images, are available at http://en.wikipedia.org/wiki/Wire_wrap.

41. There's a monumental library of AGC and *YUL* documents (and more) preserved online by Ron Burkey at http://www.ibiblio.org/apollo/links.html. In his notes, Ron uncomfortably observes that many sources call it "the infamous AGC4 Memo #9" (at http://www.ibiblio.org/apollo/hrst/archive/1689.pdf) but he'd like us to understand he himself doesn't consider it infamous at all. Burkey's archive has become the reference library for the small but global community that now builds hardware or software emulations of the Block II AGC as a hobby.

Chapter 21

42. After a few months of testing ever-larger AGC programs with the increased complexity of longer and more ambitious missions, it became clear that the 360's standard memory size wasn't going to be enough. We leased an additional unit, just about a cubic yard, containing one Mbyte. How many of today's multi-Gbyte flash drives would fit in that box? The reason System/360 elements were so huge was that in the mid-'60s IBM wasn't quite ready to embrace integrated circuits (ICs). What they felt confident with, they called Solid Logic Technology (SLT), in which each individual transistor or resistor was made on a tiny chip of its own, about one-eighth inch square, though made in the same way ICs are made. SLT chips sat on ceramic substrates with legs around the edges, a dozen or so per substrate, welded to metal interconnections printed on the substrate's top. It wasn't until the '70s that IBM computers were made of ICs, almost a full decade behind the Lab.

Chapter 22

43. Michael Collins, CM Pilot in Apollo 11, wrote what I consider the best-written book by an astronaut. In *Carrying the Fire,* he fills in some hilarious details of this scene.

Chapter 23

44. The number of symbols listed was around seven thousand, alphabetically ordered in three columns per page over dozens of pages. Each symbol was accompanied by its numerical definition, usually a memory address, and the number of the page on which it was defined—very useful for looking up "What is this symbol even all about?" Also displayed was the number of times it was referred to, and the first and last pages where such references appeared. Most symbols were reasonably mnemonic, so you didn't need further interpretation except perhaps at the point where it was defined. As an example, AXISCTR named a variable used in the Digital AutoPilot (DAP) as a subscript to allow each execution of a DAP program loop to control the RCS jet pairs that would rotate the LM about a different axis. The name AXISCTR signified "Axis Counter," referring to the LM's X, Y and Z body axes respectively. Its symbol table entry:

AXISCTR E6,1505   133   3   1234   1501

identifies AXISCTR as the symbolic name for the memory location addressed as word 1505 in Erasable bank 6, defined on page 133, and referred to in three other places on pages ranging from 1234 through 1501.

To find all the places a given symbol was used, you'd turn to the page of the final reference, here 1501. Scanning it bottom to top, you'd find "REF 3 LAST 1500" on the line where AXISCTR was used for the third and final time. Since it named the previous page for the previous reference, you'd turn back a page and scan up to find "REF 2 LAST 1234" on the line where AXISCTR was used for the second time. Then skipping straight to page 1234, you'd find the first line where AXISCTR was referenced, tagged simply "REF 1."

The "backward" sequencing of the list was simply due to the way *YUL* developed the data. Building the listing page by page, it could always get from the internal symbol table the current serial number and the last reference page encountered so far. It put those in the listing and then updated the symbol table entry with the new previous-page number and the incremented serial number.

There were other tables, sorted by ascending memory addresses, to show how fixed memory was allocated to native and interpretive instructions, and how erasable memory was allocated to variable and constant data. The other generally useful feature while reading through the code was two levels of page numbers. The top-level numbers were for the listing as a whole, used in all the summary tables. The lower-level page numbers applied within major parts of the program that were like chapters in a book. On every page, the second line of print gave the "chapter" title along with the local page number.

45. The flaw in our understanding came from a shocking foul-up, by one of Grumman's subcontractors, in maintaining the Descent engine documentation. The software controlling this engine's throttle had to compensate for its "lag time," how long it took to achieve the new

thrust level after receipt of a control pulse. The document stated the lag time as 300 milliseconds, but the Lab's Don Eyles decided to set the compensation by a systematic process. His experiments showed that setting the compensation to only 100 milliseconds gave much smoother operation, and his boss, Allan Klumpp, accepted that result. In Apollo 12, telemetry data showed the throttling oscillating back and forth between two values, not quite unstable but close to it, so NASA asked the Lab to investigate. That's how we discovered that the Descent engine contractor had improved the lag time to 75 milliseconds, *but had never told us or anybody else about the change.* If Don had just compensated for 300 milliseconds instead of taking the initiative to find the correct value, the engine would have gone unstable and aborted missions, probably as early as Apollo 9. See also note 48 below.

46. It would have been nice to be able to tell the crew how much time should elapse between powering up the AGS and powering up the PGNCS, but no such luck. Unlike the seacoast tides with their cycle period of 12½ hours, the 800 Hz supplies had a cycle period of one 800th of a second, or 1250 microseconds. Within that period, there were two slivers of about 60 microseconds each that corresponded to the critical phase difference. The time at which a finger pushes a button can be consciously controlled to within about one second at best. There's just no way to stay away from such tiny slivers of time.

It's pure coincidence that my analogy using the Cape Cod Canal tides shows the same phase difference, one-quarter cycle, as the critical values for the LM's 800 Hz supplies. Quarter-cycle differences in general are interesting enough to have a special name, "being in quadrature," but they have no universal property of causing trouble. The canal tides would present much the same problems to boaters if the phase difference were, say, a third of a cycle.

CHAPTER 24

47. The term "exegesis" isn't wrong here, but it's certainly unusual in technical writing. Usually, it refers to a lengthy and deeply scholastic explanation of passages from the Torah or other sacred texts. It's a perfectly good ancient Greek word, well known to such scholars—and to a few word nuts like George Cherry and me. George chose the word to make his letter stand out from all the other documents (such as memos, explanations, and reports) filling up NASA files, and he surely succeeded. I have been unable to find the letter on the Internet, so I've included all of it, except for some very technical tables, as the Appendix. It's a good example of George's intense and thorough style, leaving nothing to be guessed at.

48. Don Eyles presented his paper, *Tales From The Lunar Module Guidance Computer*, to the American Astronautical Society in 2004, and then posted it on his web site: http://www.doneyles.com/LM/Tales.html. He describes system integration problems in three missions: Apollo 5, the unmanned test of LM-1; Apollo 11, the first Moon landing; and Apollo 12, the second Moon landing.

In Apollo 5, he relates how a ground control procedure change prevented the LGC from starting LM-1's Descent engine (Chapter 22).

In Apollo 11, he details what the time-wasting glitch in the Rendezvous Radar interface logic did to SERVICER and other guidance modules in the LGC software.

In Apollo 12, he shows what an obsolete specification document did to endanger the stability of the Descent engine—an effect we then realized had also applied to Apollo 10 and 11. See also note 45 above.

Chapter 26

49. Wikipedia's article on *Fallen Astronaut* lists all the names and the circumstances of their deaths, and shows a photo of this first art installation on the Moon (http://en.wikipedia.org/wiki/Fallen_Astronaut).

Chapter 30

50. When Intermetrics (founded around 1969 by several of the Lab's software stars) came to define a new compiler language for use in the Space Shuttle's computers, they made it an upgrade of *MAC* and named it *HAL* in honor of Hal Laning's role in developing *MAC* as well as *George*. Don't let anybody tell you it was for the talky computer in *2001: A Space Odyssey*, and its sequel *2010*. The name HAL in those films was an acronym for *Heuristically programmed ALgorithic computer*, as explained in chapter 16 of Arthur C. Clarke's *2001* book. A fanciful urban legend explains it as derived from applying an absurdly simple encryption scheme to "IBM"—the scheme (usually credited to Julius Caesar) being to substitute for each letter the one just preceding it in the alphabet. Strictly speaking, the *HAL* variant used for the Shuttle was appropriately tagged *HAL/S*, but I don't know whether anybody ever bought the version without the *S*.

51. There was another set of wires that interconnected all five GPCs, data buses called ICC for Inter-Computer Communication, but they were used for somewhat more high-level data exchanges rather than for synchronization as such. By the nature of data bus communication protocols, they couldn't perform synchronizing and in fact had to be supported by the discrete-driven sync scheme. Incidentally, NASA's official history site, *Computers in Spaceflight: The NASA Experience*, in Chapter Four, *Computers in the Space Shuttle Avionics System*, under *Computer synchronization and redundancy management*, Item 106 (*Box 4-2: Redundant Set Synchronization: Key to Reliability*) confuses the ICCs with the discretes, among other small discrepancies. That chapter is available at http://history.nasa.gov/computers/Ch4-4.html.

52. Our scheme, at this base level, was a rather simple implementation of a fairly complex idea. Every job was required, at intervals no greater than a millisecond, to include a "sync point" by calling a routine that looked around to see whether any timer expiration or any I/O completion was pending, and verifying that all other GPCs in the RS had noticed the same kind of event. The three kinds of event had inherent priorities, from programmed sync point (lowest) to I/O completion (highest), so the purpose of the "looking around" was to wait, within limits, until all GPCs in the set agreed on the highest-priority event experienced by any one of them.

This synchronization logic resolved any race conditions. For example, if one GPC came to a sync point at the same time two other GPCs saw a timer expiration, and yet another GPC saw an I/O completion, the first three would wait until they too saw the I/O completion. At that point, all four GPCs would proceed in unison to raise the priority of the job that was waiting for that event. Then they would re-enter the sync point to achieve agreement on the timer expiration, which would also raise the priority of its appropriate job. If (as was likely) the priority of the job that entered the programmed sync point was lower than that of the most highly-promoted job, FCOS would redirect control of all four GPCs to the latter, assuring complete uniformity of the control switch. All that was driven by exchanging just two of the three discrete signals to encode the four possibilities:

➤ 00: not in a sync point,

➤ 01: in a programmed sync point,

➤ 10: in a timer expiration sync point, or

➤ 11: in an I/O completion sync point.

Such uniformity could be spoiled in either of two ways. One GPC might fail and set its discretes to a code that remained in disagreement with the others for too long, thereby violating the rule about waiting "within limits." Or faulty input data might appear in some GPCs but not others. These situations were called "sync failures," and they turned on lights in a crew display called Computer Annunciation Matrix (CAM) so the crew could decide whether to shut down the odd-computer-out. We couldn't imagine under what circumstances they might opt *not* to do so, and would have been happy to do the shutdown automatically for them. However, the astronaut corps told us that was the sort of irrevocable deed they wouldn't allow any automation to commit.

53. Isolating faulty input data was where the third discrete came in as an indicator. Combined with the other two discretes, it identified which of the four input strings contained data found by built-in tests to be faulty, and that was the key to pinning the tail on the right donkey. If all GPCs signaled each other that they saw a fault in the same string, then the GPCs were working and the subsystem or its MDM had failed, but if just one GPC reported a fault, then the subsystem was probably OK, and the GPC's input-processing hardware had failed. When a subsystem on one string failed, the FO-FS rule required all GPCs in the redundant set to ignore data from that source until further disposition by the crew—often enough, they could fix the problem by cycling the faulted unit's power off and on again.

54. The Space Shuttle didn't suffer radio blackout on entry because its airplane-like shape left a hole in the ionization, through which it communicated via a Tracking and Data Relay Satellite.

Epilogue

55. The *GAP* assembly listing of LGC program *Luminary* is accessible through http://www.ibiblio.org/apollo/ScansForConversion/Luminary131/, which is a list of 1,742 links. Each link leads to a jpg image of a single page of the assembly listing. Although the clarity of these images is

compromised by the color bars on the paper being scanned (stripes of light green alternating with stripes of white, three lines each), they're quite readable when zoomed in. For a clearer image of an earlier version, made from paper with no green stripes and more readable without zooming, see http://www.ibiblio.org/apollo/ScansForConversion/ Luminary099/.

56. In 1981, my final year at the Lab, I worked on mathematical analyses of ways to stabilize vibrations in such a large spacecraft.

PHOTO CREDITS AND PERMISSIONS

Cover:

Front: Description and Performance of the Saturn Launch Vehicle's Navigation, Guidance, and Control System, from klabs.org; Courtesy of NASA

Saturn 5 liftoff: Apollo-launch-8909250; Courtesy of NASA

Lunar base scene: Apollo_15_flag,_rover,_LM,_Irwin_wikipedia; Courtesy of NASA

Apollo 11 crew portrait: https://en.wikipedia.org/wiki/Apollo_program#/media/File:Apollo_11.jpg; Courtesy of NASA

Back: Flag of Soviet Union SSSR: Depositphotos_2290897_m-2015

USA-flag-Depositphotos_4964272_m-2015

Spine: moon: Depositphotos; by korionov Image ID: 4916760

MIT Bldg 10: web.mit.edu722 × 308; Courtesy of MIT

NASA Logo:http://pics-about.space/nasa-logo-transparent-background?p=1; Courtesy of NASA

Interior stock images:

Chapter opener image: Rocket-Earth-depositphotos_25665141

Part opener image: "Go-to-Space:" Rocket-depositphotos_43451851-Rocket

Figure 5-1: A three dimensional Cartesian coordinate system © Jorge Stolfi, used by explicit release into the public domain.

Figure 7-1: Photo # NH 96566-KN (Color) First Computer "bug", 1947 © Naval History and Heritage Command, used with permission.

Figure 8-1: Harvard Mark IV memory register; Courtesy of the Collection of Historical Scientific Instruments, Harvard University.

Figure 8-2: IBM 650 Installation © IBM Corp.; Courtesy of IBM Archives.

Figure 8-3a: IBM 407 Accounting Machine © IBM Corp.; Courtesy of IBM Archives.

Figure 8-3b: IBM 407 Control Panel 1949 © IBM Corp.; Courtesy of IBM Archives.

Figure 11-1a: Apollo Astronauts in Command Module © Draper Laboratory, used with permission.

Figure 11-1b: Apollo Astronauts in Command Module © Draper Laboratory, used with permission.

Figure 11-2: Apollo Guidance Computer and DSKY © Draper Laboratory, used with permission.

Figure 13-1: G19276P – Charles "Doc" Draper: Scientist, MIT, engineer, aerospace, father of inertial navigation, sitting in the Apollo mockup © Ted Polumbaum collection at Newseum, used with permission.

Figure in Chapter 14: Saturn V Launch Vehicle and Apollo Spacecraft © NASA via Kipp Teague's Apollo Archive, declared by Teague to be in the public domain.

About the Author photo: © Hugh Blair-Smith.

Appendix: Exegesis of the 1201 and 1202 Alarms Which Occurred During the Mission G Lunar Landing © NASA, in the public domain.

GLOSSARY OF ACRONYMS AND ABBREVIATIONS
USED IN APOLLO AND THE SPACE SHUTTLE

AGC Apollo Guidance Computer (also did Navigation and [Flight] Control)

AGS Abort Guidance System (backup in LM, never needed)

APS Ascent Propulsion System, LM (ascent from Moon to rendezvous)

BFS Backup Flight System (non-IBM software for fifth GPC in Orbiter)

CAM Computer-Aided Manufacturing (see YUL below)

CM Command Module (gumdrop-shaped reentry spacecraft, Apollo)

CMC Command Module Computer (the AGC in the CM)

CSM Command and Service Modules while joined

DEU Display Electronics Unit (three in Orbiter, includes screen and keyboard)

DPS Descent Propulsion System, LM (descent and landing on Moon)

DSKY Display and Keyboard (two in CM, one in LM)

ET External Tank (supplies fuel & oxidizer to Orbiter main engines in boost)

FO/FS Fail Operational, Fail Safe (fault tolerance criterion for Orbiter avionics)

FSD Federal Systems Division of IBM (built GPCs and programmed PASS)

GAEC Grumman Aircraft Engineering Corp. (built LM)

GB Gigabyte[s]: 1,073,741,824 (= $1,024^3$) eight-bit bytes of data

GPC General Purpose Computer (five in Orbiter, by FSD)

HAL aka HAL/S, spacecraft version of MAC (in honor of J. Halcombe Laning)

JSC Johnson Space Center/Houston (NASA; named MSC prior to 1973)

KB Kilobyte[s]: 1,024 eight-bit bytes of data

KSC Kennedy Space Center/Cape Canaveral (NASA launch facility)

LGC LM Guidance Computer (the AGC in the LM)

LM Lunar [landing] Module (spindly-legged spacecraft with descent stage and ascent stage); formerly LEM (Lunar Excursion Module)

MAC MIT Algebraic Compiler (converts algebraic equations to object code)

MB Megabyte[s]: 1,048,576 (= $1,024^2$) eight-bit bytes of data

MSC Manned Spacecraft Center/Houston (NASA; renamed JSC, 1973)

NAA North American Aviation (built CM and SM; also see RISD below)

NASA National Aeronautics and Space Administration

OMS Orbital Maneuvering System (medium rocket engines, two on Orbiter)

Orbiter Space Shuttle vehicle, excluding booster elements SRBs and ET

PASS Primary Avionics Software System (FSD-supplied GPC software; see BFS)

PGNCS Primary Guidance, Navigation, and Control System ("pings," AGC and other MIT-designed equipment, and operating software therein)

RCS Reaction Control System (small rockets or "jets" for attitude control, on SM, LM, CM, and Orbiter)

RISD Rockwell International Space Division (ex-NAA, built Orbiter)

RR Rendezvous Radar (in LM ascent, gives CSM position to LGC or AGS)

SM Service Module (cylindrical spacecraft with SPS rocket engine at one end, and CM attached at the other until reentry; supplies electricity)

SPS Service Propulsion System (medium rocket engine for entering and leaving Lunar orbit, also retro-fire for Earth reentry)

SRB Solid Rocket Booster (two strapped onto Orbiter for boost)

YUL Assembler/CAM/version control for AGC series (named for 1959 "Christmas Computer"); CAM made punched tape to control core rope memory weaving

TOP-DOWN NOMENCLATURE OF MANNED SPACECRAFT SOFTWARE

➤ Complete Software Suite (AGC: core rope)
- System Software
  - ◆ Operating System (like the kernel in modern OS products)
    - − Multitasking Control
    - − User Interfaces (display, keyboard, network)
  - ◆ Library of useful functions (AGC: available via Interpreter)
- Mission Software (Apps)
  - ◆ Navigation
  - ◆ Guidance
  - ◆ [Flight] Control

Each bottom-level element above breaks down further into:
- Modules (functions, subroutines, memory allocation for data)
  - ◆ Object code from compiler statements (not in AGC) or assembler
    - − Machine instructions, one per word of program memory

TOP-DOWN NOMENCLATURE OF EMBEDDED COMPUTER HARDWARE

➤ Computer System

- High-level modules with backplanes (AGC: logic tray and memory tray)

  ◆ Central Processor Unit (CPU) logic modules

    − Frame with pins to plug into front of backplane

    − Multilayer printed circuit board with connections to pins

    − Logic chips with legs welded to circuit board

      • Integrated transistors, diodes, resistors

  ◆ Memory modules

  ◆ RAM (AGC: Erasable)

    − Coincident-current cores (AGC: 2,048 16-bit words)

    − Discrete transistors, diodes, resistors to control RAM

  ◆ ROM (AGC: Fixed)

    − Core rope module (AGC: six @ 6,144 16-bit words)

      • Two module halves, 256 cores each

        • 192 bits (twelve 16-bit words) per core

    − Discrete transistors, diodes, resistors to control ROM

➤ Peripheral Units

- User Interface Display and Keyboard (AGC: DSKY; Orbiter: DEU)

- Digital Communications with Ground (AGC: downlink, uplink)

- Subsystem Signal Conditioning (AGC: Coupling Data Units = CDUs)

  ◆ Inertial Measurement Unit interface

  ◆ Optical Subsystem interface

  ◆ Radar Subsystems interface (not in Apollo CM)

- Rocket controllers: engines and RCS attitude-control jets

- Air data sensors and aviation navigational-aid receivers (Orbiter)

- Control surface hydraulics controllers (Orbiter)

- Magnetic tape drives for program loading (Orbiter)

Appendix

The following, courtesy of NASA from the files of the late George Silver of MIT, is with one exception the complete letter written by George Cherry to NASA explaining the program alarms in the Apollo 11 landing. The exception is the omission of the tables of software jobs and their assigned priorities referred to in two places in the letter. PDI = Powered Descent Initiation. ECDU (Electronic Coupling Data Unit) is the full name of the Block II CDU.

MASSACHUSETTS INSTITUTE OF TECHNOLOGY
DEPARTMENT OF AERONAUTICS AND ASTRONAUTICS
INSTRUMENTATION LABORATORY
CAMBRIDGE, MASS 02139

C. S. DRAPER
DIRECTOR

AG# 370-69
August 4, 1969

National Aeronautics and Space Administration
Manned Spacecraft Center
Houston, Texas 77058

Attention: Mr. W. Kelly
              Project Office PP7
              Guidance and Navigation
              Mr. Christopher Kraft, Jr. FA

Through: NASA / RASPO at MIT/IL

Subject: Exegesis of the 1201 and 1202 Alarms Which Occurred
              During the Mission G Lunar Landing

Gentlemen:

Background

During the mission G lunar landing five LGC Executive overflow alarms occurred. They were with approximate times of occurrence,

1202 at PDI + 316 seconds

1202 at PDI + 356 seconds

435

1201 at PDI + 552 seconds

1202 at PDI + 578 seconds

1202 at PDI + 594 seconds

The first two alarms occurred in P63; the last three occurred in P64. A later section of this letter gives more detail on the other DSKY activity during landing.

These alarms arose because of a computer overload caused by a high frequency train of "counter increment requests" from the RR ECDU's. Each "counter increment request" requires one LGC central processor memory cycle. Consequently, the other computational tasks and jobs of the LGC are effectively slowed down. The slow-down was so bad at times that some repetitively scheduled jobs (like SERVICER, the navigation and guidance job which is done every two seconds) were still running when the time arrived for their succeeding cycle of computations to begin.

This phenomenon (requesting the EXECUTIVE program to start some particular job before the previous request of the same job has been completed) is a feature of the way the LGC guidance cycle is structured and the way successive repetitive jobs are scheduled. The execution of jobs may be slowed down by RR ECDU memory cycle robbery but the clock which schedules jobs like SERVICER and LRHJOB (the job which reads LR range) is scarcely affected. The clock (TIME3, the WAITLIST clock) we use to schedule these jobs ineluctably counts down to the time for the next repetition of a job to begin whether the previous repetition is complete or not. This is not the only way to structure our programs but it is the simplest and most natural way. There is, of course, danger in this structure, a danger well understood and, we thought, provided against. Some computations may never be finished if the basic cycle period is too short for the load on the central processor. Worse yet, the EXECUTIVE program may be deluged with requests for jobs — the new ones and the old still unfinished ones. The EXECUTIVE must supply a unshared set of erasables for each job's execution from the moment it is started until the moment it is completed. The EXECUTIVE has only so many sets of these erasables at its disposal. After it has allocated all its sets the next requestor of a job asks for the impossible. The EXECUTIVE responds to the impossible request by turning on the PROG light (program alarm), storing the 1201 or 1202 alarm code, and transferring control to the BAILOUT routine which tries to bail the program out of trouble by stopping all jobs and tasks and restarting only the absolutely required (in the programmer's limited fallible viewpoint) jobs and tasks. Thus, certain astronaut requested activity like extended verbs and monitor displays are preemptively terminated (he can call them back). This cleaning out of the temporarily dispensable can cure a temporary overload. A permanent overload is the very dangerous situation. If there is a danger in this simple natural philosophy the danger can be reduced to an acceptable level. We try to do this by simulating all the known sources of computer load and then to be safe impose a safety margin. We simulate an unknown source or sources of memory cycle loss (we call it TLOSS) and insist that a certain TLOSS be tolerable (no 1201's, no 1202's). The margin has a price — it can be obtained by lengthening the navigation, guidance and display period and by trading off execution speed against storage in the coding technique. We insisted on a tolerable TLOSS of about 10% during landing. The coding and the guidance period were therefore massaged until 10% TLOSS was tolerable (with a monitor verb running). Unfortunately, the RR ECDU's stole about 15% (most of the time).

The balance of this letter gives a simple explanation of the EXECUTIVE program and the job structure during landing, the interesting hardware interface between the RR shaft and trunnion angle resolvers and the LGC when the RR switch is in AUTO TRACK or SLEW, and also what we are doing in LUMINARY 1B about this interface. Finally, it is not this specific problem which we thoroughly understand and have several ways of avoiding that really concerns us now. As you asked me in your office last Thursday, how can we prevent a similar presently unknown thing from happening? The last part of this letter explains some precautions we are taking and some disciplines we are invoking.

The Executive Program and How 1201 and 1202 Alarms Can Arise

The job scheduling and job supervising program in the LGC is called the EXECUTIVE. When the landing programs must schedule a job they call the EXECUTIVE program and give it the address of the job to be run and the priority for running it. Examples of jobs which are scheduled repetitively during landing are SERVICER, LRHJOB, and LRVJOB (the job which reads the velocity measurement from the LR). An example of a one shot job scheduled at HI-GATE and therefore called HIGATJOB, is the LR antenna re-positioning program.

People sometimes talk about jobs running "simultaneously". This cannot literally happen since there is only one central processor in the LGC and only one job's computations can be done at a time. However, jobs can be simultaneously waiting to be run, and these jobs can be waiting in various stages of completion.

How does the EXECUTIVE decide which one of a group of waiting jobs actually gets control of the central processor? That is the purpose of the job priority rating which the caller of the EXECUTIVE program must specify along with the address of the job. If a priority 20 job is running and a priority 32 job request is made to the EXECUTIVE, the EXECUTIVE will temporarily suspend (put to sleep) the priority 20 job (at a convenient point of suspension of the suspended job) and initiate the priority 32 job. Evidently, there must be an inviolate unshared set of erasable registers for each suspended (sleeping) job where its intermediate results are stored until it can be re-awakened to finish its computations. Even the simplest job requires a certain minimum set of erasables — this is called a coreset (twelve erasable registers per coreset). More sophisticated programming jobs, which perform matrix and vector computations and therefore use the INTERPRETER, need an additional set of erasables called a VAC area (43 erasable memory cells per vac area). (VAC stands for vector accumulator).

Therefore, every job needs a coreset and some jobs need a VAC area. Furthermore, every job must be allocated its required set of unshared erasable registers from the time it begins its computations until the time it concludes its computations and does an ENDOFJOB — even if it is temporarily suspended and waiting to be awakened in order to finish its computations. Jobs which use coreset storage only are called NOVAC-jobs; those which require a "vector accumulator area" also, are called VAC jobs. A table of the jobs which may run during landing, their priority, and their type (VAC or NOVAC) is given below.

Obviously, the EXECUTIVE program cannot respond to an arbitrarily large number of requests to schedule jobs. For that would require an arbitrarily large number of erasable registers. The LUMINARY 1B EXECUTIVE program has enough erasable memory to provide 8 coresets and 5 VAC areas. (COLOSSUS only has 7 coresets.) If the EXECUTIVE is requested to schedule more than eight jobs altogether or more than five VAC type jobs it cannot comply. There are several actions which the EXECUTIVE could take in this overload condition. One possible action would be for the EXECUTIVE to terminate abruptly the lowest priority waiting job and pre-empt its erasables for the newly requested job (or ignoring the request for a new job if its priority is lower than the priorities of the already waiting job). Of course, in this kind of scheme, a NOVAC job could not be preemptively "de-scheduled" to accommodate a VAC job. This philosophy is not really realistic. The EXECUTIVE program then might be making mission affecting decisions. It could conceivably ignore the execution of a low-priority but nonetheless crucial job. The EXECUTIVE, then, should not make a decision to abort or kill a job.

How, then, can an EXECUTIVE overload reasonably be handled? To understand how we handle EXECUTIVE overloads we have to understand how the computer handles software or hardware restarts. A restart causes, among other things, a cleaning out of the EXECUTIVE program's queue (and also the WAITLIST program's queue). The RESTART program then consults "phase tables" to see what jobs and tasks should be restarted. The phase tables are updated by the mission programs as the computations proceed. The phase tables do not necessarily start a given job over at its beginning; they are more likely to restart the cleaned-out program at some point conveniently prior to the point at which the restart interruption occurred. If we think of the programming job as being composed of blocks or chunks of functional coding, operations and computations, then we see that logical points for a restart to begin (that is, a logical place to insert a phase change) would be at the beginning of the logical block or chunk which the computer is currently executing. Note that the advantages of causing a software restart following an EXECUTIVE overload are twofold.

1) Old jobs which were not finished before their successors were requested are cleaned-out; i.e., the backlog, the logjam, is cleaned up. Because SERVICER does its navigation first in its cycle and then its guidance computations and then its DAP output computations, the state vector maintenance is not likely to degrade but the DAP outputs may be old if the SERVICERs begin to accumulate. The philosophy of cleaning out the old unfinished SERVICERs and restarting the current one is therefore a good idea.

2) When a restart is executed only the programs, jobs, and tasks which the programmers provided for in the "phase tables" are restarted. (This, of course, is a two-edged sword, for the programmer may forget to provide for a crucial job or task.) Temporarily dispensable items like astronaut requested monitor verbs or extended verbs are not automatically restarted. Thus, there is likely to be an immediate reduction in the computer load. The astronaut may subsequently re-request his preemptively terminated monitor or extended verb.

Reference to the Table of Jobs and Priorities below shows that there are only 8 jobs which can run during lunar landing and that only three of these are jobs which use a VAC area. Furthermore, some of these jobs, like HIGATJOB and LRH JOB (or LRVJOB) cannot run simultaneously. Therefore the 1201 alarm (not enough VAC areas available) and the 1202 alarms (not enough coresets available) must have occurred because of multiple scheduling of the same job. Obviously, then, if there was a 1201 EXECUTIVE overflow some job like SERVICER was scheduled two and possibly three or four times. In effect, the tail end of SERVICER was not being finished before a new SERVICER was scheduled.

The software restarts which accompanied the 1201 and 1202 alarms kept the program from becoming hopelessly snarled up. However, the unusually high frequency of unanticipated "counter increment requests" caused the program to require three software restarts within about 40 seconds in P64.

Long-Range Safer and More Flexible Software

It has been proposed by several people at MIT/IL (Peter Adler and Don Eyles) to provide a variable DT SERVICER program which starts a new cycle of computations as soon as the old cycle is finished. Our present SERVICER has a fixed DT of two seconds and the AVERAGE G, FINDCDUW and PIPA and GYRO compensation routines take advantage of this value of fixed integral number of seconds chosen for DT. Therefore, this programming change is not trivial. Such a mechanization has tremendous advantages however. By running all non-SERVICER jobs (like, extended verbs and monitor verbs) at a higher priority than SERVICER, we can get every job done that is requested in one SERVICER cycle by making the end of one SERVICER cycle schedule the next SERVICER cycle. The computer is continually busy this way but the programs never overburden the EXECUTIVE job scheduling capacity. In effect, you have the shortest DT possible for the number of tasks and jobs you are trying to do. This also allows new computations (PCRs) to be inserted with the simple consequence of increasing the average DT. The undesirable effects are that the DT varies and verification of stability due to sampling frequency of PIPA reading and output-command frequency to the DAP is more difficult.

How the RR Can Rob 15% of the LGC

The 1201 and 1202 program alarms which occurred during the mission G landing were due to computer overload caused by high frequency shaft and trunnion angle "counter" incrementing from the RR ECDU's. The spurious erratic high frequency output from the RR ECDUs can occur whenever the rendezvous radar control switch is in SLEW or AUTO TRACK (rather than LGC) because then the ATCA provides a 15 volt 800 cps signal to the angle resolver primaries which has a random phase relationship to the 800 cps which the PSA provides for a reference to the RR ECDUs. The consequence is that the ECDUs may count at their maximum rate, 6400 cps, in their futile attempts to null the ECDU "errors". The loss of computation time for the two ECDUs counting at maximum rate is $12.8 \times 10^3 \times 11.72 \times 10^{-6} = 0.15$ seconds/second or 15% of the LGC time since each involuntary "counter" increment takes a memory cycle (one memory cycle $= 11.72$ microseconds).

The Apollo 11 crew checklist specified that the RR switch be in AUTO TRACK immediately before calling P63. We were unaware of the effect this would have on the computer execution time load.

Preventing Future LGC Memory Cycle Robbery by the RR Ecdus

When the RR mode switch is in either the AUTO TRACK or SLEW positions the RR Ecdus obviously cannot digitize the signal transformed from the shaft and trunnion angle resolver primaries to the input to the Ecdus. The only time the LGC is interested in the ECDU signal is when the RR mode switch is in LGC. Therefore, a PCR has been written, approved, and implemented in LUMINARY 1B to monitor the discrete (the RR Power On/LGC Mode discrete) which the LGC receives when the RR switch is in the LGC position. When the LGC does not receive this discrete, it sets the RR ECDU zero command which stops the Ecdus' attempt to digitize the analog voltage from the resolvers. This action effectively prevents "counter increment requests" from the Ecdus and prevents central processor execution of these meaningless interrupts.

It should be mentioned that if the RR DC circuit breaker is pulled the LGC does not receive the RR Power On/LGC Mode discrete, and therefore the LGC will zero the RR Ecdus. This action is correct since the LGC is not interested in the shaft and trunnion angle of the RR when its circuit breakers are pulled.

We may modify our all-digital simulator to send 6400 pps from each RR ECDU to the LGC if the RR switch is not in LGC and the LGC has not set the RR CDU ZERO bit. Of course, if the simulator had this feature for our software verification tests we would have detected the computer overload during our testing.

In addition to the above PCR, other actions have been taken. PCR 814, for example, provides for a modified V57 which incorporates a display of N68 and avoids the need for a monitor verb and job (MONDO).

The separate call of MAKEPLAY has been eliminated by incorporating this job into SERVICER.

A Program to Keep Similar Events From Occurring in the Future

There were folks who knew about the RR resolver/ECDU/LGC interface mechanization. There were also a great many people who knew the effect which a 15% TLOSS would have on the landing program's operation. These folks never got together on the subject. Therefore we need to improve communications.

There are various simulations throughout the country which might have detected this problem if they had simulated the RR resolver/ECDU/ LGC interface with enough fidelity. Therefore, we might look at our various simulator configurations to see whether we are leaving anything significant out. We have just started a new Simulator Configuration Control Board at

MIT/IL which will function like your own Apollo Software Configuration Control Board. This board will adjudicate the approval of SCRs (simulator change requests). We will encourage the writing of SCRs which can increase the fidelity of the simulator in significant ways. I hope to constitute this board with hardware personnel as well as software personnel so that important hardware/software interface features are not overlooked.

Our anomaly prevention plan includes the following steps:

1. "What if" sessions between hardware and software personnel.
2. Orientation lectures by hardware personnel for the benefit of software personnel so that programmers and mission support personnel better understand the hardware.
3. A review of the adequacy of the simulator we use for mission verification. Perhaps we can get hardware personnel from GAEC, MSC and MIT/IL to review our current models.
4. Scrutiny of the crew checklist by the hardware personnel. (This could have prevented the alarms.)
5. An insistence that anyone who knows anything peculiar about the hardware, the hardware/software interface, or the software [must] document his information in the appropriate place (AOH, GSOP, Program Note, etc.) and tell the appropriate personnel.

Very truly yours,
George W. Cherry
Luminary Project Director

cc:

R. Ragan	K. Glick	W. North, CF
D. Hoag	T. Fitzgibbon	D. Cheatham, EG 2
L. Larson	B. McCoy	W. Goeckler, PD 8
R. Battin	C. Schulenberg	E. Kranz, FC
N. Sears	R. Covelli	H. Tindall, FM
F. Martin	D. Eyles	S. Bales, FC
A. Laats	P. Adler	R. Gardiner, EG
G. Silver	K. Greene	F. Bennett, FM 2
P. Felleman	L. Dunseith, FS	J. Hanaway, EG 412
R. Larson	T. Gibson, FS 5	R. Chilton, EG
J. Nevins	T. Price, FS 5	W. Heffron (Bellcomm)
W. Marscher	N. Armstrong, CB	C. Tillman GAEC
M. Hamilton	A. Aldrin, CB	G. Cherry (20)
A. Kosmala		

ACKNOWLEDGMENTS

In a history with a strong first-person component, acknowledgment could logically be made to everyone I've ever known who helped me to become the "rocket scientist" who could write this book. And since a good deal of what's here is a history of science, I could equally acknowledge a host of scientific and engineering pioneers. But that's a bigger "telephone book" than I can put into this section, so I'll have to leave it to the text to recognize people in those categories.

I'll start with some people who gave me confidence that a book about the Space Race events of half a century ago will be relevant and interesting to a twenty-first century readership. Professor David Mindell of MIT reached out, in 2001, to many of the Apollo graybeards and asked us to gather in oral-history sessions for the Dibner Institute's project in History of Recent Science and Technology, now archived at the Huntington Library, California Institute of Technology. Professor Mindell also asked Don Eyles and me to be occasional guest lecturers for his MIT course in history of technology. The students' response was most encouraging. At NASA's Goddard Space Flight Center, Rich Katz's Office of Logic Design sponsored a series of annual conferences on Military-Aerospace Programmable Logic Devices (MAPLD), for which he invited some historical contributions to the Lessons Learned sessions (2004–2006). Rich then encouraged me to present a paper at the 2008 Digital Avionics Systems Conference (DASC) on the work I did for him on the Lunar Reconnaissance Orbiter, and I have found DASC attendees also responsive to papers I've presented every year since then, which discuss parallels between the MIT/NASA experience in the Apollo/Space Shuttle programs and the problems facing digital avionics today. Among the supportive DASC leaders are Chris Watkins, Tom Redling, Glen Logan, and Benjamin Levy. Many Apollo "veterans" from MIT, Raytheon, and NASA still get together to swap astonishingly detailed memories of those exciting times. I'll acknowledge here three names—that do not appear in the book—of those who have led or supported these gatherings: Wayne Tempelman, Peter Volante, and Norm Sears. And Rob Stengel pointed me to Cyrano de Bergerac's research into Earth-Moon travel.

I know it's supposed to be a little *infra dig* to acknowledge the assistance of Google and Wikipedia, but in this century it's wonderfully easy to find first-rate material on any subject if you know what to ask for. And though I don't remember all the right answers, I *do* remember nearly all the right questions.

443

Besides, NASA's archives, especially the Lunar Surface Journal, are an unprecedented resource. Where else can you find such exhaustive recordings of the words and deeds of great historical events as spoken and done by the immediate participants—not as rearranged later by spinmeisters?

My wife, Vicki, suggested librarian colleague Anne Speyer as a preliminary freelance editor, and Anne coined a neat acronym for the larger part of my intended audience: Literate Interested Non-Scientists (LINS). With that in mind, she helped me craft writing that picks a careful path between the scientific and LINS readers. Another early manuscript reader, Gary Helmstetter, pointed out that what I was writing was not just a techno-memoir but an entertaining history of technology, which inspired me to shift much of my focus in that direction.

I have benefited greatly from membership in the Cape Cod Writers Center (CCWC) and, within it, exchanges of constructive criticism in a small Mid-Cape Nonfiction Writers Group, from which I'll mention the longest-running member besides myself: Barbara Sillery. Annual CCWC conferences, organized by Nancy Rubin Stuart, Kevin Symmons, and Janet Gardner among others, feature a wealth of expertise in courses taught by authors, professors, and literary agents. Also, a CCWC workshop put me in touch with my independent publishing house, SDP Publishing Solutions, headed by a most knowledgeable and helpful lady, Lisa Akoury-Ross. From her office in East Bridgewater, Massachusetts, she reaches out to editors and designers wherever they may be. I gratefully acknowledge the developmental editors she found for me: Gregory Crouch, a California-based book editor and author of action-packed nonfiction about mountaineering and aviation, and Kellyann Zuzulo, a Philadelphia-based book editor and best-selling author of romantic suspense. Anne and Greg and Kellyann deserve great credit for getting topics into a more sensible order, putting obese sentences on diets, and generally keeping things as graceful as they can be, considering who wrote them! Lisa's production team, proofreader Karen Grennan, and graphic designer Howard Johnson of Howard Communigrafix, Inc. have expertly done the things no author can do, and I particularly commend their patience with my relationship to the software tools.

In a book full of historical statements (and reconstructions) of fact—most of which are better known to other people than to me—there must be some errors and off-target simplifications, and I take responsibility for them.

BIBLIOGRAPHY

Bell, C. Gordon, and Allen Newell. *Computer Structures: Readings and Examples*. New York: McGraw Hill, 1971.

Brooks, Frederick Jr. *The Mythical Man-Month: Essays on Software Engineering*. Reading MA: Addison-Wesley, 1975.

Chaikin, Andrew. *A Man on the Moon: The Voyages of the Apollo Astronauts*. New York: Penguin, 2007.

Clarke, Arthur. *2001: A Space Odyssey*. Millenial Edition. New York: New American Library, 1999.

Collins, Michael. *Carrying the Fire: An Astronaut's Journeys*. 40th Anniversary Edition. New York: Farrar, Straus and Giroux, 2009.

Hall, Eldon. *Journey to the Moon: The History of the Apollo Guidance Computer*. Reston VA: American Institute of Aeronautics and Astronautics, 1996.

Hansen, James. *First Man: The Life of Neil A. Armstrong*. New York: Simon & Schuster, 2005.

Jones, R. V. *The Wizard War: British Scientific Intelligence 1939-1945*. London: Hamish Hamilton, 1978.

Kelly, Thomas. *Moon Lander: How We Developed the Apollo Lunar Module*. Washington: Smithsonian, 2001.

Kidder, Tracy. *The Soul of a New Machine*. New York: Avon, 1981.

Maass, Arthur, et al. *Design of Water-Resources Systems: New Techniques for Relating Economic Objectives, Engineering Analysis, and Governmental Planning*. Cambridge: Harvard University Press, 1962.

Mindell, David. *Digital Apollo: Human and Machine in Spaceflight*. Cambridge: MIT Press, 2008.

Murray, Charles, and Catherine Bly Cox. *Apollo*. Burkittsville MD: South Mountain, 2004.

O'Brien, Frank. *The Apollo Guidance Computer: Architecture and Operation*. Chichester: Springer-Praxis, 2010.

Oreskes, Naomi, and John Krige, eds. *Science and Technology in the Global Cold War*. Cambridge: MIT Press, 2014.

Sobel, Dava. *Longitude: The True Story of a Lone Genius Who Solved the Greatest Scientific Problem of His Time*. New York: Walker, 1995.

445

INDEX

ABOUT THE AUTHOR

Hugh Blair-Smith grew up in the cities of the Northeastern Megalopolis that stretches from Washington to Boston, always wanting to become an engineer—which he then understood was about building bridges. Studying electronic engineering and applied physics at Harvard, he learned that computers are much more fun than bridges, and making them do six impossible things before breakfast was even better. As the Space Race began, he joined the engineering staff of MIT's Instrumentation Laboratory, founded by Charles Stark "Doc" Draper to develop self-contained inertial navigation for missiles, aircraft, and spacecraft.

That timing gave him a ground-floor spot with Apollo's Primary Guidance, Navigation, and Control system, where he became the software specialist on the Apollo Guidance Computer design team, and the computer hardware specialist on the AGC programming team. Halfway through a 22-year career at MIT, he refocused on fault tolerance logic for the Space Shuttle's onboard computer system. Direct contact with astronauts included Buzz Aldrin (studying rendezvous science at MIT), Dave Scott (among the first to fully embrace the AGC way of flying), and Bob Crippen (a team member on the Shuttle work).

Leaving MIT at the end of 1981, he produced special-purpose software for two startup companies, became a migrant worker (software division), and joined a company founded by an Apollo colleague. One startup (Interactive Images, later Easel Corporation) pioneered touch screens before the world was ready for them. The other (International Treasury Systems) put touch screens to work in foreign-exchange trading rooms of international banks, which had to be ready for that field's "Big Bang" in the mid-1980s. His final "cubicle farm" (Programart, later bought by Compuware) made a software tool to identify poor performance in mainframe computers caused by inefficient programming.

After retiring to Cape Cod in 2005, he worked a one-year contract with NASA on reliability software for an instrument in the Lunar Reconnaissance Orbiter, thereby placing thousands of his own ones and zeros in orbit around the Moon.

Hugh and his wife Vicki, married since 1968, have two grown children, who are successful professionals. There are also two teenaged grandchildren and approximately twenty-five granddogs. When he's not sailing or preparing a paper to give at the next Digital Avionics Systems Conference, he enjoys teaching boating skills, reading (mostly history and other non-fiction), avoiding watching television, taking medium walks and thinking long thoughts, and puzzling out the meaning in a busy life. He has followed through on a decades-long threat to write a book that will appeal to educated readers who may or may not be scientists.

Left Brains for the Right Stuff

Computers, Space, and History

Hugh Blair-Smith

www.mitrocketscientist.com

Publisher: SDP Publishing

Also available in ebook format

TO PURCHASE:

SDPPublishing.com

BarnesAndNoble.com

Amazon.com

 **SDP Publishing**

www.SDPPublishing.com

Contact us at: info@SDPPublishing.com

CPSIA information can be obtained
at www.ICGtesting.com
Printed in the USA
LVOW13s1440091216

516588LV00008B/862/P

DEC 23 2016

9 780996 434539